Mysteries of the Gods

Great Mysteries

Aldus Books London

Mysteries of the Gods

by Stuart Holroyd

Series Coordinator:	John Mason
Art Director:	Grahame Dudley
Design:	Ann Dunn
Editorial:	Damian Grint
	Nina Shandloff
Research:	Marian Pullen
Series Consultant:	Beppie Harrison

SBN 490 004326
© 1979 Aldus Books Limited London
First published in the United Kingdom
in 1979 by Aldus Books Limited
17 Conway Street, London W1P 6BS

Printed and bound in Hong Kong
by Leefung-Asco Printers Ltd.

Introduction

No other area of human experience is more full of mystery than man's long relationship with his God or gods. In this book, the author explores some of these mysteries. The result is fascinating. What, for example, is the basis for the numerous creation myths that men have used over the centuries to explain their being here on this earth? What exactly is the role gods play in enabling man to come to terms with his own nature, with society, and with death? Why do many of the world's great religions—Christianity, Judaism, Islam—worship one god, while so many others—Hinduism, in particular—worship numerous deities? There are chapters that look at the newest evidence for the story of the Flood, and at the real life stories of the Old Testament prophets. The author also tackles the intriguing quest for the historical Jesus, uncovering a wide range of evidence from New Testament and other early writings to the most amazing object of all among Christian relics, the Shroud of Turin. Other chapters explore the nature of the sacred in both primitive and sophisticated religions and societies, and the true meaning of ritual and its place in religion. A final chapter, "The Unresolved Mystery," looks at the fundamental question that has teased and troubled mankind from the earliest times to the present day—is there a God or gods?

Contents

Chapter 1
Myths of Creation

"In the beginning God created Heaven and Earth." The familiarity of the words of the Book of Genesis often obscures the fact that every human culture, no matter how unsophisticated, has devised some mythic framework to account for the existence of the universe and of man. Sumerians, Babylonians, Hebrews, Greeks, Egyptians, Hindus, Persians, Japanese—how do their creation myths compare? Why are they all so different and yet so alike? The author examines this variety on a basic theme, and shows how, rather than mere "once upon a time" stories, these myths represent symbolic truths about the universe and man's place in it.

In the south of France there is a famous paleolithic carving dating from about 30,000 B.C. known as the Venus of Laussel, a female figure with great breasts and hips and a protruding belly. The many similar pictures and statuettes found throughout the world point to a widespread diffusion of a cult of the naked pregnant female—a cult that continued right down to later neolithic times (about 3500 B.C.). Unlike the male in later pictures and statues, she needs no regalia or magical vestments to intensify her mystery. Her body itself is magic and mystery; it is creative; it is the door through which souls come from the other world into this one.

On the basis of the evidence of the Laussel Venus and of other prehistoric pictures and carvings, and taking into account what is known of present-day primitive peoples in a similar stage of evolution, historians have suggested that worship of an earth goddess as the embodiment of fruitfulness and creativity was probably man's first religion. Also, primitive males probably had an inferior social role to the females, for it seems very likely that there was a stage in human history when males were unaware of the part they played in procreation and in consequence held the reproductive female in awe.

Whether there ever was a stage in the history of mankind when society was entirely matriarchal is a much-debated question, but scholars are agreed that the absolute ascendency of the male was a comparatively late development that came about around the

Opposite: the 30,000-year-old rock carving known as the Venus of Laussel. Found in France, it is probably the oldest representation of a deity yet discovered and represents woman as the mother goddess—a symbol of creativity and fruitfulness.

Below: a Pre-Columbian figure of a mother and child from Mexico. A pregnant woman or a woman with child or children is a constantly recurring theme in the art of primitive peoples.

Right: a West African woman from the Niger with several of her children. There is much evidence for believing that primitive males did not at first realize the part they played in the procreation of their offspring and in consequence motherhood was a source of wonderment to them. Through the mysterious female the tribe was renewed. She became the image of the renewal of all life around them.

time of the first city-states in Mesopotamia in the period 3500 to 2500 B.C. Before then, throughout the nomadic food-gathering and animal-hunting stage (down to about 7500 B.C.) and the following grain-cultivation and stock-breeding stage of human civilization, it was the female that was identified with the forces that created and sustained life.

There are no written records with which to date prehistoric revolutions in thought but it is not difficult to imagine how the male's status would have changed when the connection between sex and the production of young eventually dawned on him. He would have realized that he too was a creator, a partner in the miracle of birth; that he was as the sun to the earth, pouring forth his life-giving energy; that he was awesome in his way, too, with all the power and pride of his sexual endowment. In his mythological thinking mother earth now would be complemented by father sky, the earth goddess by the sky god. And it would hardly be surprising if the male tended to compensate for

Earth Mothers

Left: grass sprouts after rain falls on the barren ground. Much of primitive man's early thinking and discovery were expressed in his myths. As soon as the male discovered the part he played in procreation he transformed his function into that of a sky god that fertilized, through rain, the earth mother. From considering himself inferior to the mysterious, fruitful female, the male now sought a share in the power of the earth goddess.

Father Figures

Right and opposite: pictures illustrating
types of creation myths. The New Guinea
house-door painting of an X-ray view of a
pregnant woman (right) illustrates the first,
and earliest, type of creation myth that
makes the female earth mother the unaided
creator and renewer of the world. Opposite
left: a Bronze-Age rock painting from
Sweden showing the disk of the sun
depicted as the sky god, his maleness
expressed through the ceremonial warrior's
ax and erect phallus. The sky god now takes
an equal share with the earth mother in
creation—just as the primitive male
realized that he, too, shared in the
procreation of his own kind.

Far right: a wooden figure from Indonesia
of the "Father of the Tribe." The
exaggerated genitals of the figure are a
flamboyant comment on the male's later
conception of his role in creation. He is now
the dominant factor, only his all-powerful
seed can make the barren fruitful.

his former inferior position by belittling that of the female.

It is in mythology that scholars find support for the view that a
prehistoric revolution occurred in the understanding of the
sexual roles of the male and female. Although writing was not
developed until the period of the city-state, when society was
already dominated by the male, far earlier attitudes of mind can
be detected in the recorded myths, particularly the myths of
creation. Joseph Campbell, an American historian of mythology,
has distinguished four types of primitive creation myth: in the
first the world is born of a goddess without the aid of a consort;
in the second the world is born of a goddess after sexual union
with a consort; in the third the world is fashioned from the body
of a goddess by a male warrior-god; and in a fourth type the

world is created by the unaided power of a male god alone.

In the form that they have come down to us the earliest creation myths are complex tales often containing seemingly contradictory elements from different periods of a culture. Rarely do myths fit Joseph Campbell's categories exactly, but his analysis does help to break down the structure of the creation myths and make them more understandable—as well as helping to roughly date their component parts. In the myths in his first two categories the world is spoken of as being "born;" the second two speak of it being "fashioned" and "created." The word "born" suggests a natural process, "fashioned" and "created" suggest a willed and purposeful process; and this is another distinction that helps to clarify the variety of creation myths. Some of them try to explain how the physical world came into existence, how something came from nothing, how diversity came from unity, order from chaos, while others put forward the idea of an "Unmoved First Mover" standing outside his creation, a god

God the Creator

who created the world and man by an act of will and for a specific purpose.

By applying some of these categories and distinctions to some of the world's creation myths we can look behind the myths and into the minds of the people who created them.

The myths best known to Western man are those from the Bible as related in the Book of Genesis. European literature and art are full of reconstructions of these stories, such as the English poet John Milton's *Paradise Lost*, the German-born composer Handel's *Creation* and Italian Renaissance artist Michelangelo's paintings in the Sistine Chapel, and they have helped make the Genesis stories a fundamental part of Western culture and consciousness. But to this day many people do not realize that the Bible gives us two different and in some ways incompatible accounts of the Creation. In Chapter 1 of the Book of Genesis there is the story of the Six Days of Creation, and in Chapter 2 the story of Adam and Eve and their expulsion from the Garden of Eden. The second is in fact the older account, dating from about 950 to 850 B.C., whereas the story of the Six Days of Creation comes from what is known as the priestly source dating from some 400 years later. Both accounts, however, come under Joseph Campbell's category, "the world created by the unaided power of a male god alone," which

Right: the creation of man, from the biblical story of the Creation in the Book of Genesis. It was painted by the 16th-century Italian artist Michelangelo for the ceiling of the Sistine Chapel in the Vatican, Rome. Michelangelo's picture illustrates the fourth type of creation myth in which all creation is accomplished through the unaided power of a male god. No sexual act is involved—the whole of creation comes into being at the command of God.

indicates that they are of fairly late composition, the product of a male-dominated culture that had obliterated the much earlier concept of the earth goddess. Indeed, all analogy to human sexuality has been removed from its thinking about the Creation, and a concept of creation through the Word—the command—has been substituted.

"In the beginning," Chapter 1 of Genesis tells us, ". . . the earth was without form, and void; and darkness was upon the face of the deep. And the Spirit of God moved upon the face of the waters. And God said, Let there be light: and there was light." This idea of "creation from nothing" is fundamental to the Jewish-Christian tradition, and it is vividly symbolized in an engraving by Robert Fludd, the 17th-century English mystic and artist, in which the Spirit of God, represented by a dove, is released by creative command and establishes an area of light in the enveloping darkness. Before the divine command was issued, however, according to the later Genesis story, there existed the primeval waters, "the deep," and this is an idea we find in other mythologies. Indeed, in the Babylonian Creation Epic, the *Enuma Elish*, the primeval waters are identified with the goddess Tiamat, a name from which scholars have maintained that the Hebrew word for "the deep," *tehōm*, was derived. Another idea common to many creation myths is that of the separation of

Above: an engraving by the artist De Bry from a book published in 1617 by the English physician and mystic Robert Fludd. It depicts Chaos, in which hot, cold, moist, and dry "elements" seethe in confusion and out of which God created the universe and everything in it including man himself.

The Six Days of the Creation

heaven from earth. On the second day, according to Chapter 1 of Genesis, "God made the firmament, and divided the waters which were under the firmament from the waters which were above the firmament." The priests who composed this chapter of Genesis in the 5th century B.C. certainly did not invent the story, for it incorporates ideas and mythical motifs that were already of great antiquity in their day.

The account goes on to tell how on the third day God separated the land from the sea and created vegetation. On the fourth day he created the sun and the moon—and therefore day and night. On the fifth day he created fish and birds and on the sixth all the animals and finally man and woman, who he created "in his own image" and commanded to "Be fruitful, and multiply, and replenish the earth, and subdue it." Then he surveyed his creation, felt satisfied with it ("behold, it was very good"), and withdrew to rest from his labors.

The much older Chapter 2 of Genesis appears to take up the story where the priestly first chapter left it, only shifting the focus of interest to man. God, we learn, "formed man of the dust of the

Right: these scenes from a French Bible of about 1250 depict the Creation according to the version laid down by the Jewish priests in Chapter 1 of the Book of Genesis. Top row: on the first day of Creation God divides light from dark (left), on the second, he makes dry land in the middle of the waters (right).
Center: on the third day God creates seed-yielding herbs (left) and on the fourth day he makes the sun, moon, and stars (right). On the fifth day of creation, illustrated opposite from a 16th-century French stained glass window in the church of La Madeleine, Troyes, God makes the fish and birds. On the sixth day, illustrated on bottom row, right, he makes all the land animals (left) and finally mankind (right).

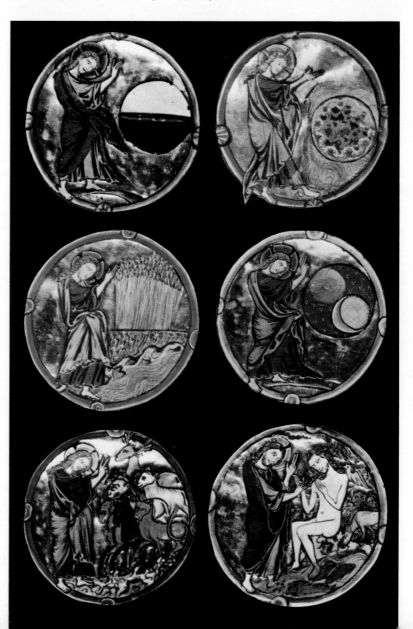

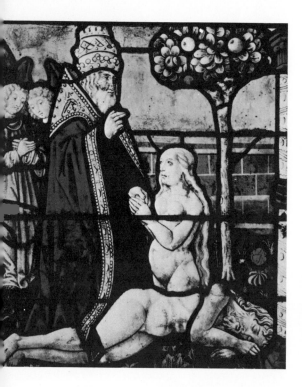

Above: Eve, the mother of the human race, rising at God's command from the side of the sleeping Adam. The illustration is from a stained glass window in the church of La Madeleine, France. In the Jewish creation story Eve is created to be Adam's helpmate and partner. Man and woman together with the whole of creation come into being at the command of God, unlike the creation stories of civilizations around the Hebrews, which were rooted firmly in fertility myths.

Right: *The Temptation* by the 15th-century Dutch painter Hugo van der Goes. Adam and Eve are created to be immortal and live in a paradise of plenty. There is one proscription, however. They must not eat of the tree of the Knowledge of good and evil. Through the wiles of the serpent—a symbol of fertility connected with the worship of the Canaanite goddess Astarte—Eve eats the fruit and gives some to Adam who also eats. For woman's prime part in the disobedience of God's command she is made man's inferior: "thou shalt be under thy husband's power and he shall have dominion over thee," says God. Both the fertility religions and cult of the supremacy of the female are here condemned in two of the many strands of this ancient story.

ground, and breathed into his nostrils the breath of life"; then he put him in the Garden of Eden, "to dress it and to keep it," and to give him company he created first of all the animals and then the female, Eve, whom he fashioned out of Adam's rib. The first man and the first woman were meant to be immortal, it seems, living in eternal bliss, without pain or toil—provided they obeyed God's command not to eat the fruit of the tree of the knowledge of good and evil. But they did eat it, urged on by the serpent. As soon as they had eaten the fruit they became conscious of their nakedness and God punished their disobedience: He made them mortal and expelled them from the Garden into the world where they had to work, breed, and die.

In this myth the animals are created after man, and woman is fashioned from his rib, whereas in Chapter 1 the animals appear first and man and woman are created simultaneously. But it is not only in such details that the two Genesis myths are different. They set out to explain different things: the origins, respectively of the physical world and its life forms, and of man and human nature. What they have in common, and where they differ from earlier creation myths, is that there is no female principle involved in the act of creation. Indeed, in the second Genesis story Eve is created as an afterthought and is portrayed as the first to disobey God's prohibition, which suggests that the myth comes from the time when the earth goddess was being denigrated and devalued. The fact that the first man became an agriculturalist after being expelled from paradise is historically significant too, for the change from a nomadic to a settled crop-tending way of life, which occurred when the Hebrew tribes settled in the land of Canaan, resulted in a change to religious practices that the pastoralists deplored, such as the practice of fertility cults in which crude sexual symbolism was used and sexual licence indulged. Like all great myths, that of the Fall of Man in the second chapter of Genesis has several levels of significance, and it has been of particular interest to men throughout the centuries largely because it contains overtones of man's uncertain attitudes

The Fall of Man

Left: the expulsion of Adam and Eve from the garden of paradise from a painting by the 16th-century artist Lucas Cranach. By disobeying God Adam and Eve lose their immortality and death enters the world. Instead of abundance all around them, Adam must toil to make the ground fertile, while his wife's fertility is achieved through pain and, at times, even death.

The Sumerian Myth

to sex, woman, work, and death. It also contains, in symbolic form, a censure on the consequences of the change from the nomadic pastoralist's to the settled agriculturalist's way of life, which was one of the great changes in human history.

Both Genesis myths are silent on God's purpose for creating the earth and man. In Chapter 1 there is the injunction to "be fruitful and multiply," but in Chapter 2 man does not discover sex or begin to reproduce until after the Fall, which is another discrepancy between the two accounts. Man, according to Chapter 2, was put into the Garden of Eden "to dress and to keep it," and some scholars have taken this statement to be an echo of an even older Sumerian creation myth in which man was created by the gods as a servant species. There are in fact many themes in Genesis, found also in Sumerian, Babylonian, and Egyptian creation myths dating from as far back as 2000–3000 years B.C., and when we examine these it becomes clear that the Hebrew myths derived from sources older and more widely distributed than their own.

The Sumerian myth begins by relating how the air-god Enlil tore apart the cosmic mountain, the base of which was the female principle, *Ki*, and the summit the male principle, *An*, and which hovered above the primal watery abyss. This tearing apart was the creation of heaven and earth, and it was followed by the appearance of the gods, who in their heavenly homeland lived as men do on earth, enjoying physical pleasures and cultivating their fields. They found the cultivation of fields too much of a burden and there came a time when, because of their neglect, the crops failed. At this the old water-goddess Nammu suggested to

Right: part of an Assyrian boundary stone of about 1120 B.C. showing symbols representing the Sumerian and late Babylonian gods Anu (left) and Enlil (right). Both were sky gods. Anu, the supreme controller of the Universe, had little to do with worldly affairs. Enlil, a storm and wind god, was more immediately involved with mankind as bringer of violent storms and the life-giving rains. It was Enlil, in the older Sumerian creation myths, who separated heaven and earth and so began the process of creation.

the god Enki that he should create servants to carry out the tasks of the gods. Enki was the lord of the watery abyss and his wife was the earth-mother. It was from the earth-mother's substance that he fashioned man, and when the marvelous creation of the servant race had been accomplished, Enki threw a celebration party for all the gods, who of course were delighted at being set free from tedious labor by their colleague's clever invention. It was a wild party and Enki and his wife became drunk and began to entertain themselves and their guests with a curious competitive game. One of them would create a human being that was defective in some way, and the other had to find an appropriate place and function for it. Enki won the game by producing a series of human beings afflicted with terrible diseases or with madness and for whom the earth-mother was unable to decree

Left: a green-stone carving of between 2360–2180 B.C. of the god Enki, or Ea, Lord of the Watery abyss. He stands to the right of two mountains, between which the sun god rises. Water and fish flow from Enki, confirming that he is indeed the water god. To the left of the sun god stands a winged vegetation goddess. From her shoulders sprout branches ending in leaves or fruit and in her hand is a bunch of dates. To her left is another figure with a bow and accompanied by a lion. Beneath Enki sits a young bull—identified with Marduk "the young bull of the sun." It was Marduk who brought order to the cosmos.

any place or function. But she was so enraged by her failure and by Enki's malicious creations that she promptly debarred him from access to earth or heaven and condemned him to live for ever in the abyss.

This Sumerian myth is complex and attempts a great deal. It not only explains the origin of the physical world, employing the very earliest motifs—those of the waters that existed from before the creation and the violent separation of heaven and earth—but it also seeks to explain the origin of man's many afflictions. In common with the earliest of the Genesis stories and many other myths, it conceives of man as made from earth, and it is notable that in it the earth goddess is a formidable figure endowed with considerable power, which is an indication of its antiquity.

Sumer was a city-state of Mesopotamia, the land of the two great rivers, the Tigris and the Euphrates, that flow into the present-day Persian Gulf. Another, and later developed, city was Babylon, which lay south of Sumer and with which the great creation epic known as the *Enuma Elish* was associated. In this myth the original gods, Apsu and Tiamat, are conceived respectively as male and female and as personifications of the river waters and the sea, and as in Chapter 1 of Genesis, the original state of things is thought of as a watery chaos. From the waters, and the union of Apsu and Tiamat, the great gods were born, but because they behaved like boisterous children rampaging around the heavens they annoyed Apsu, who wanted only to sleep, and

Below: an Assyrian seal depicting the god Marduk about to kill the monster Tiamat—the goddess of the ocean of salt water. From her union with Apsu, god of the ocean of fresh water, the gods were born. Their father Apsu planned to kill them, but was himself slain by the youngest, Ea.

Below: the emasculation of Uranus. The Greek creation myth has many aspects of the old Babylonian creation epic. It too begins with chaos, from which comes Ge, the earth mother, and from her Uranus, who becomes her husband and deals savagely with the children of their union. Eventually the young gods rebelled and Cronus, unmanning his father with a sickle, takes his position as supreme god.

he resolved to kill them. But the gods found out about his intentions and the leader among them, Ea, devised a plan to kill Apsu and carried it out successfully. Ea then settled down to a peaceful life with his wife Damkina, and of their union was born Marduk, "the wisest of the wise, most knowing of the gods, the Lord himself."

The goddess Tiamat, meanwhile, was angry that Apsu had been supplanted by Ea, and she planned revenge. She, the personification of the sea and the original chaos, spawned a brood of terrible monsters, the firstborn of which, Kingu, she made her husband. Then she gathered them all together for a great battle against the gods. In an early skirmish the minor god Anu was defeated by Tiamat, so the elders among the gods called on Marduk to lead the fight against her. He agreed, on condition that he should be supreme among the gods if he defeated Tiamat. A titanic struggle, described vividly in the epic, ended with Marduk's victory and Tiamat's death. Marduk took the defeated goddess's body and split it "like a shellfish" into two halves, one of which he suspended above the other, thus creating heaven and earth. Then, because he was now supreme god and his word unalterable law, Marduk proceeded to dictate the stations and motions of the stars, the sun, and the moon, and when the universe was created he had the idea of creating man as a servant for the gods. To accomplish this he needed some raw material. The captive Kingu, the monstrous son and husband of Tiamat, was brought before Marduk and the gods bound and

The Greek Myths

Left: the birth of Aphrodite, goddess of love and beauty, part of a Greek relief of around 460 B.C. showing two nymphs helping Aphrodite from the sea. According to the 8th-century Greek poet Hesiod, Aphrodite sprang from drops of blood or seed that fell into the sea from the wound of Uranus.

held him while Marduk "slashed the arteries of his blood and with his blood created mankind."

In the *Enuma Elish* we find elements of both the second and third of Joseph Campbell's categories. From the union of Tiamat and Apsu the first gods come into being, and then from the slain body of the goddess Tiamat the warrior-god Marduk creates heaven and earth. So Tiamat, the great primeval goddess is despised and regarded as the personification of chaos and the mother of monstrosities, but she is still credited with power and acknowledged as something to be feared and overcome. What we have in this Babylonian Creation epic is an allegory of man's conquest of nature and his establishment of order in the world. It has some obvious parallels with the Book of Genesis, but its closest correspondences are with Greek mythology. The 8th-century Greek poet Hesiod, who attempted to solve conflicting accounts of the Greek gods in his *Theogany*, left an account of the Greek creation myths.

According to Hesiod, in the beginning there was only open and empty space. Then appeared the first divinity, Gaea, the earth goddess, who is addressed by the poet as "the deep-breasted." She was followed by Eros, representing the force of attraction that brings things together. Through the influence of Eros Gaea produced Uranus, the sky god with his crown of stars, and from the mating of the earth goddess and the sky god were born the 12 Titans, followed by the three one-eyed Cyclopes and three monsters. Uranus was horrified with his offspring and shut them away in the depths of the earth, which made Gaea so angry that she plotted with her son Cronus, the last-born of the Titans, to mutilate Uranus while he slept. Using a sickle, the son emasculated the father and threw his bleeding genitals into the sea. He then liberated the other Titans and the work of creation proceeded apace. But an oracle had predicted that Cronus would be supplanted by one of his children, so he tried to preserve his position by swallowing each child as it was born. His wife, Rhea, managed to bear a son in secret, however, and gave him to their mother, Gaea, to bring up. The son was Zeus, who when he had attained manhood drove Cronus from the sky and imprisoned him in a region beneath the earth and the sea, first making him

Above: Cronus was worried by an oracle that predicted that he, too, would be supplanted by one of his own children. To preserve his position Cronus swallowed each of his children as his wife Rhea gave birth. When the youngest, Zeus, was born Rhea gave Cronus a stone to swallow and reared Zeus in secret.

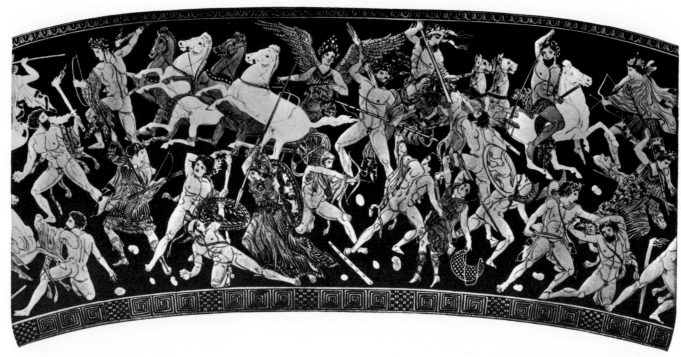

Above: part of a Greek wine jar from the 4th century B.C. depicting the war between the Titans and the Olympians. In the center is Zeus about to strike a Titan with his thunderbolt. Zeus was the youngest of the supreme god Cronus' children and the only one to survive being eaten by their father. With his mother Rhea's help Zeus gave Cronus a potion that made him disgorge his five other children who now joined Zeus against their father and the old Titan gods. The Titans were eventually defeated after a 10-year war. Some scholars see this myth as reflecting the age of conquest and the great tribal migrations on earth. Zeus, the sky god, the cloud-gatherer, is not a creator-god, but a warrior god who seized the sky kingdom from Cronus and rules the other gods as a high king rules his vassals.

disgorge the gods, his children, whom he had swallowed. But now the brothers of Cronus, the Titans, became jealous of Zeus and the new generation of gods, and a mighty war was waged that resulted in the defeat of the Titans. This was followed by another war against a race of Giants who had sprung from the earth where the blood of the mutilated Uranus had fallen. The Giants attacked the home of the gods, Mount Olympus, with fury, tearing up mountains and piling them one upon the other in order to reach the summit of Olympus, but they too, in turn, were eventually vanquished by the gods. Gaea, the earth mother, would not accept the defeat of her children, and in a final attempt to overcome Zeus she produced a terrifying 100-headed monster, Typhoesus, who was taller than the tallest mountain. At the sight of the monster all the gods except Zeus trembled with fear and fled. Zeus came off worst in the first round of the struggle with Typhoesus, but he finally overcame the monster with his thunderbolts and crushed Typhoesus beneath Mount Etna in Sicily.

There is much in this saga that echoes the Babylonian Creation Epic. While the primeval male god, Apsu, planned to murder his children, his Greek counterpart, Uranus, imprisoned his. Apsu was killed by his son, Ea, and Uranus was mutilated by his son, Cronus, and both of these were in turn usurped by their sons. In both mythologies there is an original great female goddess (Tiamat and Gaea) who attempts to resist the establishment of the new order and who breeds monsters in order to help her to attain her end, and in both cases the monster is defeated by the god-hero, Marduk or Zeus.

These myths are a symbolic account of how order originally emerged, by degrees and after many struggles, out of chaos. The mythologies look back to a time when the elements were wild and unpredictable, when the earth heaved, the mountains quaked or crumbled or hurled volcanic materials out of their depths, and the seas seethed and swelled in tumult. Aspects of the rebellious elements are represented by the titans, giants, or monsters, and the elements themselves by the sea- and earth-goddesses, and the stories tell of the ultimate triumph over them of the shining god-hero figures, bringers of harmony and law.

If we regard these myths in the context of the change-over from the hunter-gatherer to the herd-raising, pastoral social order, we see that they express the opposite attitude to the one found in Genesis, for they represent the change as a positive thing, an advance in civilization, an overcoming of lawlessness and an establishing of the foundations of orderly government. They and Genesis agree on one point, though: the degrading of the female as the representative or the bringer of disorder.

The female doesn't get much credit in early Egyptian mythology, either. According to the Pyramid Texts, written about 2400 B.C., which record the teachings of the priesthood of the city of Heliopolis, the Egyptian center of sun-worship, there was a time when nothing existed except boundless water and enveloping darkness. Then the water began to subside and a small hill appeared that afforded a foothold for the sun-god Atum-

Gods and Giants

Below: the monster Typhoesus who was produced by the original great earth mother Gaea. He had 100 dragons' heads issuing from his shoulders and his eyes breathed fire. Zeus overcame the monster and buried him beneath Mount Etna.

Above: a 5th-century bronze figure of Zeus with his thunderbolt. Zeus is thought of as one of the best examples of a sky god and belongs firmly to the stage of man's development that ascends over the female and reduces her to the bringer of chaos and disharmony.

Creation Myths of the Egyptians

Right: an ancient Egyptian painting shows the primordial ocean Nun raising the boat of day with the sun god Atum in the form of a scarab beetle rolling before him the ball of the sun. According to Egyptian creation myths Atum was the first god to emerge from the chaotic wastes of Nun. He appeared on a hill (on which was later built the temple and city of Heliopolis—the "City of the Sun"). After creating himself, Atum's next act was to create further gods. As he was without a mate, he produced his offspring from his own semen. In this way he created Shu, god of air, and Tefnut, a female god to be Shu's wife. So, according to the ancient Egyptian Pyramid texts, creation began.

Khepera. In time the hill became the site of the temple of Heliopolis. The sun-god Atum then created the twins Shu and Tefnut from his own semen. According to another version in the Pyramid Texts, he created the male and female twins Shu and Tefnut from the spittle of his mouth. They in turn begat the sky-goddess Nut and the earth-god Geb (in most other mythologies there is an earth goddess and a sky god) who completed a pantheon of nine divinities by producing two sets of opposed twins, Isis and Osiris and Nephthys and Set. The motif of the physical act of separation of earth from sky is found here, though. A papyrus sketch shows the air-god Shu raising the sky-goddess Nut from the embrace of the earth-god Geb.

A large basalt stone found on an Egyptian beach was sent to the British Museum in 1805. In the preface to its hieroglyphic text it states that the slab is a copy, made in the 8th century B.C. by order of the pharaoh Sabakos of an ancient document that had been "devoured by worms." The text expounds the teaching of the priesthood of Memphis, a neighbor city of Helipolis, and it challengingly exalts the god Ptah above Atum, stating that whereas Atum created the nine gods of Heliopolis from his own

body, Ptah created by "pronouncing of every thing its name." It maintains that everything came into existence through Ptah's "heart's thought and tongue's command," and in this it anticipates by some 2000 years the account of God's creation in the first chapter of Genesis. Furthermore, the text states that Ptah "was satisfied when he had made all things and every divine word," just as the God of the Book of Genesis was when he surveyed his creation and "saw that it was good."

There is no account of the creation of man in the Pyramid Texts or the recorded Memphite teaching, and the only indication we have of how the Egyptians conceived of this event is on a low relief sculptured monument to Amenhotep III (1405–1370 B.C.), where the god Chnum is shown fashioning the infant king and his double on a kind of potter's wheel, and the goddess Hathor is animating him with the *ankh*, the symbol of life. This also is reminiscent of the Genesis account of the creation of man: "God formed man of the dust of the ground, and breathed into his nostrils the breath of life." In fact there are so many parallels between the Egyptian and Hebrew myths of creation that we must conclude that the former influenced the latter, which would not be surprising since the nomadic Hebrew tribes were long held captive in Egypt.

It is not easy to be sure whether correspondences between the creation myths from the Near and Middle East are due to the diffusion of cultures throughout those areas or arise because a concept is *archetypal*. Archetypal concepts and images are ones that arise spontaneously in the human mind and are found widely distributed among cultures that have had no direct contact with each other. The Pyramid Texts' account of the act of creation from a god's semen is an archetypal concept, for instance. It is a symbolic representation of an idea that we also find in Indian scriptures: that in the beginning God poured himself physically into his creation. In Eastern religions significant consequences follow from this idea that identifies God with his creation, just as they do in Western religions from the

Above: the separation of earth and sky. To the right stands Shu, the air god, who raises the sky goddess Nut from the embrace of the earth god Geb.

Below: the Egyptian creator-god Chnum fashioning man on his potter's wheel while the goddess Hathor (standing behind his chair) brings the figure to life. This relief from a monument to the Pharoah Amenhotep III is the only Egyptian reference to the creation of man, who seems to have been created solely to provide temples and offerings for the gods.

opposite idea that he is distinct from it and that the act of creation was not physical but mental.

The idea of creation from semen spilt upon the earth is found in a hymn in the 3000-year-old Hindu *Rig Veda*. The end of the hymn declares: "Heaven is my father, the engenderer. . . . My mother is this wide earth, my close kin." So we are back with the familiar myth of the coupling of the sky god and the earth goddess.

In the *Upanishads*, sacred essays composed between the 6th and 8th centuries B.C., the imagery of the *Rig Veda* is elaborated upon and developed philosophically. One of them contains the most delightful of all creation myths:

"In the beginning, this universe was soul (*atman*) in the form of the Man (*Purusha*). He looked around and saw nothing other than himself. Then, at first, he said 'I am,' and thus the word 'I' was born." Then suddenly Purusha was afraid, but he reasoned that as nothing existed except himself, there was nothing to fear. Then he felt lonely and "lacked delight," and as "he was of the same kind and size as a man and woman closely embracing," he divided himself into two parts, and from the later sexual union of these two parts mankind was produced. But then the female felt the shame of incest and reflected, "How can he unite with me, who am produced from himself," She decided to hide and became a cow, but Purusha "became a bull and united with her, and from this all the cattle were born." Then she became a mare, he a stallion; she an ass, he a donkey; she a sheep, he a ram; and so on until they had "poured forth all pairing things, down to the ants." Then Purusha had a novel thought: "I, actually, am creation, for I have poured forth all this."

The idea of a Primal Being as an androgyne (male and female combined) and of creation proceeding from the separation of the two parts is a variant of another creation myth of the *Rig Veda*, in which Purusha is sacrificed and dismembered and from his parts both the physical universe and the social order are formed. Mircea Eliade, the Romanian-born historian of religions, has remarked on the extremely wide distribution throughout the world of this theme of the creative violent death, the sacrifice of a living being so that "the life concentrated in one person overflows that person and manifests itself on the cosmic or collective scale." He specifies some variations on the theme: "A single being transforms itself into the Cosmos, or takes multiple re-birth in a whole vegetable species or race of mankind. A living 'whole' bursts into fragments and disperses itself in myriads of animated forms. In other terms, here we find the well-known cosmogonic pattern of the primordial 'wholeness' broken into fragments by the act of Creation."

This widely distributed myth corresponds with one of the main theories of the origin of the universe held by modern astronomers, the so-called "big bang theory." The significance of it in the context of religion, however, is that it implies that the divinity is at one with his creation. Whether the god pours himself into his creation with sexual exuberance or is dismembered and his parts distributed as the component elements of the universe and its life, the consequence is that he is an inseparable part of all that has been created, and can be sought and found both in man himself and in the physical world. It is in fact only

Below: 18th-century popular religious painting from India of a half-male half-female deity, identified as Shiva and Parvati. The idea of the first being as composite male and female (an androgyne) is contained in Hindu creation myths of the Upanishads. The androgyne is known to scholars as an *archetypal* concept, that is, an idea or image that arises spontaneously in the human mind all over the world among cultures that have no direct contact with each other. In some myths creation comes about from the separation of the two parts of an androgyne; in others, creation comes about from the dismemberment of a primal god. In both, god is identical with his creation.

in the religions of Semitic origin, Judaism, Christianity, and Islam, that we find the idea of a creator distinct from his creation, of God set completely apart from the world. This is the fundamental difference that lies at the heart not only of the creation myths of East and West, but also of their religions, their arts, their psychology, and their attitudes to nature. Western theologians have scorned as primitive pantheism belief in a god that exists only as long as he can be comprehended, but throughout the centuries this conception of the deity has kept creeping back in various heretical forms of Christianity and in art and literature inspired by Christianity, just as the religion of the original goddess-mother, who had been defamed and defeated by her sons in the patriarchal creation myths, comes back in occasional outbursts of Mariolatry—that is, excessive veneration of the Virgin Mary.

Another worldwide archetypal concept is that of the origin of the universe as an egg—the cosmogonic egg. Mircea Eliade has traced it in ancient Indian, Polynesian, Indonesian, Iranian, Phoenician, Greek, Scandinavian, South American, and Japanese mythologies. The Japanese creation myth, in fact, has many motifs in common with the myths so far considered that it will be useful briefly to summarize it in order to illustrate how similar ideas arise in quite unconnected cultural contexts.

The ancient Japanese heaven and earth divinities, Izanagi and Izanami, were said to have been originally intermingled, making up a chaos in the shape of an egg. In the middle of the egg was a germ, which in time became a reed, around which an island gradually formed. From this reed the first three celestial gods

The Myth of the Cosmogonic Egg

Below: an 18th-century Indian painting of the primary divisions within the fertilized "world egg"—the cosmogonic egg. Although the idea of the cosmos starting in the shape of an egg is found worldwide, there are many different versions of how the universe and the world were created from the egg.

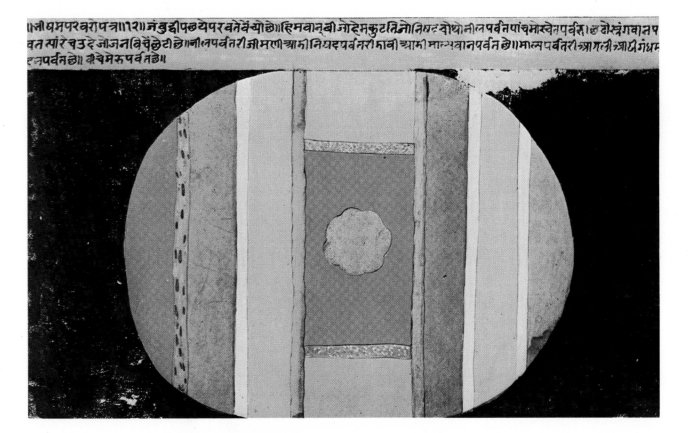

Above: a late-19th-century Japanese illustration of the sky god Izanagi and the earth goddess Izanami. They separated out from the cosmic egg and are seen on the "floating bridge of heaven." The sky god plunges a jeweled spear into the waters of chaos and stirs until the waters thicken and congeal into an island. On this island, the "central pillar of earth," the two gods performed the ritual of marriage and from their union all the gods were created.

were born, and at the same time the original divinities became separated into heaven and earth and manifested themselves in human form: Izanagi as man and Izanami as woman. These beings were instructed by the celestial gods to complete the Creation, and from their union came first the whole Japanese archipelago and then a host of gods. The last born of the gods was Fire, and in bearing him Izanami's womb was burned and she died; while in her death throes she gave birth to the gods of water and agriculture. She then descended beneath the earth and Izanagi went to search for her, as Orpheus sought Euridice in the Greek myth. When he found her she was in a state of decomposition, so he fled. As he emerged from the earth he sealed the chasm with a huge rock, and then went back to heaven. So earth and heaven were finally completely separated, and earth became the realm of the great goddess.

If, as it seems, the older creation myths tend to exalt the function of the female and the later ones that of the male, and that this change is accompanied at the same time by the historical change from the nomadic to the agricultural and finally to a city-dwelling way of life, then the question arises as to whether these myths do not tell us more about the development of the world and of man in historical times than about their origins in primordial times. Is there, in fact, anything to learn about the Creation from them, or must they be dismissed as mere imaginings, or rationalizations from hindsight. Must we turn to science for enlightenment?

The sensible answer to this question is that mythology has a great deal to teach scholars about what men throughout the ages have thought about the subject of the Creation. Science, too, certainly has something to say and should be matched against what we learn from mythology.

All myths look backward to a time before creation when there existed only composite matter, the most common symbol for which was water—which agrees with the scientific evolutionists' claim that life originated in the sea. The basic question, then, is how this original composite matter became differentiated, and to explain this, mythology puts forward the idea of a spontaneous division within the original unified matter into two opposite but complementary principles, which is what microscopic science has observed occurs in the process of *mitosis*, in which a single cell divides and becomes two. In mythology this division has two aspects: into male and female as generative principles on the one hand, and into heaven and earth on the other, and the two aspects are often combined in the symbolism of the sky god and the earth goddess. In many myths the separation is portrayed as a violent act, a tearing apart. There is often violence, too, in the process of order emerging from or being imposed upon chaos. It is a symbolism that could equally well refer to events of geological time on earth or to the violence involved in establishing harmony and the rule of law in human societies.

When they come to man, mythologies generally agree in regarding him as created out of the substance of the earth itself, but they differ on the question of the portion of divinity that he has in him. The later mythologies of the patriarchal societies show a concern for explaining the origins of good and evil in the world, particularly in man. In the creation myth of the Zoroastrians—named for the 6th-century B.C. Persian priest Zoroaster—for instance, the wise Lord Ahura Mazda, is opposed by the Evil One, Angra Mainyu, who creates an imperfection in every creation of Ahura Mazda's, and although the first man, Gayomart, remains incorruptible, his offspring succumb to the Evil One's guile, and through their fall the Evil One manages to introduce himself into human nature as he has into all other aspects of creation.

This myth has much in common with that of the Fall of Man in the second chapter of Genesis. In both myths there appears to be a strong element of speculation about the origins of things based of facts available in the present observable world. It cannot be otherwise of course, unless man is to receive a direct revelation of the origins of things from outside his experience. Or unless the archetypes of man's collective unconscious, as projected into his mythologies, contain truths about the origins of things that have been preserved in the racial memory. That may be; it is also possible that the general view of the Creation as found in the myths comes very close to the truth.

Japanese and Persian Myths

Below: the Temptation of Man in Zoroastrian creation myth depicted in a Persian manuscript of the 14th century A.D. According to the beliefs taught by this ancient Persian religion the god of Evil, Angra Mainyu, plans revenge on the god of good and wisdom, Ahura Mazda. This he does by tempting Mashye and Mashyane, the father and mother of the human race. Through their succumbing to evil, wickedness was introduced into the world.

Chapter 2
Gods of Good and Evil

Most primitive religions see their gods as all-powerful and, if not malevolent, at least to be placated. Even the more sophisticated religions still have to find some way of accounting for evil and the wretchedness of the human condition. Generally, the spirit of evil is personified—the Egyptian Hathor, the Hindu Kali, the Christian Satan, the Buddhist Mara, the Moslem Iblis—the range is wide and fascinating, but the principle is the same. Here then is a far-ranging examination of the place that evil occupies in mankind's long relationship with his gods.

Osiris, the fourth of the divine pharaohs, was a wise and good ruler who civilized Egypt, giving its people agricultural know-how, just laws, and a formalized religion. During the 28th year of his reign he journeyed abroad to spread his principles of wise government. On his return his brother Set gave a banquet, in the course of which he gave orders for a beautifully ornamented chest to be brought into the room. His guests all admired the marvelous creation, and, as if spontaneously and as a party jest, Set promised to give it to anyone present whose body fitted exactly into it. One after another the guests lay down in the chest, but none fitted it exactly. Osiris was the last to try, and he did fit the chest, for in fact Set had had it secretly made to Osiris's measurements. Set had long been jealous of his elder brother and secretly aspired to the throne. While his brother was abroad he had recruited 72 fellow conspirators, who were all present at the splendid returning-home banquet. As soon as Osiris lay in the chest they rushed forward, closed the lid, nailed it down and sealed it by pouring molten lead over it. Then they took the chest down the Nile to the sea, where they dumped it.

The story so far is of a squalid political murder like something thought up by a Renaissance prince following the unscrupulous principles of Macchiavelli, the 15th-century Italian statesman. The difference, however, is that Osiris and Set were the first and second sons of Geb and Nut, the earth-god and the sky-goddess, and the outcome of the story, as befits one dealing with the

Opposite: Osiris, firstborn son of the sky god and earth goddess, is the god who brought civilization to the Egyptian people. He is seen here holding the crook and flail, traditional emblems of Egyptian royalty. His brother Set, by a trick, sealed him in a casket and threw it in the sea and so claimed Osiris' throne for himself.

activities of gods, is appropriately marvelous.

The chest was carried across the sea to the Phoenician city of Byblos, where the waves cast it ashore and it lodged in the branches of a tamarisk tree, which then grew so rapidly that soon the chest was enclosed in its trunk. One day the king of Byblos had the immense tree cut down and used the trunk as a prop for the roof of his palace. Soon the king found that he had an extra benefit from the giant trunk, for it gave off an exquisite scent.

When Osiris's sister-wife, Isis, heard what had happened to her husband, she wandered all over Egypt in search of the chest. Eventually news of the wonderful tamarisk trunk at Byblos reached her, and she immediately understood its significance. Isis went to Byblos, where she was engaged by the queen, Astarte, as nurse to her newborn son. One day she was discovered by the queen bathing the baby in flames, which was part of a ritual to make the child immortal, but the mother was understandably alarmed, and Isis had to reveal that she was really a goddess and explain her reason for being at Byblos. She was given the tamarisk trunk, and from it she took the chest containing Osiris's body, which she then took back to Egypt and hid in a swamp.

Set, now at last the pharaoh, by chance found the hidden chest while out hunting, and in order to get rid of the body of Osiris for

Above: Isis, the sister of Osiris and chosen by him to be his queen. She is depicted here holding a sistrum, a ritual object in the form of a musical instrument, which was used to drive away evil spirits.

Right: Isis, helped by her sister Nephthys, restores her husband Osiris to life. According to one version of the myth Isis recovered her husband's body after he had been entombed in a casket by his brother Set, and she hid it in a swamp. Set, however, discovered her hiding place and dismembered the body of Osiris and scattered it throughout the land. The faithful Isis recovered the pieces and reunited them and brought the body back to life long enough for her to conceive a son to avenge his father.

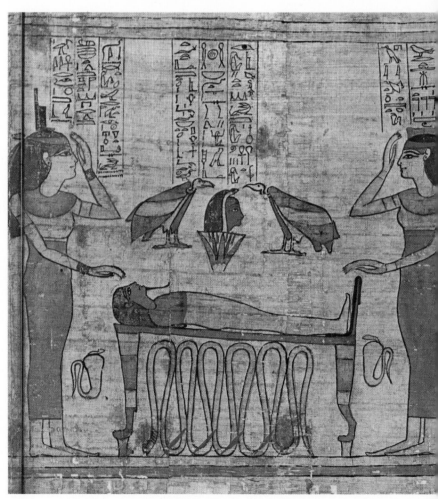

good he dismembered it and scattered it in 14 pieces far and wide throughout his lands. Once again Isis went on to a patient search and eventually recovered all the parts of Osiris's body, which she then reconstituted and by magical means brought him back to life for a short time after which he went down to the underworld to become ruler of the kingdom of the dead. Isis bore Osiris a posthumous son, Horus, who, though frail at birth, grew up protected by his mother's sorcery and instructed by the ghost of his father in the use of weapons, so that when he reached manhood he could wage war on and overthrow his uncle Set.

That is the bare skeleton of the Osirian legend, which was at the heart of ancient Egyptian religion. It was a legend that could be interpreted on several levels. Osiris is associated with a primitive vegetation god, repeatedly reborn as the crops are each year. He is also associated with the Nile, which regularly floods and fertilizes the plains of Egypt (which are represented by Isis); with the sun, which daily rises and sets; and in later Egyptian mythology he changed from being the god of the underworld to becoming the greatest of the gods who could confer upon his devotees the gift of eternal life.

As Osiris took on the characteristics of other gods to become the personification of good, so Set became the personification of evil. Originally Set was a god associated with the desert and with

The Legend of Osiris and Set

Below: bronze statuette of the 3rd–4th centuries B.C. of the goddess Isis holding her infant son Horus. Isis brought Osiris' son up in secret so that he would eventually avenge his father's murder by his uncle Set.

The Osiris Cult

Below: a "corn Osiris," symbol of the resurrection of the pharaohs, from the tomb of the pharaoh Tutankhamen. The cult of Osiris was one of the oldest and most popular in ancient Egypt and he symbolized a theme found in many religions—the dying and the rising god.

Right: Set, the brother of Osiris, as the personification of evil. He is seen here in the form of Apophis, the "dragon of darkness" that daily threatens the sun god with extinction. The goddess Tefnut, in the form of a lioness in this Egyptian papyrus illustration of around 1300 B.C., is seen severing Apophis' head.

the violent aspects of nature. Then he became identified with animals into which it was believed that the spirits of evil had sought refuge from the conquering Horus: the ass, the hippopotamus, the boar, the crocodile, and the scorpion. He also manifested himself as Apophis, the dragon of darkness that every day menaced the life of the sun-god. He became the eternal adversary, the god of death standing in opposition to Osiris, the Lord of life.

This polarization of the gods into personifications of good and evil is found in most of the mythologies and religions of the world. Hinduism, however, has a unique variation of the theme, in that the two opposites are often embodied in one god, who on different occasions manifests different aspects of himself. The entire Hindu mythology emphasizes the way good and evil, creation and destruction, light and dark, life and death complement each other.

The greatest Hindu scripture is the 3rd-century B.C. poem, the *Bhagavad-Gita* (Song of the Blessed One). The poem takes the form of a dialogue between a prince, Arjuna, and his charioteer, who he discovers is Krishna, an incarnation of the great god Vishnu, in disguise. The dialogue takes place on the eve of a battle that Arjuna is reluctant to take part in, for the thought of the slaughter that will result appals him. When he realizes the identity of his charioteer, Arjuna asks the god to reveal his true self. Vishnu-Krishna agrees to do so, and Arjuna is overwhelmed by a vision of the splendor, greatness, and benevolence of the

creator of the universe. But he feels that the god is not revealing himself in his entirety, and begs him to do so. In spite of a warning that he should not ask for this, he insists, and the vision he experiences strikes terror into him. He sees all created things going to destruction in the multiple and awful mouths of Vishnu, and he cries out:

Thy mighty form with many mouths beholding,
O mighty-armed, with eyes, arms, thighs, and feet,
With many bellies, and many dreadful fangs,
The worlds all tremble, even as I do also.

Then Vishnu explains:

Know I am Time, which makes the worlds to perish,
When ripe, and come to bring on them destruction.

In Hinduism, then, as well as the Creator being integral with his creation—a part of every aspect of existence—Arjuna's vision shows that he is also ambivalent, the Destroyer as well as the Creator, and in his role as Destroyer he is identified with Time. The thinking behind this idea is fairly sophisticated, and

Above: an illustration inspired by the great religious epic of Hinduism the *Bhagavad-Gita*. The poem is written in the form of a dialogue between a prince, Arjuna, and his charioteer, who he discovers is Krishna, the great god Vishnu in disguise. Arjuna begs Vishnu to reveal himself in all his glory. Vishnu allows Arjuna to see him in his splendor as the creator of the universe. Arjuna, at the left of the picture, is deeply impressed by the cosmic vision. He feels, nevertheless, that Vishnu has not revealed all. Although warned not to request the final revelation, he persists and is shown Vishnu as the great destroyer Time.

Kali, Goddess of Destruction

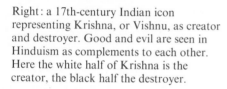

Right: a 17th-century Indian icon representing Krishna, or Vishnu, as creator and destroyer. Good and evil are seen in Hinduism as complements to each other. Here the white half of Krishna is the creator, the black half the destroyer.

is a far cry from primitive man's identification of evil with the violent and destructive forces of nature. Good and evil are two sides of the same coin, interdependent and inseparable in anything that exists in time; and because in time the Creation-Destruction-re-Creation cycle is unalterable and endlessly repeated, the Destroyer is as important and as deserving of worship as the Creator. Whereas in primitive religion people sought to appease the gods of destruction, the Hindu celebrates them as aspects of the supreme God.

The Sanskrit word for "time" is *kala*, and the feminine form of the word is *kali*, which is the name of the most awesome goddess in the Hindu pantheon. Kali, who is also known as the "black mother," is the goddess of destruction, and she is usually represented as a woman of very dark complexion, with wild flowing hair and with four arms. She carries a sword in one hand, a severed head in a second, a third is raised in a gesture of peace and with the other she encourages her worshipers. Adorned with a necklace of human heads, a girdle of two rows of hands, and two corpses as ear-pendants, she has hideous fangs and her tongue hangs out to lick up the world. She is often depicted as trampling on the body of the god Shiva, her husband, and there is a story behind this convention. Kali once fought a battle with the chief of the army of demons, Raktavija. She attacked him with terrible weapons, but from every drop of his blood that she shed a thousand giants sprang up to join the fight against her. She could only defeat Raktavija finally by drinking all his blood. When she had done so, she performed a wild dance of joy which made the whole earth quake. The gods sent her husband to beg

Left: an 18th-century Punjabi artist's impression of Kali, goddess of destruction. The word "kali" is the feminine form of the Sanskrit word "kala" ("Time"). The goddess is always depicted as demonic. She is seen here seated in intercourse on the body of her husband Shiva, who she trampled to death in a frenzied dance.

Below: a 15th–16th-century Indian bronze statuette of Shiva, a god of good and evil seen as King of Dancers. He dances in a circle of flame, his upright hand holding the drum by whose rhythm everything is created. His upper left hand holds the fire by which all is consumed. He is dancing on the body of Forgetfulness. His raised foot signifies Release.

her to stop, but in her frenzy Kali did not recognize Shiva, and she hurled him down among the dead and trampled on his body.

For all her ferocity and repulsiveness, Kali is a popular goddess in the Hindu religion, and she inspires devotion as well as fear. Her worshipers are not seeking to appease her, but to acknowledge how intimately linked with life and creation are the principles of time and destruction.

Shiva, who tried to stop the goddess's dance with such calamitous results to himself, is a god of both good and evil. The cult of Shiva absorbed the traditions of the god Rudra, who in the *Vedas* (the oldest sacred books of India, composed between 1000 and 600 B.C.) personified the destructive powers of nature. In later traditions Shiva's symbol was the *lingam*, or phallus, representing generation, abundance, life, power. And many of

Below: an 18th-century Indian painting depicting "The Churning of the Ocean of Milk." The gods—the Devas—are on the left and hold the tail of the serpent, while the demons—the Asuras—hold the head. The serpent is coiled around a mountain resting on the god Vishnu in the form of a tortoise. The tug of war between demons and gods produces a churning action that thickens the milky ocean and turns it into ambrosia, the food of the gods and a symbol of all that is good in life.

the legends about him emphasize his devotion, his self-sacrifice, and his asceticism. But on the other hand he appears sometimes as a ghoulish god, as in the following description spoken by Daksha, one of the lords of creation, whose daughter Sati had been enticed by Shiva: "It was against my will that I gave my daughter to this sullied personage. . . . He frequents horrible cemeteries, accompanied by crowds of spirits and ghosts, looking like a madman, naked, with disheveled hair, wearing a garland of skulls and human bones . . . a lunatic beloved by lunatics, lord of the demons whose nature is wholly obscure." Again, in the cave-paintings at Elephanta, Shiva is portrayed with many arms, holding in his several hands a sword, a human figure, a basin of blood, and a sacrificial bell, and with two other hands he is extinguishing the sun. No wonder early Christian missionaries in India saw Shiva as the Devil and Kali as his female counterpart; but when Europeans began to study the Hindu culture in depth it became clear that such simple parallels could not be drawn. The ambivalent Shiva, it seemed, was a concept that represented a profound insight into reality.

Daksha's ghoulish description of Shiva is in his incarnation as lord of demons. Hinduism has a rich demonology, which is different from the Christian one in that the line between gods (or angels in Christianity) and demons is not easily drawn. The gods are called the "Devas" and the demons the "Asuras," and the two are supposed to be deadly enemies. On the other hand, one of the supreme gods, Varuna, is sometimes referred to as an "Asura" and in one of the oldest myths, which tells the story of how the first ocean, "the sea of milk," was churned to obtain ambrosia from it, the gods have to ask the demons to help them with the work, and while it lasts Devas and Asuras are in harmony. But when the ambrosia is finally extracted gods and demons quickly start fighting and mountains and thunderbolts are hurled about. In the end the gods rout the demons and return in noisy triumph to the heavens to enjoy their ambrosia, while the demons go into the earth and the ocean.

Although the other major religion of the East, Buddhism, does not have a god in the sense of a suprahuman eternal Being, it does dramatize in its legends the continuing struggle between good and evil. A favorite theme in Buddhist art is the Prince Siddhartha's efforts to attain Buddhahood and the attempts to thwart him by Mara, the Buddhist "lord of demons," whose title is *papman*, "the evil one." The legend states that when Siddhartha sat under the Tree of Wisdom and declared that he would would not rise until he had obtained his utmost aim, the whole world rejoiced, but Mara was afraid. He summoned his three sons, Confusion, Gaiety, and Pride, and his three daughters, Lust, Delight, and Thirst, and told them: "This sage . . . sits yonder intending to conquer my realms. . . . If he succeeds in overcoming me and proclaims to the world the path of final bliss, all this my realm will today become empty." So to distract Siddhartha from his meditation he first sent his daughters, who sang and danced erotically before the sage's eyes, but he remained unmoved, his mind steadily on his pursuit of Enlighten-

Siddartha, the Buddha

Left: part of an Indian stone frieze of around A.D. 150 showing the victorious Buddha enthroned as the "enlightened one." He has just overcome the temptations of Mara, the lord of the demons, and an attack by the evil one's army (symbolized by the fallen soldiers under his throne). Around him are gods, mankind, and nature to witness his enlightenment.

Above: women worship at the shrine of the reclining Buddha in Sri Lanka. Founded some 560 years before Christianity, Buddhism was originally conceived as a religion without a personal concept of God and without any theory of salvation for mankind, only salvation from the continual cycle of rebirth, which is extinction. Eventually Buddhism developed, from a spiritual yearning for extinction by throwing off both suffering and pleasure and avoiding life itself as a source of all evil, into a cult religion of temples, statues, candles, incense, and rich vestments. Buddha himself was translated into a hero figure who, through countering the temptations of the evil Mara, found the path to Enlightenment.

ment. Then Mara called up his army of demons, who swarmed around in numerous grotesque forms, some with the faces of animals, others with multiple limbs or heads, with "protuberant bellies and speckled bellies," with half-mutilated faces and monstrous mouths. The demons clamored around the Tree of Wisdom, threatening and trying to frighten Siddhartha, but he remained resolute in his purpose and Mara finally had to admit defeat. When Siddhartha attained perfect Enlightenment and became a Buddha, he had to choose whether to enter Nirvana at once or to put off his own deliverance so that he could pass on to mankind his knowledge of the causes of suffering and the way of release from it. At this moment of choice Mara intervened again, urging him to enter Nirvana and leave the world, but the Buddha resisted Mara's arguments as he had resisted the lord of demons' delectable daughters and his terrifying demons, and chose to remain on earth and preach the Law.

The theme of the Evil One as the Tempter, who tries to subvert the mission of the man-god, is found in several traditions. The legendary life of the Persian Zoroaster, or Zarathustra, in many ways parallels that of the Buddha as well as that of Jesus Christ. His birth was accompanied by marvels and in his early years his life was in danger because of the fears and jealousies of the priests and followers of the many ancient Persian gods. At the age of 20 he left home to go in search of the man who most followed the paths of moral virtue. After some wanderings, he settled down to seven years of extreme self-denial, abstinence, and religious exercises, living alone in total silence in the depths of a cave. At the age of 30 archangels conferred upon him a revelation that gave him control over the various elements of the universe. He then began a life of wandering and preaching, which eventually made the Evil One, Angra Mainyu, seek him out to protest and attempt to bargain with him.

"Do not destroy my creatures, O holy Zoroaster.... Renounce the good religion of the worshipers of Mazda, and thou shalt gain such a boon as Vadhaghua gained, the ruler of the nations." The offer of worldly power was, of course, one of the temptations that Jesus rejected. Zoroaster's refusal, and his declaration of eternal opposition to the tempter's creation, brought the proud and challenging question: "By whose word wilt thou strike, by whose word wilt thou repel, by whose weapon will the good creatures strike and repel my creation, who am Angra Mainyu?" Zoroaster replied that "the Word taught by Mazda" would be his weapon: "By this Word will I strike, by this Word will I repel, by this weapon will the good creatures strike and repel thee, O evildoer." Agra Mainyu made one final attempt on Zoroaster's uprightness and honesty by sending a demon in the guise of a "golden-bodied, full-bosomed," female who asked for Zoroaster's "companionship, conversation, and cooperation." But Zoroaster recognized the demon for what she was and saw through her seductive charms. He made her turn her back, and: "the fiend turned her back, and she was seen by Zoroaster behind in the groin; and when matter was exuded, it was full of serpents, toads, lizards, centipedes, and frogs."

The Temptation of Zoroaster

Above: a 19th-century engraving of a Zoroastrian priest. Zoroaster was the 6th-century founder of a religion that replaced worship of the many gods of ancient Persia with the worship of a single god, Ahura Mazda, god of purity, truth, and wisdom (though later many of the old gods were incorporated into Zoroastrianism). In the priest's left hand is a bundle of barsom twigs, apparently an essential part of Persian ritual. The book in his right hand is probably the *Vendidad*, the law book setting out the prescribed rites for purification from demonic possession. Zoroastrianism was deeply concerned with the twin concepts of good and evil, which ran through the whole world of gods and men—the constant struggle between Ahura Mazda and Angra Mainyu, the Evil One. Left: a relief from a temple at Persepolis, the ancient capital of the Kings of Persia. It is in the form of a symbol of Ahura Mazda, "the Wise Lord." Mazda became supreme god of the Persian Empire, and Zoroastrianism eventually spread as far as western China in the north, Abyssinia in the south, the Indus River to the east, and the Aegean Sea to the west.

The religion that Zoroaster gave to the world was a new development in the evolution of the world's religions. Whereas earlier religions had just grown, and the multitude of ideas and of divinities in them had often had to undergo drastic changes for the sake of the accommodation, now one man had founded a religion on the idea of good and bad. The earlier stage is represented by the Osiris legend, in which the ideas of good and evil, and of justice and retribution, are superimposed on an ancient fertility myth. They can be seen as having their roots in the processes of creation and destruction in nature. It is in Zoroastrianism that we first find the idea of a cosmic contest between good and evil, and that good and evil existed side by side from the beginning. Consequently Zoroastrianism did not hold out an offer of salvation to man if he fulfilled certain requirements, but instead demanded that he take sides in the cosmic contest, that he actively join with Ahura Mazda to overcome Aingra Mainyu. Most other religions, by contrast, put forward the idea of an original state of goodness, one that man either fell from or had to work toward through spiritual evolutions. Later Zoroastrianism predicted a final and decisive battle between the two forces which would take place after a long struggle that would last for 9000 years, and that the forces of good under Ahura Mazda would ultimately prevail.

This idea of a final cosmic contest is found also in the Book of Revelation in the Bible, and in Teutonic mythology, where the gods and warriors assemble in Valhalla to prepare for the day when the demons and giants of the underworld launch their attack upon the gods. In fact the Zoroastrian concept of evil as a mighty independent uncreated force, unconnected with the known forces of nature, and whose existence confronted man

Above: a copy by a 19th-century artist of a painting from Persepolis depicting the triumph of Ohrmazd (the figure on the right) over Ahriman. After Alexander the Great's conquest of the Persian Empire Zoroastrianism declined until the 9th century A.D. when a new form of it was established with Ohrmazd (the Zoroastrian Ahura Mazda) and Ahriman (Angra Mainyu) as co-equal spirits that had existed from the beginning of time.

Right: the god Mithra slaying the cosmic bull. Mithra, a god of light and the sun, had been repressed by Zoroaster's religious reform but gradually gained in importance as Zoroastrianism waned. He was worshiped as the god who was in perpetual conflict with powers of darkness and had a wide appeal far outside the Persian Empire. By slaying the cosmic bull life was released on earth in great abundance. From the bull's tail ears of corn germinate, from the wound the flowing blood becomes the vine.

Mithra and Mani

Left: the martyrdom of Mani, the
Babylonian founder of the Manichaean
religion, from a 14th-century Persian
manuscript. The flayed body of Mani lies
on the ground; his skin, stuffed with straw,
hangs from a palm tree. Manichaeism
evolved from Zoroastrianism, and taught
that there were two principles—one good
and spiritual, the other bad and material.
Mani, who lived from A.D. 216 to 277,
regarded himself as the last of the prophets
and bringers of salvation after Buddha,
Zoroaster, and Jesus.

with a moral choice, was an immensely important concept in
the history of religious ideas. It was to spread far and wide
throughout the Western world in the ensuing centuries.

Two of the religious cults in direct competition with Christianity in the first four centuries A.D. derived directly from
Zoroastrianism. One was the cult of the sun god Mithra, which
was immensely popular with the soldiers of the Roman armies.
In Mithraism evil was represented as Time and symbolized by a
monstrous being with a human body and a lion's head, and
endowed with wings to signify the flight of time. In the creature's
hands are held a scepter and keys, which represent authority and
destiny. Around its body coils a serpent, symbolizing the tortuous
course of the sun through the zodiac. The monster, which has
many of the attributes of "Time the Destroyer," is associated
with Ahriman (the Zoroastrian Angra Mainyu) who stands in
opposition to Ohrmazd (formerly Ahura Mazda), who represents Eternity. Between these two stands the god Mithra
through whom salvation from the dominion of Time the
Destroyer can be obtained, rather as in Christianity salvation can
be obtained through Jesus Christ.

The second offshoot of Zoroastrianism, Manichaeism, seriously and vigorously rivaled the Catholic Church's missionary
efforts in the early centuries of the Christian era. Its founder,

Yahweh and His Adversary Satan

Mani, was born in Babylonia about A.D. 216, and he claimed that he was the successor of Buddha, Zoroaster, and Christ, each of whom had preached aspects of the faith that he had come to preach in its fullness and purity. Mani's teaching was basically that the material, physical world was under the rule of Ahriman, and therefore evil, and that man's purpose was to rise above it by following a life of self-denial and self-discipline and constant struggle against the Prince of Darkness.

For people in Western cultures, whether they are religious or not, the Bible has been the most influential of the ancient scriptures, and the personification of evil that they are most familiar with is Satan. The name can be traced back to the Hebrew word meaning "to oppose," and means "the Adversary." It is directly related to, and probably also derived from, the Persian Ahriman. The idea of an Adversary to God, who is supreme ruler over the forces of evil, was foreign to the ancient Hebrews and did not enter their religion until after the return from the Babylonian Exile (about 530 B.C.), so it is reasonable to suppose that it was an idea that they acquired from a foreign source during the Exile.

The great theological problem of how to explain the presence of evil in a world created by a good god did not apparently worry the ancient Hebrews. Their god Yahweh was omnipotent, and therefore it followed that things men conceive as evil must be done at his bidding. The account in Chapter 18 of the First Book of Samuel of how Saul, the first king of Israel, had an attack of insanity and tried to murder David mentions "the evil spirit from God" that came upon Saul. The raving king charged around his palace and while David was playing the lyre—as he did each day—Saul took a spear and threw it at David hoping to pin him to the wall. But David managed to evade him. Another

Opposite: David playing the harp for Saul by the 16th-century Dutch painter Lucas van Leyden. An evil spirit from God was said to have come upon Saul who tried to kill David. The doctrine of good and evil so deeply rooted in ancient Persian religious thought gradually made an impact on the Hebrew religion. At first Yahweh was sole Lord and Creator of the Universe who loved righteousness and hated evil-doing. There were, indeed, multitudes of demons, but there was no powerful Evil One to oppose the omnipotent Yahweh. It was after the Babylonian exile that the idea of an all-powerful Adversary of Yahweh developed.

Right: King David of Israel instructing Joab, the commander of his army, to take a census of all the tribes of Israel. The census was considered by many to be an act of tyranny designed to turn the free citizens of Israel into the servants of the state and introduce forced labor. The evil genius behind the idea, however, is given in the second book of Samuel as God himself, whereas a later writer in the first book of Chronicles ascribes the idea to Satan.

DAVID INSTRUCTING JOAB TO NUMBER THE PEOPLE.

Satan and the Fallen Angels

significant example is the story told in the Second Book of Samuel, of how "the anger of the Lord was kindled against Israel, and he moved David against them to say, Go, number Israel and Judah." David obediently took the census, but then Yahweh punished him for doing so by sending a pestilence upon Israel. Seventy thousand men died, the Book relates, and then "when the angel stretched out his hand upon Jerusalem to destroy it, the Lord repented him of the evil." Scholars date the composition of the Second Book of Samuel as early as the 10th century B.C., yet by the 3rd century B.C. when the First Book of Chronicles was composed, the story retold there almost verbatim has a significant change in the opening verse: "Satan stood up against Israel and provoked David to number Israel." Clearly, the later author was embarrassed by the apparent capriciousness of the Almighty in the earlier account, and has made Satan responsible for the idea of the fatal census. The same thing happened with the story of the Fall of Man. In the Book of Genesis there is no mention of Satan, who first appears in the Book of Job—and then not as a wicked spirit. It is only in later Christian theology that the serpent is equated with him.

The most extended treatment of the problem of suffering and evil in the Old Testament is found in the Book of Job. In it a council is held in heaven in which Satan appears as one of the angels or councillors. When God asks him whether he has noticed the incomparable Job, "a perfect and upright man, one that feareth and escheweth evil," Satan replies that Job's uprightness is really due to self-interest and to the fact that in everything he has done he has prospered. To this God says, "Behold, all that he hath is in thy power; only upon himself put not forth thine hand." So the misfortunes and tragedies that Satan heaped upon Job were not willful malevolence on his part but really tests of Job's integrity thought up by Satan on God's instructions and with his consent. Satan is not yet the cosmic

Right: "Satan smiting Job with sore boils," by the English artist and poet William Blake, painted around 1825. Job is the innocent man who is allowed to suffer a series of calamities to prove his loyalty to God. In the biblical story Satan is seen merely as God's agent. It is God who is the real author of his misfortunes.

Adversary, and God is *still* the fount of both good and evil.

There are, in fact, only five references to Satan in the Old Testament itself, and they are brief, but in the writings of the period that were not included in the Bible the concept of Satan was developed in various ways that gave later Christian writers plenty of traditional material to draw upon. The idea of Satan as the fallen angel emerges in the *Book of Enoch*, which was written some time between the 2nd and 1st centuries B.C. In it the curious passage in Chapter 6 of Genesis that tells how the "sons of God saw the daughters of men that they were fair; and they took them wives of all which they chose," is taken as an explanation of how evil came into the world. The angels, the *Book of Enoch* maintains, were being punished for rebellion by being sent to earth, but they only increased their crimes against God by uniting with women and by passing on to them knowledge of occult arts. Other sources develop the idea of a war in heaven and Satan being cast down from heaven to earth, which was later taken up with powerful effect by the author of the New Testament Book of Revelation and by the 17th-century English poet John Milton in his *Paradise Lost*. In the *Book of the Secrets*

Above: *The Fall of the Rebel Angels* by the 16th-century Flemish painter Pieter Brueghel. The story of the fall of the angels appears in the *First Book of Enoch*, a collection of writings from the 2nd–1st centuries B.C. The writer interprets the reference in Chapter 6 of Genesis, to the "Sons of God" who took the daughters of men to wife, as the angels who were driven from heaven. For passing on to humans knowledge to which they were not entitled, the fallen angels were condemned to eternal punishment.

Christ Tempted

Below: *The Three Temptations of Christ* by
the late-15th-century Florentine painter
Sandro Botticelli. According to the Gospel
writers, Satan tempts Jesus at the start of
his public ministry, presenting himself as the
master of the world. Satan, described in
Chapter 10 of Luke's Gospel as "fallen as
lightning from heaven," has no power over
the God-man Jesus. At the top left of
Botticelli's painting: Jesus is tempted to
turn stones into bread, to satisfy his
hunger. Top center: Satan tempts Jesus to
throw himself from a pinnacle of the
Temple to put God to an arbitrary test and
stage a spectacular miracle. Top right:
Satan shows Jesus all the kingdoms of the
world, which he will give him if only Jesus
will fall down and worship him—the
temptation of power unworthily
accomplished. Behind Christ are the Angels
of God who comfort him when he
overcomes all the temptations.

of Enoch, which dates from around the 1st century A.D., the
name Satanial is given to the leader of a host of angels whose
functions are to control the forces of nature and regulate the
stars in their courses. He becomes envious of Adam and seeks
to extend his rule over the world as well. All these writings are
attempts to explain the existence in the world of a power of evil,
an adversary of God, and they all ultimately derive from the
Persian concept of the eternal opposition between Ohrmazd and
Ahriman, the Lords of Light and of Darkness. In a passage in
the *Manual of Discipline*, one of the ancient scrolls found in a
cave at Qumran near the Dead Sea in 1947, the influence of
Zoroastrian belief in two independent divine beings, one good
the other evil, stands out particularly clearly: "In the abode of
light are the origins of truth, and from the source of darkness are
the origins of error. In the hand of the prince of lights is dominion
over all sons of righteousness; in the ways of light they walk.
And by the angel of darkness is all dominion over the sons of
error; and in the ways of darkness they walk. And by the angel
of darkness is the straying of all the sons of righteousness, and
all their sin and their iniquities and their guilt."

It was in Christianity that these streams of thought came
together and the idea of the cosmic Adversary was developed to
the full. Jesus' mission, according to the teaching laid down by
the Church, was to usher in the Kingdom of God, which involved
accomplishing the final overthrow of Satan and his followers. In
the Gospels Satan is personalized, vividly portrayed, and
credited with great powers. In Luke's version of the temptation

of Jesus, the Devil offers him all the kingdoms of the world, saying "All this power will I give thee and the glory of them: for that is delivered unto me; and to whomsoever I will I give it." This implies that Satan is the undisputed lord of this world. In another vivid image of Satan's untiring efforts to undo all the good man does, Jesus represents him as going about sowing weeds among the wheat.

A good deal of Jesus' own work consisted in casting out devils from people possessed, and in the 10th Chapter of Luke's gospel, when his disciples returned from a successful mission they reported to him joyfully, "Lord, even the devils are subject unto us through thy name." Jesus replied to this with a cryptic reference to Lucifer as the fallen angel: "I beheld Satan as lightning fall from heaven."

After Jesus was crucified and his mission had apparently come to a stop, it must have looked to his followers as if Satan had won the great contest. But then along came Saul of Tarsus, later the apostle Paul, a man of ingenious intellect, to carry on the mission and build it into a theology. It was Paul who conceived and propagated the ideas of Jesus as the Savior of mankind, and of his death as a sacrificial triumph. These ideas raised the questions: from what had man been saved? and to what or whom had Jesus been sacrificed? In Chapter 4 of his Epistle to the Galations Paul answered that man was subject to demonic forces: "We . . . were in bondage under the elements of the world" until God sent His Son into the world, tricking the Devil into engineering Jesus' apparent downfall in a manner that would separate men's loyalties from Satan and win them over to the suffering and sacrificed Christ.

These ideas of Paul's became fundamental doctrines of the Christian faith. They were immensely successful in winning converts to the new Christian religion, as was Saint Augustine's later refinement that all men inherited the evil of Adam's original sin and could only be absolved from it by taking part in the atonement of Jesus Christ. Early theologians represented the significance of Christ in the cosmic contest between God and Satan in the simile of God fishing for Satan with the hook of Christ's divinity disguised by and baited with his humanity. But although these images implied that God had triumphed over Satan through Christ, His Satanic Majesty was to lead a very vigorous and prosperous life in the coming centuries of Christian culture. Vivid and enduring testimonies have been created to Satan and his minions' reality, as can be seen in the harrowing paintings of the 15th-century Flemish artist Hieronymus Bosch, the medieval cathedral sculpture with its gargoyles, the Faust legend, the Black Mass and other occult rituals associated with witchcraft, and innumerable works in all the arts, ancient, medieval, and modern. Those who accept reasoning as the supreme authority may scoff at the idea, but the advertised immense sales of a recent book by the American author Hal Lindsey titled *Satan is Alive and Well on Planet Earth* are one indication among many that the concept of a supernatural Adversary is for many people today not only plausible but essential to their understanding of the world and its ways and its possible ultimate fate.

Above: Paul of Tarsus, the one-time persecutor of the followers of Jesus, who became the "Apostle of the Gentiles," by the Italian artist Raphael (1483–1520). He taught (in his Epistles to the Philippians and the Colossians) that Jesus was not only the Christ, or Messiah, the Old Testament prophets foretold, but that he was also the eternal, pre-existent Son of God through whom all things were created. By his death and resurrection Jesus had freed mankind from the dominion of Satan. All who now believed in Jesus the Son of God and chose good instead of evil would rise, too, and enter into the Kingdom of Heaven whose Gates had been unlocked by God's son.

Chapter 3
One God or Many?

The ancient Egyptians and Greeks believed in great hierarchies of gods and goddesses. The Hindus, the Muslims, and the Christians all believe in one God, though many Christians see God as manifested in the Trinity of "three persons"—Father, Son, and Holy Spirit. What is the appeal of many gods rather than one? Does it somehow reflect the inner complexities of man himself? And which belief came first—the belief in one or many? This chapter examines the problem and comes to some unexpected conclusions.

About the year 1370 B.C. an odd-looking young man with a deformed body, an elongated head, and a drooping jaw succeeded his father as pharaoh of Egypt. His strangeness did not end with his physical appearance. He had a strange turn of mind, too. He was a religious genius, and, being well placed to put his ideas into effect, he tried to carry out the most radical reform in religion that the ancient world had known. He tried to make his subjects worship only one god—Aten, the sun-god.

The new pharaoh began his reign with the name Amenhotep, which meant "Amen is satisfied," but he changed it to Akhenaten, which meant "Profitable to Aten." By doing so he offended the powerful priesthood of the god Amen, the former state god, and he then proceeded to add to the offense by having the names of all other gods erased from monuments, closing temples, and sacking priests devoted to cults that he denounced as heretical. Nothing testifies so clearly to the awe with which a pharaoh was regarded and the absoluteness of his power as the fact that Akhenaten was able to impose his will and his strange creed for the duration of his reign.

There would have been nothing unusual in the new pharaoh making his favorite divinity the official state god, and simply demoting Amen. Amen had originally been a local god of the city of Thebes in upper Egypt, and he had risen in prestige and power as the Theban rulers had established their sovereignty throughout Egypt, and eventually throughout neighboring lands

Opposite: an Egyptian engraving from Tell el-Amarna of the 14th-century B.C. pharaoh Akhenaten (right) and his wife Nefertiti. They are presenting offerings to the sun god Aten, represented above them by the disk with 14 rays that end in hands. Behind the queen is probably one of the royal princesses and to the right of the group two stands support bunches of lotus blossoms. Akhenaten was deeply religious and sought single-handed to replace the centuries-old accumulation of many deities with worship of a single universal god, represented by the disk of the sun. Akhenaten's break with tradition had another aim, too. The old priesthood and bureaucracy had become immensely powerful, encroaching on the authority of the pharaoh himself. Akhenaten made the priesthood, temples, and cults of the other gods—particularly of the most powerful, Amen—redundant.

Akhenaten and the Sun God

Below: a commemoration stone in honor of the "Restoration of the Theban Temples." After the death of Akhenaten the young king Tutankhaten ascended the throne. Guided by the court chamberlain, Ay, and the head of the army Horemheb, the nine-year-old pharaoh reverted to the old religion of Egypt dominated by the worship of Amen-Ra, whose temple was at Thebes.

too. Amen was associated with Egypt's greatest era of prosperity and political power, and his priesthood had grown rich on the gifts of pharaohs grateful for the god's support of their political and military enterprises. He had become Amen-Ra, adding to his name the traditional name of the sun-god. It had been standard practice in Egypt for one god to supersede another and to take over his characteristics and sometimes his name. The new pharaoh refused to have anything to do with the practice. He declared that there was only one true god, Aten, and that Amen-Ra was an impostor. So instead of demoting him or assimilating him in accordance with traditional practice, he tried to get rid of him. Akhenaten moved out of Thebes, had a new capital, palace, and temple built about 300 miles to the north of Tell el-Amarna, and settled there spending most of his time in religious devotions. His agents meanwhile ranged the country with hammers and chisels looking for heretical inscriptions to erase. He neglected his army and his empire, he antagonized the old priesthood, he sought to impose on his people an austere belief in a single god instead of the multitude of colorful gods they were used to, and in spite of all this ruled for some 20 years. But that was the end of the religious revolution. When he died, his successor Tutankhaten changed his name to Tutankhamen and moved back to Thebes. Very soon the chisels were at work again, this time erasing inscriptions on monuments to the god Aten.

It is fortunate that some of the works of art of Akhenaten's age survived the destruction, for the pharaoh clearly had unusual ideas about art as well as about religion. There is a flowing and naturalistic line in the portraiture of the age, and instead of being depicted in the stiff poses that were traditional in Egyptian art, and shown engaged in ritual or martial activities, the pharaoh is often seen in intimate domestic situations, such as nursing one of his children. Everywhere there is the great sun-disk, symbol of Aten, emitting rays that end in hands which bestow a blessing or hold the *ankh*, the symbol of life. Religious art was revolutionary too. Traditionally the Egyptian gods were often represented as animals or birds: Horus, for instance, as a hawk and Kheper as a scarab-beetle, and the goddess Hathor as a cow. The traditional priestly hieroglyphic writing is crowded with curious figures with human bodies and animal heads. But there is none of this in the art of Akhenaten's time. No cult-image was permitted in the temple at El-Amarna, and the only symbolic representation of Aten that was allowed was the solar disk with its spreading rays.

Aten was not thought of as a god to be sacrificed to, or petitioned for favors. In the *Hymn to Aten*, a text found on a tomb and composed by Akhenaten himself, Aten is praised as the creator and sustainer of all life, and it is made clear that he is not just the "first among equals" of the Egyptian gods, but is a truly universal god. "All distant foreign countries, thou makest their life also," the *Hymn* declares, and "Thou settest every man in his place, Thou suppliest their necessities." The language of the *Hymn* is ecstatic and lyrical and its sentiments are lofty, and the only thing that jars is the sense of exclusiveness or self-conceit that comes through in the last lines:

Thou art in my heart,
There is no other that knoweth thee

Save thy son Akhenaten.
For thou hast made him wise
In thy designs and in thy might.

This was probably no more than a statement of the traditional Egyptian idea of the pharaoh's unique relationship with the deity, but the picture that emerges of the strange recluse king at El-Amarna, engaged with his queen, the beautiful Nefertiti, in religious observances that were completely new in Egypt and that had almost no following among the ordinary people, a despairing note can be detected in those lines:

There is no other that knoweth thee
Save thy son Akhenaten.

It has often been said that Akhenaten was centuries ahead of his time, and some historians of religion have seen his influence in the later development of the single God of the Hebrews. It is not, however, as simple as that. Certainly his idea of God was more exalted than that held by his contemporaries. Aten was not conceived in human form or with human virtues and vices and worship of the one God was purged of the usual gross superstition, and self-seeking, but it is a mistake to argue from this that

Above: a painted limestone plaque from an altar at Tell el-Amarna showing the pharaoh Akhenaten with his queen and their three daughters in a domestic scene. In Akhenaten's religion, only the king and his family worshiped the god Aten directly while the people worshiped the pharaoh as the god-king, "thy son Akhenaten."

Left: a brown quartzite carving of the head of Queen Nefertiti, wife of the pharaoh Akhenaten, made around 1373–1357 B.C. It is carved in the realistic style adopted during her husband's reign. Her name means "the Beautiful One is come."

How Gods Began?

Akhenaten was the first monotheist the world had known. A careful study of the history of religious ideas shows only too clearly that there is no smooth evolutionary path of ideas. In fact, instead of seeing the growth of religion as a progression from a primitive belief that all visible things possess spirits or souls, through belief in a multitude of gods to the single deity of the "higher" faiths, the puzzling fact that belief in a single, high principled, moral god has been fundamental to many so-called primitive religions. The answer, it seems, is to adopt a psychological instead of an historical-evolutionary view of religious beliefs. Then the puzzlement disappears for belief in a single god is seen as directly allied to a particular type of religious experience—an experience there is no reason to assume that the "savage" mind was closed to, as the Scottish scholar Andrew Lang was to point out.

Before turning to Lang's evidence on primitive belief in a single god the naturalistic-evolutionary view of religion should be looked at and assessed for its credibility and its limitations. The view was put with characteristic incisiveness in 1930 by the American writer H. L. Mencken in his *Treatise on the Gods*. Just as long as things were going well, Mencken maintains, primitive man would have given the gods little thought, but "when thought of them was forced upon him by their own acts, he no doubt regarded them with uneasiness and aversion, as a rat regards cats. When he approached them, either directly or through his priests, it was not to assure them of his admiration or to inquire their wishes, but to get immediate favors. . . . He wanted more blackberries or fewer mosquitoes. He wanted his dead wife to come back, or his living wife to die. . . . He craved protection against falling trees and rocks, against storms and floods, against snakes and venomous insects, against the beasts he hunted, against other men, and, perhaps after a while, against ghosts. Thus his religion was no more than a scheme of propitia-

Above: a medicine man from Dahomey, West Africa. Men approach the "other" world of gods and spirits through particular individuals, some endowed from birth with special powers and an understanding of the forces that aid or harm mankind. They are important, often powerful members of the community.

Right: a medicine man of the Congo with members of his village.

tion, and the first priests who served him were simply champions who professed to know better than he did how to stay the malignancy of evil forces. These forces . . . were the first gods." They were mainly weather gods, deities who manifested themselves as lightning, thunder, flood, wind, and rain, or, at one remove of abstraction, in fire, water, or air, and eventually, Mencken argues, gods began to multiply when different personifications were required for the beneficial or the harmful aspects of these natural forces as they affected human life. Priests eagerly fulfilled the need, for "the more [gods] they had at their command, the better they could meet the demands of any professional call; and the more they had to say about the idiosyncracies of this one or that one, the more entertaining their discourse was, and the higher their repute."

Early man was a hunter, and as the population of the world increased he became also a warrior, and in course of time an agriculturalist, and these developments further swelled the number of gods. Gods to assist in wars and battles, and gods to protect the crops and make the harvests prosper, were required. The deity of crops and harvests was nearly always a female, for

Above: a rainbow in Kenya. It is easy to imagine the effect a rainbow must have had on primitive people especially as it is nearly always connected with life-giving rain. There is much evidence that weather gods were among the earliest deities worshiped by man.

Right: Quetzalcotl, the wind god. His importance to the Aztecs was as "the breath of life," who came to sweep the way for the rains that made the earth fertile.

Below: Olokun, the Benin peoples' god of the sea, who lives in a great palace under the sea and was said to have tried to conquer the earth with a great flood. He is the son of the supreme being Osanobwe. Peoples throughout Africa are remarkably consistent in their beliefs in a supreme being, and in many cases he is associated with rain. Often he is remote and little is known of him and there has grown up a pantheon of lesser gods, and below them spirits and ghosts.

the way woman brought forth children was seen to correspond with the way the earth brought forth food, and so the earth goddess came into being. For a time she was supreme, until the male sun god usurped her. With his supremacy and the cult of fatherhood and male dominance, Mencken maintains, religion took its first step toward monotheism. But: "The concept of a single omnipotent god, reigning in the heavens in solitary grandeur, had to wait for long ages, and when it came in at last it was probably devised, not by theologians, but by metaphysicans. They proved that there could be but one god, not by bringing up any overt evidence to that effect, but simply by appealing to what they conceived to be the logical necessities. The human race, on its more refined and exalted levels, has accepted their proofs with the head, but never with the heart. All the great religions surround their chief deity with lesser presences, some of them potent enough to defy him."

A similar argument to Mencken's had been put some 60 years before in the English anthropologist E. B. Tylor's *Primitive Cults*, published in 1871. Tylor was more specific about the "logical necessities" that led to monotheism, and argued that "the instinctive craving of the mind after simplification and unification of its ideas" caused man by degrees to unite his many gods until eventually he arrived at the idea of one all-powerful, all-seeing, just and righteous Supreme Being, the Lord of Creation, who had laid down the laws of human conduct and supervised their observance. Tylor defined religion as "belief in spiritual beings," and it was he who coined the word "animism" for the belief that individual spirits animated "every nook and hill, every tree and flower, every brook and river, every breeze that blew and every cloud that flecked with silvery white the blue expanse of heaven." Out of this multiplicity of spirits, Tylor demonstrated with formidable scholarship how man, as he progressed from primitivism to civilization, distilled first a hierarchy of godlings and finally the One God.

Tylor's thesis was in line with 19th-century evolutionary theory, but unfortunately it was wrong, and one man who saw

Supreme Beings and the Lesser Gods

Left: a Japanese print of the spirits of the pine tree, Jo and Ubu. Pine trees symbolize fidelity in marriage and there are many Japanese myths of devoted lovers being turned into pine trees. Belief that every tree and flower, brook and river, wind, cloud, and shower was animated with spiritual beings is known as "animism," and has played a part in very many of the cultures so far investigated by historians of religion.

where it was wrong and who was not daunted by Tylor's scholarship was Andrew Lang, who in his book *The Making of Religion*, published in 1898, put forward conclusive anthropological evidence for the view that primitive man was no stranger to the idea of a moral and just Supreme Being. The argument and the data presented by Lang were largely ignored by scholars and there is certainly no evidence that Mencken had come across them when he wrote his *Treatise on the Gods*, but they are crucial to any discussion of the origins and history of religion.

Tylor's entire argument, Lang pointed out, had rested on the idea that primitive peoples thought of their gods as spirits, for they were alleged to have imagined all nature to be animated by spirits and to have reduced this multiplicity to a few deities for practical purposes. But, Lang argued, "there is no reason why we should take it for granted that the earliest deities of the earliest men were supposed by them to be 'spirits' at all. These gods might most judiciously be spoken of not as 'spirits,' but as 'undefined eternal beings.' . . . Not being ghosts, they crave no food from men, and receive no sacrifice, as do ghosts, or gods

developed from ghosts, or gods to whom the ghost-ritual has been transferred."

Lang gives some examples in a chapter titled "High Gods of Low Races." The god of the Andaman Islanders, Pulinga, is thought of as "like fire" but invisible. "He was never born, and is immortal, By him were all things created, except the powers of evil. He knows even the thoughts of the heart. He is angered by sin, or wrong-doing, that is falsehood, theft, grave assault, murder, adultery. . . ." He is the Judge of Souls, but he is compassionate toward those in pain or distress and will sometimes help them. The Kamiloroi tribe of Australia had a similar god, Beiame, who was believed to have created the world and men and women, taught them everything, and laid down the laws for their guidance before he returned to the sky. Another Australian "high god" is Daramulun, who was also believed to be the Creator and to have lived on the earth long ago and given men their knowledge and their laws. Anthropologists found that the pattern of beliefs was virtually the same in all the Australian aboriginal tribes. Lang found that in all their religions: "An all-knowing being observes and rewards the conduct of men; he is named with reverence, if named at all; his abode is the heavens; he is the Maker and Lord of all things; his lessons 'soften the heart'." In all this, says Lang, "the moral element is conspicuous, the reverence is conspicuous: we have here no mere ghost, propitiated by food or sacrifice, or by purely magical rites." and moreover, when the aborigines first began to come into contact with Christians, the elders among them were often deeply concerned that the association caused their youth to backslide from the high morality taught by their god.

So anthropological evidence suggests that the monotheistic "higher" religions did not evolve by degrees as man became more civilized, but on the contrary that "the Supreme Being was succeeded in advancing civilization by ruthless and insatiable ghost-gods, full of the worst human qualities." The Dinkas of

Above: Tangaroa-Upao-Vahu, the Polynesian creator god. This wooden statuette shows him creating the gods and men. The body is hollow, with a door at the back. Inside the body are a great many small idols. Like many primitive peoples, the Polynesians, the Aborigines, and the Maoris had their myths about an original cosmic creator god—the "High God"—to explain the existence of the world and themselves, but he was not worshiped in the sense known to Europeans. Priests and shamans would contact various lesser gods and spirits to secure supernatural help.

Right: a group of Dinkas in their Sudan homeland. Their supreme being was Dendid, who being incapable of evil (and thus of doing them harm) did not need worship—which was reserved for the evil spirit.

The Importance of Lesser Gods

Left: Yorubas of southwestern Nigeria formerly owed their allegiance to the priest-king of Oyo. They have a pantheon of some 400 gods most of whom are former ancestors or nature spirits. Over all the gods is Olorun, the supreme deity and creator of the world. Like many "High Gods," however, Olorun withdrew from earthly affairs and left humans to lesser gods.

the Upper Nile, for instance, in theory paid homage to an all-powerful Being called "Dendid," who lived in heaven, but as they believed him incapable of doing evil and that he did not need human gratitude, their prayers were reserved for the evil spirit, to whom they also offered sacrifices. The Zulus, too, had a tradition of a Creator who had ceased to exist, called Unkulunkulu, and one Zulu told an anthropologist, "In process of time we have come to worship the Amadhlozi (spirits) only; because we know not what to say about Unkulunkulu." And the Yorubas of West Africa, according to Mircea Eliade, "believe in a sky god called Olorun, who having started to create the world handed over the finishing and governing of it to a lower god, Obatalla. Olorun himself withdrew from earthly and human affairs, and though he is a Supreme God, he had neither temples, statutes nor priests. He is, however, called on as the last resort in time of calamity."

This tendency for the high god to be elevated to a higher sphere beyond the affairs of ordinary mortals, is explained by Lang as a consequence of the emergence of the belief in spirits. In many

Right: granaries in a Dogon village in Mali, West Africa. The Dogon believe in a supreme being known as Amma, and in a host of other lesser gods headed by twin divinities known as the Nummo, and the deified Eight Ancestors. The Eight Ancestors were brought to earth in a model granary which also contained the first plants and animals.

Below: a carved door from a Dogon granary which served as a blessing for the contents of the granary and as a protection against evil spirits. The figures represent clan or village ancestors.

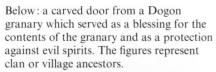

mythologies, he points out, including the Genesis Garden of Eden myth, an original state is put forward in which both man and the Creator were deathless. Then a taboo is breached, death enters the world, followed by a belief in spirits, which soon leads to the belief that God is a spirit, and then a priesthood arises professing to know how to appease the spirit-god. As for the original Creator god, he becomes a redundant divinity, for: "A moral creator in need of no gifts, and opposed to lust and mischief, will not help a man with love-spells, or with malevolent 'sendings' of disease by witchcraft; will not favour one man above his neighbor, or one tribe above its rivals, as a reward for sacrifice which he does not accept, or as constrained by charms which do not touch his imnipotence. Ghosts and ghost-gods, on the other hand, in need of food and blood, afraid of spells and binding charms, are a corrupt, but, to a man, a useful constituency."

Lang's argument, which has been supported and elaborated by contemporary historians of religion, has three major implications: first, that the idea of a straight line of evolution of religion from animism through polytheism to monotheism has little evidence to support it; second, that the high, moral God was not a very late development but a very early one; and third, that belief in the One Supreme Being is a deeply rooted, religious response to the sudden perception or manifestation of the divine in the world. This is not to say, however, that there ever was such a thing as a pure, primitive, coherent religion of the One God that denounced all other divinities as imposters and persecuted their devotees as heretics. It is Akhenaten who must be credited with having first brought this idea into the world, and it was in the higher monotheistic religions, Judaism, Christianity, and Islam, that the idea was made not only an essential article of faith but also a battle cry.

The attractions of polytheism on the one hand and mono-

Yahweh and the "False Gods" of the Babylonians

Left: a 15th-century stained glass window from Great Malvern Priory, England depicting God or Yahweh appearing to Abraham. He tells Abraham to leave his country and journey to the land he would be shown. Abraham took his wife and nephew and when they reached Canaan, Yahweh appeared again and said to Abraham, "To your descendants I will give this land." Scholars believe that the command to leave the Babylonian city of Ur and travel to Canaan with his family was because of the temptation to worship the "false gods" of their pagan surroundings in Babylonia. Abraham was to be the restorer of true religion—the worship of Yahweh alone. His sterile wife Sarah would bear him a son, Yahweh promised, although both Abraham and his wife were very old. Thus through Abraham and his son the land of Canaan would be populated with worshipers of the true high God as he had promised.

theism on the other, and the nature and various changes of fortune during the historical contest between the two systems of belief, is most clearly and dramatically illustrated in the story of the Hebrews as it unfolds in the Old Testament.

In Chapter 12 of the Book of Genesis, the first ancestor of the Jews, Abraham, is promised by the god Yahweh that his descendants will become a great nation and will occupy the land of Canaan. Canaan, or Palestine, was in fact occupied by other tribes, but this did not deter the Hebrews from regarding it as their own land from then on, because Yahweh had promised it to them. Over the centuries the descendants of Abraham and the

Above: nomads in the desert of Judaea live hard, spartan lives eking a meager living from an inhospitable land. It was in such a setting that the ancient Israelites spent 40 years during their escape from Egypt. The ancient Israelites had migrated to Egypt and had been settled in a district in Lower Egypt. As their numbers increased, successive pharaohs, particularly Rameses II and his son Mernephtah, enslaved the Israelites and used them for forced labor. They escaped Egyptian oppression and were led into the desert by Moses. It was here in the desert that the older generation, dispirited and depressed by slavery and unaccustomed to warfare, was replaced by their more vigorous offspring, hardened by their frugal existence as well as by battle with desert tribes.

tribes of the Hebrews multiplied, and in the 13th century B.C. some of them were held as slaves in Egypt. A great leader, Moses, arose among them and led them out of captivity and into the desert. Through Moses Yahweh reaffirmed his covenant with the Hebrew people on Mount Sinai. After 40 years of wandering in the desert, the tribes were finally led into the land of Canaan, fulfilling the ancient promise and demonstrating to the Hebrews Yahweh's preeminence among the gods.

Such, briefly, is the Hebrews' story of their origins and early history as set out in the first six books of the Old Testament—known as the Pentateuch. Because the story is a combination of many traditions, and was only consolidated in its present form about the 5th century B.C., a certain amount of hindsight and propaganda probably went into its make up. But the facts of the Hebrews' captivity, their escape from Egypt, and their eventual settlement in Palestine are confirmed by other historical sources.

Israel's One God

Left: two Israelite spies sent by Joshua, Moses' successor, to spy out the land promised them by Yahweh. They report that the land is green and fertile and bring a huge bunch of grapes with them to prove it. It was unlikely to have been as large as this bunch depicted in the 13th-century stained glass window in Canterbury Cathedral, England, however. Some clusters of grapes from the Eschol district of Israel today weigh up to 12 pounds, so they may well have been much larger than average.

The story illustrates what was unique in Judaism: the idea of a high god who, instead of becoming remote and indifferent, involved himself in the fortunes and worldly affairs of his worshipers.

Sandwiched as they were between the powerful empires of Egypt and Mesopotamia, the Hebrews did not enjoy peaceful occupation of the promised land for long. In the 6th century B.C. the country was overrun and the cream of the Hebrew people was sent into exile in Babylon. But this turn of events only served to strengthen their faith, for the great prophets of the Exile, Ezekiel and Isaiah, told their people that the Exile itself was a just punishment imposed on them by Yahweh for their disobedience and faithlessness, and urged them to mend their ways so that they might again inherit the promised land. When eventually they did return, the prophets had yet another example of Yahweh's care, guidance, and forgiveness to hold up to their

Above: carved relief from the time of Tiglath Pileser III (744–727 B.C.) showing Hebrews being led away in carts as captives to Babylon. Above the carts, their cattle are being driven off by their conquerors. The Babylonian exile was seen by the prophets as just punishment for the people of Israel for adopting many of the gods and religious practices of the pagans around them.

people to impress them to keep faith with the One God.

It was certainly no easy task to persuade the Hebrews to keep faith. As Andrew Lang wrote: "Had it not been for the prophets, Israel, by the time that Greece and Rome knew Israel, would have been worshipping a horde of little gods, and even beasts and ghosts, while the Eternal would have become a mere name . . . like Unkulunkulu." Historical events helped the Hebrew prophets rally their people to the worship of Yahweh, but even the most biased presentation of these events, and the fear of God and the faith in God that it aroused, did not prevent the Hebrews occasionally lapsing into worship of less austere and demanding and more obliging gods.

Scholars have long speculated about the origins of the god Yahweh, but have not reached any agreement among themselves. He seems originally to have been a mountain god who manifested his power through volcanic disturbances and earth tremors. Quite early in the history of the Hebrews, in Chapter 19 of the Book of Exodus there is a description of the people waiting around their holy mountain, Mount Sinai: "And mount Sinai was altogether on a smoke, because the Lord descended upon it in fire; and the smoke thereof ascended as the smoke of a furnace, and the whole mount quaked greatly." But Yahweh also has the characteristics of a sky god, and throughout Exodus he frequently descends from the sky to give Moses his counsel or instructions or to lay down the Law. Moses even has a regular procedure for these consultations. In Chapter 33 he pitches his special tent, the "tabernacle of the congregation" at a distance from the camp and goes into it to await Yahweh's coming, and presently a "pillar of cloud" descends and stands in the door of

The Unseen God

Opposite: 18th-century stained glass window of the Israelites worshiping the Golden Calf. When Yahweh's people demanded gods to lead them Aaron compromised by making a golden calf—a young bull like the Egyptian god Apis and the Canaanite Baal. Aaron then declared a feast to Yahweh, showing that he regarded the calf as an image of their god. They were not allowed such an easy solution to their worship of the unseen god, however. Their leader Moses destroyed the calf and restored the worship of Yahweh, whose greatness and holiness could not be captured in the work of men's hands.

Left: Yahweh appears to Moses as a "pillar of cloud." When Moses went into the "tent of meeting" or tabernacle, Yahweh descended in a pillar of cloud from the sky and spoke with Moses "as a man speaks to his friend." To Moses' request to be shown the glory of God, Yahweh replies that Moses shall not see his face for man cannot see the face of God and live.

The Many Gods of the Canaanites

Below: commemorative tablet of about 2000 B.C. from a temple at Ugarit to the Canaanite god Baal Hadhad. He is depicted as a youthful god wearing a helmet that has two bull's horns in front and brandishing an ax and a lightning spear. Baal was the king of the gods in Canaan, most of whom were connected with vegetation or fertility.

the tent, and it was in this manner that "the Lord spoke unto Moses face to face, as a man speaketh unto his friend."

After the settlement of the land of Canaan, and with the change over from a nomadic to an agricultural life, a crisis arose for the Yahwist religion. In the first place there was the attraction for the new Hebrew agriculturalists of the fertility cults of the Canaanites who still remained in the land. There was also the fact that the tribes had broken up and their members were pre-occupied with the problems of settlement in their particular areas, and one of these problems was how to behave toward the local gods. Gods were associated with territories, and if you changed your territory it was normal to change your god, as Ruth the Moabitess did in the first chapter of the Book of Ruth when she and her mother-in-law Naomi returned to Naomi's home town of Bethlehem. In the Second Book of Kings, Naaman, the Syrian commander was cured of leprosy by Elisha, and declared after his cure: "Behold, I know that there is no God in all the earth but in Israel." He asked to be given enough of Israel's earth to pack onto two mules to take back to Syria so that he could carry out his ritual devotions to the Hebrews' God. The story illustrates the extent to which gods were associated with territory. What Naaman did not understand was that Yahweh was not the god of a territory but of a people. He was the God of the twelve tribes of the Hebrews with whom he had made his covenant first through Abraham and then through Moses. But after the settlement of Canaan the orthodox Yahwists had to keep reminding their people of this fact.

The crisis that was created for the religion of the Hebrews by contact with the many native vegetation gods and their cults in Canaan, which were collectively known as Baalism, can be seen in many passages in the Old Testament, such as the following from the Second Book of Judges: "And the people of Israel did evil in the sight of the Lord, and served Baalism; and they forsook the Lord God of their fathers, which brought them out of the land of Egypt, and followed other gods, of the gods of the peoples that were round about them, and bowed themselves unto them, and provoked the Lord to anger."

The struggle between the belief in the many gods of Baalism and belief in the single God of Yahwism is seen dramatically in the contest between Elijah and the 450 priests of Baal on Mount Carmel. As told in the First Book of Kings it could be described as a flagrant piece of propaganda. Elijah harangues the Baalists saying, "How long halt ye between two opinions? If the Lord be God, follow him; but if Baal, then follow him." Then he issues his challenge. Two bulls are to be slaughtered and prepared for roasting, and he on the one hand and the priests of Baal on the other must prepare an altar, and then each in turn will call on their respective gods to send fire to consume the sacrificial offering. The Baalists accept, and from morning till noon parade around their altar calling on Baal, while Elijah jeers: "Cry aloud, for he is a god; either he is talking, or he is pursuing, or he is in a journey, or peraventure he sleepeth and must be awakened." Then Elijah prepares his altar and, with a born showman's bravado, has the meat and the wood thoroughly soaked with water before calling on Yahweh to send down fire. "Then the

fire of the Lord fell, and consumed the burnt sacrifice, and the wood, and the stones, and the dust, and licked up the water.'' At that all the people fell on their faces and worshiped Yahweh, and Elijah took the 450 priests of Baal down to the brook Kishon and had them slaughtered there.

But Elijah's triumph on Mount Carmel was soon forgotten. Despite such stunning demonstrations of Yahweh's power, and despite the exhortations and warnings of the prophets, the local Baalist cults still prospered with Hebrew as well as Canaanite support. It was left to the great prophets to keep Yahwism alive right up to and throughout the Babylonian Exile. And it was they who in the period after the Exile were able to incorporate that misfortune into their philosophy of history by regarding it as a divine punishment for the Hebrews' backsliding into the barbaric worship of primitive gods. It was in the teachings of the same prophets that Yahweh developed characteristics that made him a candidate for the status of a universal god. He had come a long way. From being a god of the desert, manifesting himself in the more dramatic natural phenomena, he had become the god of a people, then a war god, and now he had become a high, remote, moral god, loving, merciful, and perfect in righteousness, the creator, sustainer, and judge of the world and of man, who had laid down his universal and unalterable law and was in his own time and through his chosen people fulfilling his purposes for mankind.

But the high gods of the more civilized races, like those of primitive races, tend to become superfluous, because they are too withdrawn, too remote, and too ethically demanding.

Above: Elijah and the priests of Baal. Once the Israelites succeeded in conquering and settling the southern and northern areas of Canaan, they had to accustom themselves to living in cities and to being full-time farmers. They came in contact with the fertility rites of the pagan peoples of the land. Elijah was just one of the prophets of Israel who constantly battled against pagan idolatry.
Below: an ivory plaque thought to represent the Canaanite fertility goddess Astarte (known as Ashtoreth in the Old Testament).

Below: an engraving after the Flemish 17th-century painter Peter Paul Rubens, illustrating the Christian doctrine of the Trinity of God as Father, Son, and (represented by the dove) the Holy Spirit. In the Trinity, God is conceived as both unity and plurality: he is one and three. God the Father is ungenerated, timeless, and changeless, God the Son is generated by the Father, and God the Holy Spirit proceeds from the Father through the Son (in the Roman and Reformed Churches, from the Father only in the Orthodox Churches).

Through its Jewish founder Christianity inherited the high God Yahweh, but, in order to make him less remote and more accessible and human, Christianity literally brought God down to earth in the person of his Son. They then took a distinct step toward a new polytheism, it could be argued, by developing the doctrine of the trinity of the Father, the Son, and the Holy Spirit. The strict monotheism of the prophets was further put in jeopardy when Jesus was represented in the teachings of Saint Paul as a risen god. Most of the doctrinal disputes and schisms and persecutions of the early centuries of Christianity revolved around the difficult problem of the nature of God and of Jesus and how the two stood in relation to each other. It was only settled in A.D. 325 by the bishops of the Council of Nicaea, who declared that Yahweh and Jesus were one and that from then on

Right: God enthroned between two altars symbolizing the Old Law of the Jews and the New Law of the Christians. From a late-14th-century French Book of Hours.

it would be a sin punishable by exclusion from the Church to teach anything else. But even while the bishops were engaged in their learned deliberations, in other parts of Christendom people had elevated Mary, the mother of Jesus, to the status of a goddess. Mary, in fact, did stout work for Christianity, winning over devotees of other popular goddesses such as the Greek Demeter and the Egyptian Isis, and similar work was done in later centuries by the legendary martyrs, heroes, and minor pagan deities who were transformed into the "community of the saints," which to a large extent was treated as a new pantheon of minor gods.

The worldwide success of Christianity was helped by the fact that it is a religion that incorporated much from the religions it superseded. Having its origins in a time and place that was fermenting with religious, philosophical, and mystical ideas, and drawing upon ancient traditions through its parent religion, Judaism, Christianity developed into a religion with something to offer every seeker—whether that seeker was by temperament or intellect disposed toward belief in and worship of a single god, a three-persons-in-one god, or a god surrounded by a court of lesser deities, or whatever.

It seems, then, that a strict and consistent belief in a single god might have been regarded as wild deviation in the established religions of the world, an exalted idea only fit for religious geniuses like Akhenaten or the Hebrew prophets, had there not arisen, in the 7th century A.D., a new prophet and a new "solitary God" religion, which was to rival Christianity in recruiting a following throughout the world. The prophet was Muhammad, and the religion Islam, and the basic simple message and belief, which is still proclaimed daily from the minarets of innumerable mosques, was: "There is no God but Allah and Muhammad is his prophet."

Like Judaism, Islam, too, came out of the desert, and perhaps there is in this fact a clue to the appeal of the idea of the One God. In the *Seven Pillars of Wisdom* the British writer T. E. Lawrence ("Lawrence of Arabia") wrote eloquently and with insight on the subject of the desert god. Speaking of the Bedouin of the desert, he said: "In his life he had air and winds, sun and light, open spaces and great emptiness. There was no human effort, no fecundity in nature: just the heaven above and the unspotted earth beneath. There unconsciously he came near God. . . . The Bedouin could not look for God within him: he was too sure that he was within God. He could not conceive anything which was not God, Who alone was great. . . . Each individual nomad had his revealed religion, not oral or traditional or expressed, but instinctive in himself; and so we got all the Semitic creeds with a stress on the emptiness of the world and the fullness of God. . . . The desert Arab found . . . luxury in abnegation, renunciation, self-restraint. He made nakedness of the mind as sensuous as nakedness of the body. . . . His desert was made a spiritual ice-house, in which was preserved intact but unimproved for all ages a vision of the unity of God."

Lawrence's analysis brings out clearly the relationship between the physical space a man inhabits, the experiences he receives from it, and the ideas of God that arise because of them.

The Holy Trinity

Below: Muhammad, withdrawing to Mount Hira, near Mecca, had a vision in which the archangel Gabriel had him memorize the contents of a scroll. At dawn the figure of the angel stood out against the horizon whether he looked to north, south, east, or west. Muhammad was at first frightened by the fourfold vision of the archangel and resisted the call to be the prophet of Allah (God). Three years later he had another vision which strengthened his faith and from then on, according to tradition, further revelations followed one another regularly.

Above: an Arab makes his way across the
vast empty wastes of his desert home. It has
been argued that the physical surroundings
in which man finds himself condition his
mind to a particular conception of the deity
he needs to satisfy his spiritual longings.
The desert, with the great bowl of the
heavens above the rolling empty expanses of
sand, encompasses and swallows up puny
man. It becomes an image of a single, lone
god, pure, simple, unchanging, eternal,
before whom man stands in wonder and
reverence. It was an environment that
helped shape the religions of both Judaism
and Islam.

It exposes the roots of belief in a single, call-embracing god in
human experience, stressing the simplicity, the grandeur, the
proud selflessness that can be its glory, and also the sterility, the
cruelty, and the uncompromisingly negative attitude to the
world and to life that can be its disgrace. The god of Lawrence's
desert Arab, however, is not yet the ethical high God of Judaism
or Islam; he is, so to speak, a skeleton still to be fleshed out with a
moral personality.

If Lawrence's statement gives us an insight into the psychological origins of the single God of the monotheists, then it also
suggests where we might look for the origins of the many gods
of polytheism: wherever there is profusion, variety, and fertility
in nature; wherever the physical world bombards man's senses
with a multitude of impressions; wherever life is overgenerous
with invitations to luxury, sensuousness, and excess—that,
surely is where we might expect to find polytheism flourishing.
And indeed we do. In the teeming, colorful, and luxuriant subcontinent of India, for instance, hundreds of gods and goddesses
prosper in a veritable riot of religious beliefs.

But in Indian Hinduism there is a strong element of *monism*,
that is, a philosophical belief in the ultimate unity of all things;
and the wise men know that all the gods and goddesses of
popular worship are really manifestations of Brahman. Brahman
"himself is all the gods," says the *Brihadaranyaka*, the most
important sacred essay in the *Upanishads*. Belief in monotheism
or polytheism, it seems, cannot be fully explained by looking
only at the environment that they flourish in. Account has to be
taken of the degree of advanced intellectual thinking attained by
an individual or a society. Although an individual or a society
may find the idea of the ultimate unity of all things acceptable,
it need not be the same as a *religious* belief. It could be, however, a

One God or Many?

Left: every year thousands of Hindus travel to the Ganges river, which, as the goddess Ganga, purifies them from sin when they wash in its waters. If monotheism is said to be conditioned by the desert, then equally it seems that the teeming, vibrant, luxuriant subcontinent of India conditions men for polytheism—the worship of many gods. Hinduism is an amalgamation of almost every form of religious life and worship. Shiva and Vishnu are the most important of the gods of Hinduism. Shiva is seen largely as a fertility god with the phallus as his symbol and the bull as his cult animal. Vishnu, a kindly god, has incorporated other gods or heroes such as Krishna and Prince Rama. The Great Mother Goddess has three forms, all cruel: Durga, Kali, and Shakti. There are many other deities but over and above all is Brahma who created all and who, many Hindus believe, is now a kind of world soul, an impersonal universal principle.

contributory factor, a factor that only needs to be combined with a religious experience, some manifestation that can only be described as an encounter with the divine, to turn the philosophical proposition that all things and all events are but different aspects of the same ultimate reality, into the religious conviction that that ultimate reality is God.

The problem of the one and the many cuts across religion, philosophy, and science, and, as with most fundamental problems that present themselves in terms of a dilemma, ultimately the "either . . . or" approach to it proves profitless and we are led to a conclusion in terms of "both . . . and." Hinduism teaches that there is one God whose many attributes and functions are manifest in different ways and may be personified under different names. That, perhaps, seems as satisfying an answer as one could hope for to the question "One God or Many?"

Chapter 4
The Hero-Man or God?

From Hercules and Prometheus in Greek myth to Samson in the Old Testament, from the Hindu Prince Rama to the Norse heroes of Valhalla—the world's mythologies are full of legendary heroes whom the gods helped or hindered, who were often descended from gods, and even came to be worshiped as gods. This chapter looks at the hero myth. Why does it seem so necessary for man the world over to create heroes? Does "hero worship" and all its modern manifestations satisfy some vital corner of human psychology? And is there a sense too in which all the world's great religious leaders, from Muhammad to Christ, from Zoroaster to the Hebrew prophets, are really heroes?

When Krishna, the human form of the Hindu god Vishnu, played his flute in the forest at night, the music awakened the Gopis, the young wives of the village of Vrindavan. They stole from their beds and their homes to seek out the divine flautist, who was known to be a prodigious lover. At first each of the women was embarrassed to find so many others in the forest, and Krishna teased them all, saying, "Where are your fathers, brothers, husbands?" But they were entranced by his beauty and his music, and when he began to move among them they all started to dance, pressing about him voluptuously. As they danced Krishna reached out his arms, "caressing their hands, their flowing locks, thighs, waists, and breasts; laughed, joked, teased; gratified them with all the tricks of the Lord of Love."

The Gopis reached a frenzy of passion, and then suddenly, in the middle of the dance, Krishna disappeared. The women, mad with desire, searched throughout the forest, and eventually one of them found his footprints and called the others. They noticed that there were two sets of footprints for some distance, but that the smaller ones suddenly disappeared, and they deduced that Krishna had led one of their number into the forest and had then picked her up and carried her. Presently they found the favored girl recovering from a faint, and she was able to confirm what they thought about the footprints but said that scarcely had she climbed on Krishna's shoulders, as he had told her to do, than he had again disappeared.

Opposite: Zeus and Thetis, a painting by the early-19th-century French painter Ingres. Thetis was one of the 50 daughters of Nereus, a sea god whose domain was the Aegean Sea. She was courted by both Zeus and Poseidon, the gods of the heavens and the seas, but when an oracle declared that the son she would bear must be greater than his father they quickly chose Peleus, the King of Thessaly, to be her husband. Their son was Achilles, one of the great heroes of the Greek myths and mentioned by the poet Homer as the greatest of the Greek warriors in the Trojan War. When he quarreled with Agamemnon, the leader of the Greeks, his mother went to Zeus, knelt before him, and clasped his knees in petition to plead her son's cause.

Khrishna, a God in Human Form

Below: Krishna, an incarnation of the great Hindu god Vishnu, playing his pipe to the village women. So enchanted were the women that they danced themselves into a frenzy at his playing and pursued him through the forest for his caresses. Krishna is believed by some scholars to have been an historical figure. His name means "the dark-colored one" and he is regarded as the fount of all sacred and profane love. The goddess earth, according to an old tradition, asked Vishnu to free her from the torment of demons, and the god came to earth and was eventually born to the wife of a herdsman as Krishna. Even as a child he rid many of the village men from attacks by demons and as he grew into a beautiful youth all the girls and women (the Gopis) fell in love with him. He had to leave them, however, to continue his mission against the demons.

But then suddenly he was among them again, laughing, and garlanded with flowers. The Gopis all took off their upper garments for him to sit upon, and they massaged his body, pressed his hands against their breasts and took his feet in their laps. Then Krishna explained his earlier conduct: "When I refuse attachment to those devoted to me, my reason is, to make their devotion more intense. I disappeared so that your hearts should be so absorbed in me that you would be unable to think of anything else."

Then the dance began again. The women became wildly abandoned and it seemed that Krishna had multiplied himself so that each of them could experience his kisses and caresses at the same time. The wives of the gods gazed down on the scene, spellbound, and showered the dancers with blossoms. Then Krishna, streaming with perspiration and smeared all over with saffron from the Gopis' breasts, plunged into the river Jumna, where he became, in the words of the poet, like "a dark blue, glorious lotus, swarmed upon by a multitude of black bees."

A king who heard this tale, in the version of it told in the Hindu scripture *Bhagavata Purana*, was shocked and asked his brahman, or teacher, how an incarnation of the great god Vishnu could behave in such a reprehensible way, seducing other men's wives. The Brahman replied: "Krishna was already present in the hearts of the Gopis and their lords—as he is in the hearts of all living beings. His apparition as a man, the form of Krishna, was to rouse devotion to that presence."

This last sentence suggests some of the reasons why heroes and heroic deeds play a significant part in all religions: because they make the divine presence felt in the world; they translate the qualities and characteristics of godhood into actions; they focus upon a representative being those feelings of awe, of wonder, of admiration and devotion that constitute worship. Worship, wrote the 19th-century Scottish historian Thomas Carlyle, "is transcendent wonder. . . . To primeval men, all things and everything they saw were an emblem of the Godlike, of some God. . . . And if worship of a star had some meaning in it, how much more might that of a Hero! . . . No higher feeling than this of admiration for one higher than himself dwells in the breast of man."

The hero may be thought of as a man become like a god, or as a god become like a man. In Hinduism the concept of the god manifesting himself in human form and engaging in action in the world, is the usual way of expressing the heroic. Krishna the voluptuary, the Lord of Love, is one aspect of Vishnu. In the scriptural *Bhagavad Gita*, where he appears in disguise as Prince Arjuna's charioteer on the eve of the great battle in which friends and families are split up between two opposing sides, Krishna shows another aspect of his divinity: his knowledge and wisdom. Arjuna is reluctant to fight, distressed by the thought of the carnage but Krishna tells him that his reluctance is unworthy of him as a warrior, and that as the soul is eternal, death is an illusion. Arjuna then asks him a number of questions, and Krishna replies in a series of profound and beautiful statements on yoga and the nature of spiritual enlightenment. Krishna, then, as exquisite and prodigious in wisdom on the field of battle as he

Left: Krishna and Radha in a grove. In his human form the god had many mistresses but Radha was his special favorite and their love for each other has inspired many stories, paintings, and carvings.

Below: the god Vishnu sleeps out his role as Krishna on the serpent of eternity. The earth goddess is above in her role of creative principle, her demon attackers to the right.

Zeus, Father of the Greek Heroes

was in sensuality in the dance with the Gopis, makes God manifest in the physical world. And if his roles of seducer and moral philosopher seem incompatible to men, they must bear in mind, as the Brahman told the king, that "what the gods teach is virtue—and that is for men to follow; but what the gods do is something else. No god is to be judged as a man."

The idea that gods are not bound by any laws they may lay down for men was clearly held also by the ancient Greeks. Their supreme god Zeus is represented in the early legends as pursuing amorous adventures with goddesses, nymphs, and mortal women, and was known to go to any length, such as masquerading as a bull, a horse, or a swan, to take them by surprise and gratify his lust. Because the early Greeks did not form a coherent nation but were broken up into pockets of people each of which had its local divinities, there was a tendency for each local group to have a legend associating it with Zeus. This may explain Zeus' reputation as a confirmed philanderer, but it does not make his conduct any more moral. On one occasion when he wanted to seduce a mortal woman he knew to be virtuous and incorruptible, he even took on the appearance of her husband. It wasn't until some time later that the woman, Alcmene, learned from the soothsayer Tiresias how she had been deceived. Zeus, like Krishna, had no scruples about enjoying the wives of mortal men; indeed, he was much more licentious than Vishnu's incarnation, and he did not have as a reason the awakening and heightening of their passion for the divine. He did have another reason sometimes, though: that he wished to create beings at once mortal and endowed with divine powers to help him order

the unruly world. The son born of his union with Alcmene was destined to be a powerful protector of both gods and men. He was Hercules, the greatest of the heroes of Greek mythology.

It is quite probable that more legends of heroic and marvelous deeds have accumulated around the name of Hercules than around that of any other hero. He was the personification of physical strength, yet this was combined in Hercules with a complete lack of moral standards, restraints, or principles. His driving force was like the force of nature, as was that of Zeus himself. As a child he was said to have killed his music teacher, Linus, in a fit of temper, and as a youth he abused the hospitality of King Thespius by seducing each of his 50 daughters in one night. He had been unfortunate in incurring the jealousy of the great goddess Hera at birth. It was Hera who sent Lyssa, the Fury of madness to drive him to murder his first wife, Megara, and their children. To atone for this crime, Hercules had to serve Eurystheus, King of Argolis, for 12 years. The king tried to destroy him by giving him a series of strenuous and dangerous tasks to undertake. He was sent out to capture or kill a number of savage beasts or monsters, such as the great Nemean Lion, the nine-headed Hydra of Lerna, and the guardian of the gates of hell, Cerberus; and on other occasions his mission was to get for Eurystheus some fabulous trophy, like the girdle of Hippolyte, the Queen of the Amazons, or the golden apples guarded by the Hesperides in their marvelous garden at the western extremity of the world. Hercules accomplished everything that was demanded of him, and sometimes more than was demanded, and was eventually given his freedom.

Opposite top: Zeus, the king of gods. Like the Hindu god Vishnu, Zeus, too, appeared among his creatures as one of them— usually to pursue amorous adventures with mortal women. In the case of Danaë, daughter of the ruler of Argos, Zeus entered her chamber in a shower of gold and seduced her (opposite below). Their son became the hero Perseus.

Left: Leda, the wife of Tyndareus, was visited and seduced by Zeus in the form of a swan. She bore twin sons, Castor and Pollux, as well as two daughters, Clytemnestra and Helen. One of the two girls, Helen, the most beautiful woman in the world, was stolen from her husband by a Trojan prince, Paris, which led to the Trojan War in which many famous Greek heroes played a part. Clytemnestra married Agamemnon, leader of the Greek forces that besieged Troy. Castor and Pollux joined the hero Jason in his quest for the golden fleece. They eventually became the constellation Gemini.

Heroic Hercules

Below: statuette of Hercules as a child strangling two snakes. Hercules was born as the result of Zeus' union with a mortal, Alcmene. The goddess Hera, Zeus' wife, furious at her husband's amorous adventures, sent the snakes to kill the child. Hercules' feats of strength and heroic deeds were worthy of a child of Zeus.

Above right: the second of the Twelve Labors of Hercules. Hera sent a fit of madness to Hercules causing him to kill his children. When he recovered, the oracle at Delphi told him that he must serve the King of Argos for 12 years, doing whatever he commanded. He was sent to bring back the skin of the huge Nemean lion, whose pelt could not be pierced by any weapon. Hercules strangled it with his bare hands and can be seen wearing its skin as he tackles his second labor, the killing of the Lernean hydra—a doglike creature with nine snakelike heads. This monster, too, he destroyed.

A glutton for challenge and adventure, Hercules soon set out in quest of more excitement. It was not long before his quick temper got him into trouble again. A king, Eurytus, had promised his daughter to anyone who could beat him in an archery contest. When Hercules won the contest, the king went back on his word, so the champion killed the king's son. For this crime, the oracle at Delphi condemned him to another year's slavery, but this time he served Omphale, the Queen of Lydia, who was so grateful when he rid her land of a number of monsters and enemies that she set him free before his time was up. No sooner was he free than he offered to rescue the king of Troy's daughter from a dragon. Again, an ungrateful father went back on his word and withheld the reward he had promised. The furious Hercules sacked Troy, killed the king and his sons and gave the rescued princess as a wife to his friend Telamon. His life of monster-slaughter, championship of the wronged, and punishment of the wrongdoers continued until the tendency to philander he inherited from his father set off a chain of events that led to his death. As the flames of the funeral pyre rose around his body a cloud descended from the sky and, amid thunder and lightning, he was taken up to Olympus. There, he was admitted to the company of the gods, reconciled to Hera, and married to her daughter Hebe.

Left: the Third Labor of Hercules, the capture of the Cerynein hind—a fabulous creature with brazen feet and golden antlers, which he had to bring back alive.

Below: Mount Olympus, home of the gods. Due to his wife's jealousy Hercules put on a shirt soaked in blood from a centaur he had killed. The shirt burned his flesh, and, in excruciating agony, he ordered a funeral pyre to be lighted and mounted it to be burned alive. Thunderbolts demolished the pyre and he was carried on a cloud to Olympus to be listed among the immortals.

Above: Bellerophon with his winged horse,
Pegasus. Bellerophon, like Hercules, was
given several tasks to perform. When sent to
destroy the chimera, the goddess Athene
helped him capture Pegasus. Shooting
arrows from his flying steed, Bellerophon
easily killed the chimera. The legend of
Bellerophon is one of many that seek to
make the divine manifest in the world, or to
magnify the deeds of ancestors so that their
heirs may share their glory.

Above right: Hermes, Eurydice, and
Orpheus with the lyre given to him by
Apollo. Hermes was the messenger of the
gods, and conductor of the dead to the
infernal regions. He is also the inventor of
the seven-stringed lyre which he gave to
Apollo in return for the snake-entwined
staff he is sometimes depicted with.
Eurydice, the wife of Orpheus, was bitten
by a serpent and died. Her disconsolate
husband was guided by Hermes to the
nether world and after charming Pluto with
his beautiful music Eurydice was allowed to
follow him back to earth—provided he did
not look back at her while making the
journey. He did look back, and Eurydice
was taken from him.

So Hercules, the man-god, the hero demonstrating in the
world the power and wrath of God, became wholly a god and
one of the Immortals. Apart from Prometheus, he was the only
Greek hero to attain this distinction, probably because of all of
them he was the most universally revered. Different parts of the
Greek world had their own heroes. In Attica there was Theseus,
who slew the dreaded Minotaur of Crete and accompanied
Hercules on some of his adventures; in Argolis Perseus, another
son of Zeus, who slew the gorgon Medusa, and rescued Andro-
meda from sacrifice to Poseidon's sea monster; in Thessaly
Jason, who led the expedition of heroes to secure the fabled
Golden Fleece; in Thrace Orpheus, son of the god Apollo, who
used his divine musical gift to accomplish miracles and triumphs
worthy of any hero; in Corinth it was the hero Bellerophon, who
like Hercules had to perform a series of tasks given him by a
king who tried to destroy him. With the aid of the winged horse,
Pegasus, he killed the fire-breathing chimera, a monster that was
part lion, part snake, part goat. These and many other heroes
throughout the Greek world made up what was virtually a whole
assembly of under-gods—the demigods. They had altars and
temples dedicated to them, and prayers addressed to them.

Scholars see in their reading of many of the creation myths,
how the earliest men represented the gradual emergence of order

out of primeval chaos in terms of battles, wars, and heroic triumphs. This tendency continued in the Greek myths at the local level and in legends that told how particular societies had acquired their institutions and their laws. Some of the legendary heroes were ancestors or former kings, while others were obviously fictitious—people created by imaginations that sought to represent the splendor and the terror of the divine as it manifests itself in the world. If tales of heroes are attempts of the human mind to comprehend the divine, then it must be admitted that early Greek ideas were not as exalted as those of the Hebrews, and that, as the Scottish writer Andrew Lang remarked, in the face of the multitude of "freakish, corruptible" Greek deities, philosophy "could hardly restore that Eternal for whom the Prophets battled in Israel," but on the other hand the heroic legends of Greece have remained for 2500 years as stirring and colorful allegories of the powers and potentials of the Divine Man.

It might well be asked: what about the Divine Woman? When the patriarchal age came in with the settlement of cities it produced literatures and mythologies from which the female principle was removed or in which it was devalued. This male chauvinism was exhibited to the full in the legends and cults of heroes. The physical beauty of Aphrodite, goddess of love, the wifely faithfulness of Penelope, who waited for her husband Odysseus for 20 years: these were the qualities valued and admired in the female. They were qualities which, of course, have no relevance except in relation to the male. The religion of the Hero has no place in it for a woman in her own right, and it is in this that its weakness and its limitation lies.

The attitude to women in the Age of Heroes can be seen by looking at the start of that greatest contest of heroes, the Trojan War. The three goddesses, Hera, Athene, and Aphrodite, all laid claim to a golden apple inscribed "For the fairest," and Zeus ordered that the dispute should be settled by a mortal. Paris, the son of King Priam of Troy, was chosen to be the judge, and the goddesses paraded before him and each tried to bribe him. Hera offered to make him lord of all Asia, Athene promised to ensure that Paris was always successful in battle, and Aphrodite undertook to give him the most beautiful of mortal women, Helen the wife of King Menelaus of Sparta. Paris gave the golden apple to Aphrodite and was rewarded with the ravishing Helen—but with the prize came 10 years of war against her husband Menelaus and the heroes of Greece, which ended with the destruction of Troy and its royal family. In the war itself great feats of heroism were performed on both sides, and there were many opportunities to display the masculine virtue of pride in excellence. The fact remains, however, that the war was caused by a vain goddess who won a vulgar beauty contest by offering to procure another man's wife for the judge's pleasure. As with Aphrodite, so with another great story from the literature of the patriarchal age, that of the expulsion from the Garden of Eden: the blame is put on the irresponsibility of a woman.

Homer's *Iliad*, a 49-day episode in the 10-year battle for Troy, is followed by his *Odyssey*, the story of the long and adventurous return home of the most gifted of the Greek heroes, Odysseus.

An Age of Heroes

Below: a marble statue of the goddess Aphrodite. She was the goddess of love and desire, though her cult went back far beyond Hellenic times to when she was worshiped as the Great Mother Goddess. She was a fertility goddess at Paphos in Cyprus (where this statue was found) and from there her cult was taken to Corinth and to Sicily. She possessed a magic girdle that made whoever wore it irresistibly lovely. Her physical beauty alone made her worshiped.

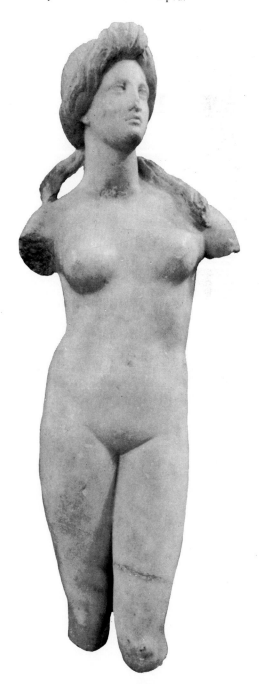

The Trojan War and Heroic Ideals

Left: a frieze depicting the war between the Greeks and Trojans. The greatest of manly virtues among the ancients were physical courage and fortitude in the face of death. The larger the portion of these "virtues" a man had, the greater hero he was judged.

The virtues and talents demanded of the heroes beneath the walls of Troy were few: physical courage, true manliness and fortitude in the face of death. The nature of the challenge the hero would be called upon to face was known. But Odysseus on his homeward journey found himself in many unforeseen situations in which survival depended on his excelling not only in courage and the art of warfare, but also in cunning, the skillful use of speech, or in the skills of boatbuilding, sailing, competitive plowing, discus-throwing and wrestling. His journey was a learning experience as well as a testing one, and it is significant that in the course of it he met and had to come to terms with three women, Calypso, Nausicaa, and Circe, who were themselves embodiments of different female qualities. The voyage could be said to have been a recovery of a whole dimension of life that the male had sacrificed when he adopted the patriarchal ideals of heroism. Although ignored, a whole range of female qualities such as gentleness, self-sacrifice, and self-effacement patiently awaited rediscovery when the male had done with his fighting, pomp, and boastfulness.

Opposite: the *Judgment of Paris*, by the early-16th-century Swiss painter Nikolaus Manuel Deutsch. Although Deutsch's conception of physical beauty would not have met with much approval among the ancient Greeks, he has succeeded in conveying the atmosphere of the beauty contest between three Renaissance goddesses and the young Trojan "judge" they sought to influence. Hera promised Paris the lordship of Asia, Athene promised fame in war, but Paris gave the apple, inscribed "to the fairest," to Aphrodite who promised him the loveliest of all women.

Left: *L'île de Calypso*, by the modern French painter André Devambez. Calypso's isle was Ogygia, and it was there that the nymph lovingly kept Odysseus for eight years until Zeus sent Hermes to command his release. It was in the wanderings of the Greek hero Odysseus that the poet Homer contrasted the civilizing female qualities with sterile male heroics. Most of the men qualifying as heroes belong firmly to the age of constant warfare, with their thrilling storybook exploits. Such men, without the compensatory feminine qualities of gentleness, self-sacrifice, self-effacement, and patience, are seen to be boorish, selfish bombasts away from the battlefield.

Teutonic Heroes

Some historians have suggested that the cult of the hero was brought to the Mediterranean by invaders from the north who settled there. Certainly there are close resemblances between Greek and Teutonic myths of the Heroic Age. For the Germans and Scandinavians as for the Greeks, pride in excellence was the supreme virtue, and prowess on the field of battle or in the sports arena was what made a hero. The gods were fashioned after the heroic mold, and the greatest among them was Odin, who held court in the great hall of Valhalla, which had walls made of spears and a roof of brilliant shields. Odin would summon outstanding mortal heroes who had fallen in battle to Valhalla, and there they spent their time feasting and engaging in warlike games while they awaited their final battle, against the race of the Giants. Meanwhile Odin, like his counterparts Vishnu and Zeus, would sometimes take on human form and go in disguise among mortals, sometimes to gratify a lust for mortal women, and sometimes to bestow favors upon or put to the test particular heroes who had come to his attention.

The most favored of human families were the Volsungs, whose founder, Sig, was born of Odin's union with a mortal woman. One night Sigi's great-grandson, Sigmund, was sitting with other warriors around a fire in a great hall when a stranger came among them, a tall old man, blind in one eye, who wore a wide-brimmed hat and a vast cloak. The stranger carried a sword which he thrust up to the hilt in a tree trunk and said that it would belong to whoever was strong enough to pull it out. Only Sigmund was able to do so, and afterward with that sword he proved unbeatable in battle and won many victories. But one day, in the middle of a fight, the old man in the hat and cloak appeared before Sigmund and pointed in his direction a wooden spear upon which the sword snapped in two. The disarmed hero fell beneath his opponent's blows. He realized that his time had come and that Odin wanted to recruit him into the select fraternity of Valhalla, and his last wish was that the two parts of the divine sword should be welded together again and the weapon should go to his son, Siegfried. The wish was granted, and the deeds that Siegfried accomplished with the sword made him the greatest of the Teutonic heroes, whose reputation as such was celebrated in the German composer Richard Wagner's series of four operas known as *The Ring of the Niblung*.

Odin was more than a warrior god. He was also the god of poetry, and a legend related how by a clever trick he had stolen hydromel, the "mead of the poets," from the Giants. This marvelous drink gave whoever drank it at once the gifts of poetry and wisdom, so that Odin became renowned for his sublime poetry and his discernment and learning. But above all he was famous for his knowledge and use of the runes, the secret writing that held the magic power that could accomplish almost anything, from stilling the waves of the sea to curing an illness or gaining a woman's love. The way Odin acquired his knowledge of the runes is the most curious episode in his story. For nine days and nights, wounded by his own spear, he hung upon the world-tree, Yggdrasil, in agony and without a visitor who would give him food or drink. There he contemplated the mysterious runes, and suddenly their secrets were revealed to him and he was

Above: a detail from a carving from a Norwegian stave-church portal depicting the repair of the Sword of Odin, greatest of the Teutonic gods. He gave the sword to the hero Sigmund who won many battles with it. Odin returned in the middle of a battle, touched the sword with a wooden spear and it broke in two. After Sigmund had been mortally wounded, he begged that the sword should be welded together and given to his son Siegfried. Thus, with the god's help, the cult of heroes was able to continue.

Left: Odin, chief among the Teutonic gods, shown with his two ravens, which every day flew around the world and reported back to him all that they had seen.

Below: a carving from a Norwegian stave-church portal shows Siegfried killing Reginn, the smith who fostered him. Reginn had persuaded Siegfried to kill Fafnir, a dragon guardian of a horde of gold, but then tried to cheat Siegfried of his hard-won prize.

Heroic Legends of North Europe

Right: the great cosmic tree, Yggdrasill. This great ash tree, which existed from the beginning of time, encompassed both heaven and earth. Dew fell from its branches, and at the tree's foot curled the huge snake Nithoggr constantly gnawing its roots. On the topmost branch perched an eagle with a hawk on its head. The eagle was the snake's deadly foe. The branches and young shoots were menaced by goats and deer. It was on the cosmic tree that Odin sacrificed himself to win knowledge for gods and men. Sacrifice of humans and animals from trees was an established part of the cult of Odin.

free. Although the story appears to have a similarity to Christ's self-sacrifice on the "tree" of the cross, it may be more relevant to consider it in relation to the story of how Prince Siddhartha heroically achieved enlightenment and Buddhahood by meditation under the Tree of Wisdom.

The 12th-century Icelandic poet Snorri Sturluson recorded a tradition that Odin had originally been a man, a prince who had ruled over a great people in the region of the Black Sea, and, accompanied by 12 other rulers and their people, had moved to the West and North and eventually conquered and settled in parts of northern Europe. Odin had then given his people their laws and institutions, and had invented letters and poetry, and eventually he and the 12 other rulers had come to be worshiped as gods. Curious as this tradition is, it fits in with modern knowledge of the prehistoric movements of people and cultures in a great crescent that embraced the lands occupied by Indian, Iranian, Slav, Greek, Italian, and Germanic peoples. Interestingly, modern scholars have suggested that the letters of the runic alphabet of the ancient Teutons developed from a form of the Greek alphabet used in the Hellenized provinces north of the Black Sea.

Left: a Norwegian painting showing the death of the blond god Balder, beloved of the gods and men, and claimed by some writers to be Odin's son; yet other stories claim him to be a hero. Because Balder was troubled by nightmares, Odin's wife made all things on earth swear never to harm Balder. The gods then amused themselves by throwing things at Balder, who was now invulnerable. The evil Loki, however, discovered that the delicate mistletoe plant had been overlooked and had never taken the oath. Loki made a dart of mistletoe wood and gave it to the blind god Hodr to throw at Balder. The dart killed Balder.

Above: the killing of the world serpent of Midgard. The serpent was one of the giants in disguise, as was also the dragon Fafnir. In all the legends the gods triumph over the giants. But the giants plan revenge. The rule of the gods was fated to end and chaos return to heaven and earth.

One thing that distinguishes the Teutonic gods from those of other religions is that they are not immortal, and there is nothing in any other Heroic Age mythology to compare with the legend of the Götterdämmerung, the "Twilight of the Gods." It is a tale of how the great ones brought about their own downfall and how they heroically faced their end when they saw that it was inescapable.

The gods lived in their mansions in the land of Asgard, which was separated from the world of man by the bridge Bifröst, the rainbow. There, originally, they had lived a busy and peaceful life, but its smooth running had eventually been upset by the gods' failure to control their passions. Out of greed they had tortured the goddess Gullveig, who was skilled in making gold by sorcery, and then they had broken their promise to a Giant who had undertaken to rebuild the wall around Asgard for them if they would give him the goddess Freya. Then among their number there arose a mischievous and spiteful god, Loki, who caused the murder of Odin's son, Balder the god of light. The gods shackled Loki in irons for this, but he escaped and joined forces with the gods' enemies, the demons and Giants, who were preparing for an all-out war.

A Warrior's Code

Below: the twilight of the gods, or
Ragnarok. It is the battle that precedes the
end of the world when the gods would be
defeated and take the world with them in
their downfall. The legends prophesy a new
world rising from the chaos left by the
passing of gods and giants. A new
generation of gods arises, this time headed
by the beautiful and good Balder, the
architect of the new world.

One of the gods, Heimdall, was posted at their end of the
Bifröst bridge as guardian and watchman, but when the Giants'
attack began Loki managed to steal his sword and delay his
raising the alarm. The Giants converged from all directions upon
Asgard. With them they brought the wolf Fenrir, whose upper
jaw touched the heavens and lower jaw the earth, and also the
great sea serpent of Midgard, who was seeking revenge against
the god Thor for once nearly hauling her out of the sea. When the
alarm was raised in Valhalla all the gods and warriors armed
themselves, and, led by Odin, who was magnificent in his golden
helmet plumed with eagles' wings, they went out in multitudes to
join battle with the invaders. But Odin was the first to perish,
swallowed by the wolf Fenrir. Gods, giants, monsters, and
warriors died in a holocaust of slaughter, and mankind, abandoned by its protectors, was swept from the face of the earth. On
the earth itself the seas and rivers rose, mountains and rocks spat
fire, and all life was obliterated. So it was, according to the myth,
that the first generation of gods and the first race of men ended.
In time the balance of nature was reestablished, the god Balder
was resurrected, and other gods joined him to rule over a new
race of men that came into the world.

This myth has much in common with creation myths, such as the Babylonian *Enuma Elish*, and also with the myths of prehistoric catastrophes such as the flood. However, in the present context, the Twilight of the Gods, like the *Iliad* and the *Bhagavad Gita,* teaches a warrior code of acceptance of the inevitability of death and of heroic bearing in the face of it. This code of grim, masculine fatalism raises further a major point on the subject of the relation between religion and the cult of the hero.

The literatures of patriarchal cultures generally take a bleak view of death. It is the end; there is no consoling myth of a return to the womb of the earth and an eventual rebirth. There is no "out-of-the-body" other self, no soul, that comes into its own in the afterlife. There are only insubstantial "shades" fretting over their flesh-and-blood bodies, often in an underworld ruled over by a sinister female, such as the Greek Persephone or the Teutonic goddess Hel. In Homer's *Odyssey* there is an account of Odysseus' descent to the underworld and his meeting with the shade of the great hero of the Trojan War, Achilles. Odysseus tries to console Achilles by telling him what a great reputation he has among men, but the former hero replies, "Nay, seek not to speak to me soothingly of death, glorious Odysseus," and says that if he could have his life again he would be content even to spend it quietly in the service of some unknown petty overlord. The implication is that where the ethic of bravery and duty is of highest importance, nothing can compensate for the loss that death entails.

If any people had an attitude to death grimmer and more uncompromising than the ancient Greeks it was the Mesopotamians, and the hero of their great *Epic of Gilgamesh* is portrayed as a man who refuses to accept the inevitability of death and who rises to heroic heights in his efforts to overcome his fate.

Gilgamesh appears to have been a historical person, a king of the early Sumerian city of Erech, and although he is described at the beginning of the poem as being two-thirds a god and one-third a man, his drama and tragedy arise from the fact that he knows himself to be mortal. He at first appears as a tyrant ruler of Erech who, like most of our heroes, is highly sexed and uses his physical strength and his royal authority to force himself on any female he desires. His subjects complain to the gods, who decide to give Gilgamesh something else to think about and to spend his demonic energy on. They create Enkidu, a wild man equal to Gilgamesh in strength, who grows up among the beasts of the desert and becomes their defender against predatory men. Eventually no man will venture into the desert for fear of Enkidu, so Gilgamesh devises a plot for his capture. He sends out a temple prostitute to await the wild man's appearance at the water-hole where he goes to drink, and when Enkidu arrives there the prostitute slips off her robe and seduces him. For six days and seven nights Enkidu revels in pleasures that he had never before experienced, and when at the end of this time he makes a move toward his friends the animals he is vexed to find that they run away from him. So he goes back to the woman, who persuades him to return with her to Erech. There he and Gilgamesh fight, and after a tremendous and prolonged struggle Gilgamesh gets the better of him, but Gilgamesh develops such

Above: an Attic vase painting of the dead hero Achilles in his armor. The literature of the cult of heroes leaves little room for belief in a life after death. The grim fatalism running through its beliefs is carried beyond the grave where such existence as there is, is in the form of ghosts or shadows. Their gloomy underworld is ruled over by a sinister god or goddess. It was no compensation to a hero to know he was remembered on earth as a hero. Only if his heroism took heaven by storm and the divine ones accepted him into their number, was the code worthwhile.

Right: Gilgamesh, who, according to
Sumerian king lists, was the fifth ruler of
Erech during the second royal dynasty after
the flood. Scholars think he certainly
existed, and probably reigned around
2600 B.C. The most complete version of his
story was found in the library of King
Ashurbanipal of Assyria (669–626 B.C.), and
is known as the Epic of Gilgamesh.
According to the epic, Gilgamesh was a
giant of a man—with giant-sized appetites.
His subjects complained about him and the
gods created a mighty wild man, Enkidu, to
contend with Gilgamesh and control his
demonic energy. But the wild man was
tamed, and he and Gilgamesh became firm
friends. They left the city and traveled far
performing many brave deeds. On their
return they insulted the goddess Ishtar and
killed a sacred bull. The gods decided to
punish them and Enkidu was chosen to die.
His death brought home to Gilgamesh the
chill fact of his own mortality. He then took
on a long search for immortality.

respect for his adversary that the two become firm and inseparable friends.

They set out on a series of adventures together, and always
triumph, but one day they make the mistake of killing a sacred
bull. The gods decide that one of them must die for this sacrilege,
and choose Enkidu. Gilgamesh mourns for the loss of his friend,
and Enkidu's death brings home to him the realization that he
too is mortal, which terrifies him. He decides to seek out the
legendary and immortal Utnapishtim and his wife, the only
survivors of a former human race that had been wiped out by a
great flood, in the hope of learning from them the secret of
immortality. The deathless couple live beyond the end of the
world, and Gilgamesh's journey is beset by many hazards, not
the least of which is the argument of the mysterious female
Siduri, the "winemaiden," whom he meets on the shore of the
cosmic sea before he emarks on the last part of his journey.
Siduri tells him that his quest is vain, that the gods are jealous
of their immortality, and man should make the most of his span
of life, enjoy to the full his physical pleasures, and accept his fate.
Gilgamesh listens to but does not heed this advice, and after
undergoing further adventures and ordeals he at last reaches the
home of Utnapishtim. He is received with kindness and allowed
a long sleep of recuperation, and on awakening given food and
drink. Utnapishtim tells him the story of his own survival, how
when he and his wife had survived the great flood the god Enlil
made them immortal. But he stresses that theirs was a unique
case, and Gilgamesh can't hope to qualify for immortality in
the same way. But there is another way, and at the prompting
of his wife, who has taken pity on Gilgamesh, Utnapishtim tells
him what he has come to learn. At the bottom of the cosmic sea

there grows a prickly plant that confers eternal youth on whoever eats it. So on his return journey across the sea Gilgamesh plunges to the bottom by tying heavy stones to his feet, and he succeeds in plucking the plant of immortality. He does not eat any of it immediately, however, but decides to take it back to Erech to share with his people. Then one day when he is resting on his journey and bathing at a water hole, a snake steals the plant and swallows it. The inconsolable Gilgamesh returns to Erech bitterly reflecting on the irony of the fact that all his heroic efforts have served only to "bring a blessing to the serpents of the world."

The *Epic of Gilgamesh* ends with a meeting between the hero and the shade of his friend Enkidu, which reminds the reader of the meeting of Odysseus and Achilles. Enkidu is at first unwilling to describe the afterlife to his friend, but he does so when pressed, beginning with a harrowing description of the decomposition of the physical body. The description of the afterlife conditions of different categories of people is unrelievedly grim, and brings Gilgamesh no consolation for the loss of the marvelous plant that he had gone to such heroic lengths to obtain.

If such are the rewards of a hero, why have they always been held up as examples to inspire ordinary mortals? The fact is that hero legends are an essential part of religion, for they represent man's attempts to conceive what is higher than himself, without which he would have neither the impulse to worship nor the impulse to rise above selfish interest in his own survival and his own pleasure—impulses that are such important aspects of religion. In a sense all the founders of the world's religions were heroes, for none of their achievements was accomplished without strenuous efforts against mighty odds and, on occasion, self-sacrifice or martyrdom. But to broaden the idea too much is to make it meaningless. What is it that the cults of such typical heroes as Hercules, Odin, or Gilgamesh lacked? They lacked what any religion must have to satisfy man's needs for an integrated personality and for a sense of belonging to something larger and more permanent than self: the recognition of the importance of the female principle, in which are locked the secrets of creation and of renewal.

A world simplified to terms of clear-cut issues that call for heroic responses is for most people a dream world, and contrasts sharply with the real world of ambiguities, conflicting demands and loyalties, and unsatisfactory but necessary compromises. That does not mean that it is unimportant or irrelevant, however. The Swiss psychologist Carl Gustav Jung, saw the hero myth as a stimulant, a half-way-house on the road to acquiring a full personality.

The heroic myth loses its relevance, Jung says, when a man achieves the full self-consciousness of maturity. And in the growth and maturing of religions, too, the Heroic Age is eventually outgrown, though it doesn't exactly pass into irrelevance. Its myths and legends remain to thrill and delight, to amaze and inspire all those who go through the experience of awakening to awareness of the portion of the divine that is in the world and in themselves, and to the realization that they have it in their power to display it—and to magnify it.

The Hero Gilgamesh

Above: a cylinder-seal of 3000 B.C. thought to depict (from left to right) Gilgamesh, the bull of heaven, and Enkidu. On the right is a lion wrestling with Gilgamesh. The story of Gilgamesh enshrined in it the religious beliefs of Mesopotamia. Unlike, say, the Egyptians, the Mesopotamians had no afterlife to look forward to, only a grim house of darkness ruled over by the queen of the underworld where, according to one of the tablets found at Nineveh, "dust is their sustenance, clay their food, clothed are they as a bird with garment of wings, the light they see not, in darkness dwelling. In the House of Dust which I entered. . . ."

Chapter 5
Facts About the Flood

"We have found the Flood!" This jubilant announcement by British archaeologist Sir Leonard Woolley in 1930 opened a vigorous controversy about the Genesis story that still lingers on. Was it really the Sumerians who lived in Mesopotamia in about 4000 B.C. whose true account of a disastrous flood provided first the Babylonians in *Gilgamesh*, then the Hebrews in Genesis with the flood myth? If so, why did the Greeks also believe in a deluge sent by gods as a punishment, a flood with only two human survivors? Is the flood a myth, part of an annual fertility ritual? Or is it the true record of a historical disaster? This chapter examines the evidence.

During World War I a Russian pilot named Roskowitzki reported that he had seen the remains of the wreckage of a ship of considerable size on the southern flank of Mount Ararat in Turkey. A search party of 150 men was sent by Csar Nicholas II to confirm the pilot's report, which it did, then returned to Moscow with photographs of the find. Unfortunately, all records of the expedition, together with the photographs, disappeared in 1917 during the Russian Revolution.

According to the Book of Genesis, Ararat is where Noah's ark was grounded when the great flood that God sent to wipe out an erring human race subsided. It is in fact a volcanic mountain mass some 25 miles long by 12 miles wide situated between the Caspian and the Black seas. The whole area is still actively volcanic, and after an earthquake in 1840 some Turkish work-men reported the discovery of the prow of an ancient vessel projecting from a glacier on Ararat. Geologists investigated, confirmed the find, and were said to have entered three com-partments of the vessel. Then in 1893 a Dr. Nouri, Archdeacon of Jerusalem, explored the mountain and returned to report that he had seen the prow and the stern of a ship made of thick wood. The outer wall of the ship was of a dark red color, he wrote. He couldn't describe the interior because it was full of snow. More recently, in 1952, an expedition climbing Ararat saw, at an altitude of 13,800 feet, what looked like the shape of a vessel about 450 feet long and with curving sides, sunk in the ice of the

Opposite: a mosaic in St. Mark's church, Venice, showing the story of the Flood.

Below: part of an aerial photograph of the mountain chain of Ararat, in eastern Turkey, showing an outline of what could be a petrified ship in a glacier.

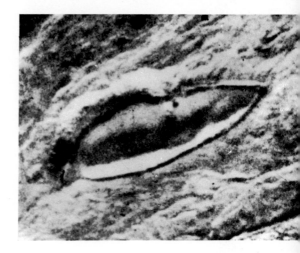

Right: some of the Turkish soldiers who took part in the 1960 expedition to search for Noah's Ark. Outlined in the ground behind them can be seen the shape of what could have been the Ark.

Below: snowcapped Mount Ararat, highest peak in the Ararat Mountains, rises majestically 16,900 feet above sea level.

glacier a few yards below the surface. Then in 1965 there appeared in the London *Daily Telegraph* an aerial photograph of a boat-like outline pointed at each end and some 400 feet long on what was said to be a section of Ararat. Geologists attributed the outline to a freak volcanic action and no further investigation was undertaken. So to this day, despite a number of intriguing travelers' tales, there has still been nothing like conclusive proof from the Ararat region of the historical truth of one of the oldest legends in the world.

There are many stories of catastrophes in prehistoric times that were sent by an angry god as a punishment on man for his disobedience and wickedness. Plato, the 4th-century B.C. Greek philosopher, tells in the *Critias* dialogue how "Zeus, the God of gods, desired to inflict punishment upon" the people of Atlantis, and caused the entire civilization to be submerged overnight. The sixth Chapter of the Book of Genesis states: "and God saw that the wickedness of man was great in the earth. . . . And the Lord said, I will destroy man whom I have created from the face of the earth." There is even a Maori legend from New Zealand that tells how God became so angry with man for his wickedness that he stamped on the crystal floor of heaven and smashed it, causing the waters of the Upper World to fall on the earth and drown it. There are many more such myths of divine punishment by means of drowning, but the biblical story of the Flood is perhaps the best known and is worth looking at in some detail.

According to the Genesis story, when God decided to punish the human race he exempted one good man and his family. He told Noah of his intentions and instructed him to build an ark of an unidentified "gopher wood," giving him precise details as to its dimensions and how to construct it and provision it to ensure the survival for the duration of the Flood of Noah and his family and two specimens of every living creature in the world. Incidentally, experts in shipbuilding have testified that the God-given specifications for the ark would have produced a perfectly seaworthy vessel, and archaeologists and geologists have confirmed the availability of the tools, the craftsmanship, and the raw materials to build a vessel to such specifications in Neolothic times. In his book *The Flood Reconsidered*, the British scholar Dr. Frederick Filby analyzes the Genesis account word by word in the light of modern historical, archaeological, geological, and scientific knowledge and comes to the conclusion that: "Not one sentence of the Biblical account, carefully interpreted in its context, can be shown to be incorrect or second hand or even to be unrealistic or unlikely." Noah built the ark following God's instructions, and when the survival party was safely assembled aboard the ark, then were "all the fountains of the great deep broken up, and the windows of heaven were opened." The waters rose until even the mountains were covered, and every thing that lived on dry land except the occupants of the ark was drowned. The rains continued for 40 days, and it was 150 days before the waters began to fall. When the rains stopped Noah sent out a dove to see whether it would find dry land. But the dove returned to the ark, having "found no rest for the sole of her foot." A week later he sent the dove out again, and it returned with a newly plucked olive leaf in its beak. When he sent the bird out a

Myths of Divine Punishment

Below: French industrialist and explorer Fernand Navarra with a piece of hand-hewn wood of great antiquity found in 1955 on Ararat. It was unearthed from the bottom of a 45-foot crevasse some 5000 feet below the summit in a glacier. Navarra used information gleaned from legends and his own calculations to direct him to the probable site of the Ark. After the successful 1955 expedition, Navarra again visited the site with the SEARCH Foundation of Washington, D.C., and again brought back more hewn wood from a small glacial pond near to the 1955 site.

Right: Noah supervises the building of the Ark. It was God who gave Noah specific instructions for the building of the Ark, including telling him to make it watertight with pitch. There are many various accounts of a universal deluge found in stories from India, Burma, China, Malaya, Palestine, and Mesopotamia, as well as Australia, most Pacific islands, Greece, Lithuania, and Wales.

Below: a 15th-century stained glass window from Ulm Cathedral in Germany showing Noah receiving the dove back into the Ark.

third time after yet another week it did not return at all. Then the ark came to rest "on the mountains of Ararat" and after some time God instructed Noah to disembark his family and livestock and replenish the earth. He promised that he would never again use the Flood to inflict such a terrible punishment on the human race.

The question whether the story of the Flood in Genesis was a historical record or just an ancient cautionary tale has been debated for years by historians and biblical scholars. Then in the middle of the 19th century archaeologists made a discovery which, though it did not solve the riddle, did seem to indicate that the Genesis story was derived from some other source. This was the discovery of the library of the 7th-century B.C. King Ashurbanipal at Nineveh on the banks of the Tigris. Some 20,000 inscribed clay tablets were found, 12 of which contained the story of the Babylonian hero Gilgamesh. When the text of the 11th tablet was translated it created a sensation, for it turned out to be the story of a man who had received a warning from God of an impending flood and had followed instructions to build a ship and stock and provision it so that life might survive the cataclysm. The text was found to date from at least 1000 years before the library was built at Nineveh, and fragments were later found indicating that the Epic of Gilgamesh probably dated back to the Sumerian civilization some 4000 years B.C., which made it very much older than Genesis and raised the question whether the story of the Flood in Genesis had been "lifted" from the Epic of Gilgamesh. There was much heated argument between scholars who proposed this view and those who maintained that the Genesis and Gilgamesh Flood stories were quite independent accounts of *the same event*.

Just how close are the two accounts, and in what respects do they differ? The name of the "Babylonian Noah" is Utnapishtim, and when the hero Gilgamesh visits him Utnapishtim tells him

One Flood or Many?

Left: Noah, his family, and all the animals leaving the Ark as depicted in this stained glass window in a church in Cornwall, England. Noah means "comfort" and he shows that God has mercy on those who obey his commands when he survives the Flood. When order is again restored to the earth, God assures Noah that he will never again wipe out all creatures of the earth with the deluge, and leaves the rainbow as his covenant with mankind.

Below: one of the 12 wedge-shaped cuneiform script tablets found at Nineveh that contain the story of the Epic of Gilgamesh. It was in the 11th tablet that the Sumerian legend of the Flood occurred. In fact, only about 100 lines of an estimated 300 original lines have survived but scholars have been able to guess, from Sumerian literary style and mannerisms, what was in the missing portion of text.

The Scholars Investigate

Above: a boat in the marshes of the River Tigris. This great eastern Mesopotamian river rises on the southern slopes of the Taurus Mountains in Turkey and winds for over 1000 miles down to the Persian Gulf. Nineveh was situated by this river.

Right: cattle crossing a ford in the River Euphrates. The longest river in southwestern Asia, the Euphrates winds for some 1700 miles before meeting the Tigris and flowing through extensive marshland into the Persian Gulf. Scholars think that the torrential rain and tidal bore mentioned in Chapter 7 of the Book of Genesis, combined with perhaps an unusually high rise in water level from the annual spring snow-melt, caused the Euphrates and the Tigris to flood the whole of the low-lying area, destroying every living thing on the plains.

that he had once lived in the city of Shurappak and had been a faithful follower of the god Ea, who had one day warned him of the gods' decision to destroy mankind by flood and had commanded him: "O man of Shurappak . . . tear down thy house, build a ship; abandon wealth, seek after life; scorn possessions, save thy life. Bring up the seed of all kinds of living things into the ship which thou shalt build. Let its dimensions be well measured."

As in the biblical Genesis, this is followed by some details of the dimensions and construction of the ship. These are not identical in the two accounts. For instance, Utnapishtim said he made a ship of six stories, whereas Noah's had three; but both include the detail that when the construction was finished it was made waterproof with thick coats of bitumen. Throughout the two accounts there are striking similarities—and striking differences. Utnapishtim takes aboard his ship not only his immediate family and the livestock specimens, but also all his kinsfolk and many craftsmen. He describes the onset of the deluge in terms recognizable by meterologists as descriptive of a cyclone driving the waters of the Persian Gulf over the low-lying land of Mesopotamia. He says that the freak weather conditions lasted six days, and that the ship eventually grounded on Mount Nisir. As the waters subsided he released a dove; which came back, then a swallow, which also came back, then finally a raven, which did not return. When at last the water level fell back to normal, Utnapishtim told Gilgamesh, "The ground was flat like a roof," and "all mankind had turned to clay." This last vivid detail, which sounds so like an eye-witness report, would precisely describe the effects of a flood in lower Mesopotamia, and it was later borne out by the British archaeologist Sir Leonard Woolley's discoveries at Ur between 1922 and 1934.

If the differences in the details of the two accounts are not enough to prove conclusively that they are independent of each other, careful study of the kind of detail given in Genesis does at least suggest that it was not derived from the Babylonian source. If Gilgamesh and Genesis are independent then there must either be another source, from which both are derived, or, more likely, there were two parties of survivors of the same Flood, so perhaps archaeologists and explorers should get to work on Utnapishtim's Mount Nisir, which has been identified as a

Below left: Sir Leonard Woolley excavating on the site of Ur, in Iraq.
Below: a completely excavated pit at Ur. The floor of the pit goes down to 2800 B.C. Below the floor—in the square opening at the foot of the stairs—is the evidence of the flood deposit.

mountain in Kurdistan and part of a range that rises sharply from the Tigris valley.

It was archaeology that produced the most convincing evidence for the historical accuracy of the Flood. In 1930 a jubilant telegram was sent from Mesopotamia to London announcing: "We have found the Flood!" The sender was Sir Leonard Woolley, who the previous year had unearthed the Sumerian treasures of the Royal Cemetery at Ur, treasures that indicated a highly evolved culture. Hoping to be able to trace the steps by which man had attained this level of culture, Woolley dug deeper. Just under the floor in one of the tombs he found in a layer of charred wood a number of clay tablets inscribed with characters much older than those on the graves. He ordered the digging to continue, and one layer after another yielded fragments of pottery of consistently high quality, showing that the Sumerians had reached a high level of civilization early and had maintained it for a long time. When his workmen had dug through these layers and called out to him that they had reached ground level, Woolley descended the shaft. He confirmed for himself that all traces of human settlement came to an end at the level the dig had now reached, but when he examined the ground on which he stood he discovered to his astonishment that it was pure water-

Above: part of the square opening in the pit floor shown in the top illustration. The light-colored layer is the flood deposit; the darker deposit beneath is black soil that contained broken pottery of a completely different kind of civilization.

Right: assembled fragments of painted pottery of the period before the evidence of flooding found by Sir Leonard Woolley at Ur. They are from a Stone Age culture.

laid mud. Woolley at first thought that the mud must be river silt, but then realized that the site was too high for this theory to be correct, so he ordered his workmen to continue digging, which they reluctantly did.

Determined, literally, to get to the bottom of the mystery, Woolley urged the men on, carefully examining the contents of each basket that was sent up out of the pit as the workmen dug three feet, six feet, then eight feet down into the solid mud. Then, at about nine feet, the layer of mud came to an end, and in the baskets of rubble that now came up there were unmistakable signs of human settlement. There were fragments of pots that had not been turned on a potter's wheel—as the fragments found above the mud layer had been—and there were primitive tools made of hewn flint. The dig had clearly penetrated to a Stone Age settlement. But what was the explanation of the thick layer of mud? Woolley had his own ideas about that, but before expressing them he asked his colleagues what they thought. "They did not know what to say," he later wrote. "My wife came

Below: Mount Parnassus in central Greece. It was on this mountain that the ark of Deucalion and his wife Pyrrha came to rest after the earth was flooded by Zeus.

along and looked and was asked the same question, and she turned away remarking casually, 'Well, of course, it's the Flood.' That was the right answer."

After this first discovery, Woolley had other shafts dug on different sites to confirm his findings, and each time the digging yielded fragments of handmade pottery lying below a layer of mud. Other archaeologists working throughout Mesopotamia took up the search for traces of the Flood, and at Kish, near Babylon, another important site was excavated. Here, however, the mud deposit was only about 18 inches thick. By plotting the thickness of the mud at various points it was decided that the Flood had reached some 400 miles inland from the Persian Gulf and about 100 miles across. "It was not a universal deluge," Woolley concluded; "it was a vast flood in the valley of the Tigris and the Euphrates which drowned the whole of the inhabitable land between the mountains and the desert; for the people that lived there that was all the world. The great bulk of those people must have perished, and it was but a scanty and dispirited remnant that from the city walls watched the waters recede at last. No wonder what they saw in this disaster the gods' punishment of a sinful generation and described it as such in a religious poem; and if some household had managed to escape by boat from the drowned lowlands the head of it would naturally be chosen as the hero of the saga."

Following Woolley's argument it seems that the Gilgamesh and Genesis Flood stories are over-dramatized stories based on a catastrophic flooding of Mesopotamia that occurred about 4000 B.C. One story written soon after the event, the other much later from preserved memories and an oral tradition of story telling. To the writers of both accounts it was an apparent universal disaster, but from the 20th-century point of view merely a localized one. The difficulty with this explanation, which comfortably reconciles scripture with reason, is that it does not account for the worldwide distribution of the Flood legend. It would be interesting to consider what some of the other records have to say—taking first those geographically closest to Mesopotamia.

Lucian, a Syrian of the 2nd century A.D., recorded that in his country there was a very ancient tradition that the gods had punished human wickedness with a deluge from which only one man, named Deucalion, and his family were saved, in an ark with many animals that became tame. Lucian's account was probably taken from Greek sources, for the name Deucalion occurs in Greek legends. According to these, the god Zeus, whose anger had been aroused by Prometheus' theft of fire from heaven, decided to destroy the human race by means of a flood. Prometheus warned his son Deucalion of Zeus' plan, and told him to build a boat to ride the waters and to take his wife Pyrrha aboard it. Deucalion did so, and in due course the torrential downpour came and lasted nine days, plunging the whole world under water. On the 10th day the waters began to subside and Deucalion's boat was grounded upon Mount Parnassus. He disembarked and made a sacrifice to Zeus, so appeasing the god, who said that he would grant Deucalion a wish. Deucalion wished for the renewal of the human race.

Deucalion, Noah of the Greeks

Below: the interior of a Greek drinking cup showing the punishment of Prometheus for stealing fire from the gods. Zeus ordered him to be taken to Mount Caucasus and tied to a rock, where for 30,000 years an eagle was to feed on his liver, which was never diminished although continually being devoured. Because Prometheus sought to benefit mankind with the fire of the gods, the enraged Zeus doomed the whole of the race of men to die in a catastrophic flood.

Right: the Egyptian cow goddess Hathor with the disk of the sun between her horns and (below) Sekmet the lion goddess of war and plagues. As the sun god Ra grew old and frail the people of the earth rebelled against his authority and Ra sent Hathor and Sekmet to subdue them. Once the bloodlust of the goddess was aroused, however, the whole of creation was in danger of annihilation. Ra then ordered the world to be flooded with beer, which the goddesses drank and so became incapable of further slaughter. This curious story is one of several Egyptian allusions to a "universal" deluge, though why it should have been of beer is unknown. The biblical story of Noah, too, has a reference to intoxication.

Egyptian records mention the Flood several times, but there is no full account of a Flood story. There is, however, a strange story about the sun-god Ra, who ordered the goddesses Hathor and Sekmet to destroy the rebellious people of the world. When they had shed seas of blood Ra relented, but he was unable to stop the goddesses' murderous rampage, so he flooded the world with beer, which they drank. They became so intoxicated that they were incapable of further slaughter. Another Egyptian Flood legend tells how Atum, the god of Heliopolis, caused a deluge to submerge the earth from which only the chosen people he took into his own boat survived. And Plato in the *Timaeus* dialogue, reports the belief of an Egyptian priest that the gods sent a flood to purify the world and all the populations of towns were swept away, leaving only a few shepherds on high mountains.

Even if all the stories from the Near and Middle East were variations on a theme that could be traced to a single source, this would not explain the existence of ancient flood legends in other parts of the world. The Aztecs, the Mixtecs, the Zapotecs, and the Mayas of South America all had such legends. In the Aztec version their chief god, Tezcatlopica, warned a human couple, Nata and Nena, of a flood that was coming and instructed them to build a ship, which they did. They became the sole survivors of the cataclysm. Flood legends have been found throughout the Pacific islands, too. The Hawaiians have an ancient tradition of a flood caused by an angry god from which only one good man and his family escaped on a boat aboard which they had taken plants and animals. In Indian mythology there is a story that the father of the human race was Manu. While washing in the river one day, Manu was visited by the god Vishnu in the form of a fish and warned that the world would be flooded in seven days' time because of the wickedness of the human race. Manu was told that he, together with seven holy men and their wives, would be saved if they boarded a vessel that would be provided, and if they stocked it with pairs of animals and adequate food. This they did, and when the flood subsided Manu's vessel was grounded halfway up a Himalayan mountain.

These are a few of the many examples of flood legends that have sprung up literally in every part of the world. Often the motifs are the same: the punishment of the human race by God and the saving of one good man and his family or associates. The distribution of this story is undoubtedly due in part to cross-cultural influences. Some of the sources are so ancient, however, and so completely unconnected that there is little doubt that they arose spontaneously. Which suggests either that the Flood is a good tale thought up independently by people all over the world, or that a tremendous planet-wide cataclysm occurred in prehistoric times, hurling the seas over the land in many widely separated areas.

Support for the theory of a prehistoric cataclysm comes from India and South America in texts that parallel the accounts in Genesis. The Sanskrit epic poem of 1200 B.C., the *Mahabharata* states: "Then men tampered with the 'Divine Fire' so that the earth split apart and 6 million people in great cities were drowned in one terrible night." And an ancient Mayan manuscript records a similar event: "The country of the hills of earth, the Land of Mu, were sacrificed. Twice upheaved, it disappeared during the night, having been constantly shaken. The land rose and sank several times in various places, and at last the surface gave way and the 10 regions were torn asunder and scattered, the millions of inhabitants sank also."

Further support for the theory of a prehistoric cataclysm comes from geologists who have found signs that point to a comparatively recent tremendous upheaval of the greater part of the earth. In the 19th century the English naturalist Charles Darwin found shells at a height of 1300 feet in the Andes and expressed surprise that they were not fossilized. At about the same altitude on Moel Tryfan in North Wales sea shells and beds of sand are to be found. In fact, according to the Irish Professor J. Joly in *The Surface History of the Earth*, published in 1925, "the most striking fact known about the mountains is that they are largely and often mainly composed of sedimentary rocks, that is, of rocks which have been deposited originally in the seas. True, these sediments may be contorted, folded, even metamorphosed almost beyond recognition, but none the less they have risen from the sea-floor to form the mountain chain. It is a universal fact. Even of the volcano-topped Andes and Caucasus it is true." In this passage Professor Joly is speaking about sediments deposited in remote geological time, but such findings as those in the Andes and North Wales of unfossilized sea shells indicate that great movements and upheavals of the earth's surface have taken place in recent times.

The word "Recent," spelled with a capital R, is used by geologists for the period after the ending of the last Ice Age, which is generally agreed to have been some 10,000 years ago. The melting of the ice at that time may have raised the level of the oceans by as much as 3000 feet, which would of course have

The Worldwide Legend of Flood

Above: part of an Aztec Codex illustrating the legend of the Earth Mother—a monstrous alligator-like creature—being tempted to come to the surface of the great waters by the god Tezcatlipoca, lord of the four cardinal compass points and lord of the nature gods. He offers the goddess his foot as bait and seizes her and takes her back to dry land. Once the earth is established, mankind is created. The god Tezcatlipoca saves mankind from being utterly wiped out by warning one human couple of a coming flood. Like the biblical Noah and his wife the couple build a ship and become the sole survivors of the deluge.

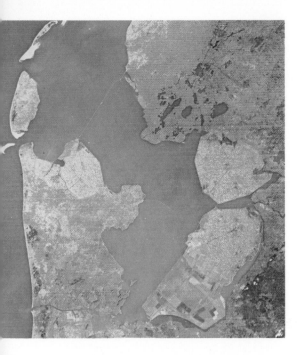

Above: a satellite view of the Ijsselmeer (formerly the Zuider Zee). The formation of the Zuider Zee, according to some scientists, belongs to a period of violent earth-movements and flooding that occurred between the end of the last Ice Age and the rise of the great empires of mankind. Western Europe experienced a vast flood well after the end of the last Ice Age, but well before historical times, possibly between 6000 to 4000 B.C. There is a growing body of evidence supplied by geological research that establishes the existence of great floods over vast areas within the period to which the flood of Noah, as related in the Book of Genesis, is generally placed.

greatly altered the distribution of land-masses throughout the world. Some scholars have found evidence that the archipelagos and peninsulas of Southeast Asia were once part of a continuous landmass, and that the subsidence happened so recently that the now underwater river valleys can still be fitted into a former land drainage system. Also, the distribution of river-fish on the islands still follows the old surface-water distribution system. Between 6000 and 4000 B.C. the great inundation that occurred in Western Europe and formed the Zuider Zee in the central Netherlands was known as the Flandrian Flood. It might well have occurred at the same time as the Mesopotamian Flood and the others recorded in legend. The fact that a great change also took place in the Middle East can be gathered from the fact that the Black and the Caspian Seas are known to have been connected at one time, but today the Caspian Sea is 85 feet below the level of the Black Sea. And between the two, of course, lie the mountains of Ararat.

Historians have often noticed that there is a distinct gap between the Paleolithic and Neolithic cultures, as if Paleolithic man was suddenly wiped out and some time elapsed before Neolithic man appeared in the world. Scholars divide the evidence for this sudden break into three types: the complete difference between Paleolithic and Neolithic art; the separation of Paleolithic and Neolithic layers in caves by a layer devoid of any signs of human settlement; and the extinction of certain Paleolithic animals. It is difficult to think of any way of explaining this historical gap except that a planet-wide catastrophe abruptly brought the Paleolithic world to an end.

The mystery of the woolly mammoths points to the same conclusion. In the cave-art of the Paleolithic period there are many pictures of this hairy relative of the modern elephant that roamed the Northern Hemisphere from Siberia to the Sahara, but none are found in Neolithic art. Nobody has been able to explain what caused their sudden extinction. Interestingly, though, scientists have observed that the state of preservation of the flesh of mammoths found in Siberia in 1799 and the fact that they were discovered with food in their mouths indicates that they were overcome in a very short time by extreme cold of the order of −150°F.

It was not only the mammoths that suffered. In France, Sicily, Malta, Gibraltar, and Yugoslavia the intermingled bones of lions, elephants, rhinoceroses, and even hippopotamuses have been found in caves and crevasses at high altitudes, which indicates that the European climate was very different when they lived. How the bones got to such an altitude is something of a puzzle. It could be that the animals were seeking refuge from rising flood waters but were eventually overtaken and drowned and their remains were swept into the deep clefts in the earth.

So the evidence for the occurrence of a planet-wide catastrophe in Recent times, and probably between 8000 and 4000 B.C., comes from many sources, both legendary and scientific. It could well be, then, that the Genesis story is neither improbable nor necessarily an exaggeration of a local occurrence. But how could such a disaster have occurred?

Scientists have put forward two possible explanations. If the axis of rotation of the earth were suddenly shifted just a single degree, the oceans would rise in a great wave that would roll around the earth. That God is quite capable of effecting such a shift is a proposition that seems perfectly in order to the pious, but science cannot suggest any known force that God could call on to implement his will if he decided to tilt the earth's axis. The second explanation is the more likely one either as a natural or a God-sent cause of the cataclysm. It is that a wandering celestial body, a small planet or large asteroid, came close to the earth. If such a body came close enough to interact with earth's gravitational field, but kept at a sufficient distance not to be captured by it, it would raise immense tidal waves on our planet. And if it carried with it, as some comets do, a quantity of frozen gas particles, these might well be captured by earth's gravity, plunging part of the planet into intense cold and at the same time "seeding" the atmosphere and causing torrential rains. In 1932 a large asteroid named Apollo came within 2 million miles of earth, and two other bodies, Hermes and Adonis, have come close in recent times, but fortunately all three were small enough and kept at a sufficient distance not to tangle with our gravitational field.

Such "near misses" do, however, show that the Genesis Flood, the extinction of the mammoths and other animals, the gap between the Paleolithic and Neolithic ages, and the depositing of sea shells and sand on high mountains throughout the world, could all be attributed to a single astronomical event. Whether that event would have been an "act of God" is a question that the rationalists will consider unreasonable and the scientists unscientific, but those who believe that the scriptures of their religion embody God's word will have no doubt about the matter.

A Climatic Conundrum

Below left: Paleolithic cave painting (of around 16,000 B.C.) on the roof of the Rouffignac Cave, Dordogne, France. The paintings are of a mammoth and ibexes, both of which appear to have been frequently hunted for food. The mammoth in particular appears many times and in many sites where Paleolithic art has been discovered.

Below: a group of Soviet scientists examining the carcass of a young mammoth found preserved in the frozen ground of the Magadan in the eastern USSR. This young mammoth, which died about 12,000 years ago, and the nine-year-old mammoth (bottom picture) are just two of the many preserved specimens of mammoths of all ages that have been found in the USSR. Examination of their blood showed they were closely related to the modern Asian elephant, and scientists have been able to open their digestive tracts to examine the remains of vegetable food they ate. The mammoths died out suddenly together with Paleolithic man.

Chapter 6
Spokesman of the Gods

The first prophets were "shamans," who by means of wild dancing and strange music became "possessed" by the gods who through them made revelations about the future. The Greek world was scattered with the temples of oracles, who similarly induced, offered frequently ambiguous prophecies. From about 700 B.C., a new kind of prophet appeared among the Hebrews—men like Amos, Isaiah, Jeremiah, Ezekiel. It was to them that the people were instructed to turn, rather than to the wizards, necromancers, and soothsayers of the Pagan tribes around them. In this context, Muhammad is simply regarded by Moslems as the last and greatest of these prophets. This chapter looks at the role of the prophets in man's religions.

God, or Yahweh, as he was known to the ancient Hebrews, became exasperated with the disobedience of his chosen people and decided that he might get his message across more effectively if he put one of his prophets in a position like his own. So he ordered the prophet Hosea to marry a prostitute. "Go, take into thee a wife of whoredom and children of whoredom: for the land hath committed great whoredom departing from the Lord," he said. Another man might have treated the divine order as a bit of flowery speech but Hosea did precisely as he was commanded, and when his first son was born he obeyed a further order to name him Jezreel, for the sinful capital of the Israelite monarchy under the infamous king Ahab. His second child, a daughter, he named Lo-ruhamah ("Not Pitied") and his third, another son, Lo-ammi ("Not my People"), again on the instructions of Yahweh, who obviously was so desperate to communicate that he would try the most outlandish means. Then Hosea's wife became an adulteress and left him, but the prophet went after her and brought her back to his home and continued to love her despite her unfaithfulness, just as God continued to love his chosen people who had forsaken him.

Biblical scholars are convinced that Hosea's story of his marriage is not an allegory of Yahweh's relation to Israel, but is literally true. He did marry a prostitute, love her in spite of her infidelities, and give his children symbolical names; and he did so because God told him to.

Opposite: a miniature from a 15th-century French manuscript depicting Yahweh surrounded by angels. God, the creator of all that is, seen or unseen, is shown here in awe-inspiring majesty. No one, said the God of Moses, may see my face and live. His commands to his followers were made known to them through specially chosen people, his spokesmen, the prophets.

EZECHIAS

Israel germinabit sicut lilium et· rumpet Radix eius ut liban osee·14·

Right: part of a tapestry from France showing the prophet Hosea, from the Tree of Jesse. There has been much controversy over the prophet's marriage to a prostitute —as commanded by God—many churchmen arguing that it is inconceivable that Yahweh should dishonor himself by ordering a marriage so repugnant to the moral sense. Everyone agrees, though, that the prophet's marriage has a symbolic meaning. When the people expressed shock at the prophet taking to himself a dishonored wife it provided him with an opportunity to insist on the evil of their faithlessness to Yahweh, in spite of Yahweh's manifested love for them.

Above: the leaders of the 12 tribes of Israel from an early-14th-century French manuscript. When the Hebrews entered Canaan they found the land divided into many different city states only nominally subject to Egypt. Joshua divided the land— still largely unconquered by him—into territories which he then assigned by lot to the various tribes. It was from among these people who comprised Yahweh's chosen followers that the innumerable prophets— greater and lesser—were selected by Yahweh himself to be the link between his people and himself.

This story of Hosea vividly and dramatically demonstrates the unquestioning faith that the Hebrew prophets had in the reality of their God. For theirs was a unique position; unlike the priests who, by carrying out sacrifices and worship on behalf of the people in a carefully prescribed manner, were intermediaries between the people and their God, the prophets were the intermediaries between God and his people. A prophet was the "mouth of God." Jeremiah, one of the 16 prophets whose writings are included in the Old Testament of the Bible, summed up the work of the prophet when he wrote: "The Lord put forth his hand and touched my mouth; and the Lord said to me: Behold I have put my words in thy mouth."

God himself had promised to select these extraordinary people from among the Hebrew tribes. In Chapter 18 of the Book

Priests or Prophets?

of Deuteronomy the Hebrews beg him not to speak to them directly as he had on Sinai, when the people were overwhelmed by the power and majesty of his voice. God replies: "They have well spoken which they have spoken. I will raise them up a Prophet from among their brethren . . . and will put my words in his mouth; and he shall speak unto them all that I shall command him." The prophets, then, were Yahweh's chosen spokesmen and leaders. And it was they, perhaps, more than any other group that had the most profound influence on the development of religion.

The word "prophet" is misleading. Today it usually means only foretelling the future, but foretelling the future was only one of the functions of these men, and by no means the most important one. In Hebrew there is a clear distinction between the *ro'eh* or *chozeh*, the seer, clairvoyant, or diviner, and the *nâbi*, the speaker called by God. When translating for the large community of Greek-speaking Jews, the word *nâbi* was always translated as prophētēs, prophet, and generally meant "one who speaks in place of another as interpreter." The Greek word prophētēs was originally used for the official at a temple who explained the myth of the god, and was later applied generally to the priests who interpreted various sounds, signs, or utterances as messages from the god.

The most famous site of prophesy in Greece was at Delphi, where there was a temple sacred to the god Apollo. People came from all over Greece to consult the famous prophet, or *oracle* who was a priestess known as the Pythia—a reincarnation of a prophetic serpent slain by Apollo. When consulted, the Pythia

Left: the ruins of the temple of Apollo, at Delphi, Greece. It is said that it preserves to this day much of the extraordinary religious atmosphere that it had in ancient times. It was one of the most important sanctuaries in the whole of Greece and contained a world-famous oracle, a prophetess known as the pythia. She sat on a tripod and inhaled fumes of barley, hemp, and chopped bay leaves burned over an oil flame. She was believed to be in direct communication with the god Apollo—slayer of the original serpent or python and possessor of that creature's powers to see into the future. For over 1000 years the oracle was consulted by Greeks, Romans, and Orientals anxious to know what the future had in store for them. Socrates was a firm believer in the oracle (which had declared him to be the wisest of mortals). It was through the oracle that Apollo operated as a moral force in Greek life. Two of his maxims, "know thyself" and "nothing in excess," are said to epitomize the awareness and moderation taken to be the Greek ideal.

Above: ruined remains of the sanctuary and oracle of Zeus at Dodona, in northern Greece. The ancient Greeks had no sacred books such as the Bible or the Koran and their priests were there mainly to carry out the ritual sacrifices or cleansings according to strictly laid down rules. They were rarely regarded as sources of wisdom or comfort. It was to the oracles that the people, from kings and generals to ordinary people, took their problems. The gods' answers to the faithful enquirers were often given by a prophet or prophetess, usually in a trance, and their replies would be interpreted by a priest. There was considerable rivalry between Dodona and Delphi. Dodona claimed to be the oracle of Zeus, father of gods and men. Delphi claimed that Apollo was the mouthpiece of his father, the almighty Zeus.

would go into a frenzy and utter weird sounds that had to be interpreted by the priests at the shrine. Second in importance only to Delphi was the ancient sanctuary of Dodona, in north-western Greece. The oracle of Dodona was sacred to Zeus, who spoke to his petitioners through the rustling leaves of a sacred red oak tree. The priests at the shrine interpreted these rustlings into often riddle-like answers to questions that had been written down on lead tablets.

The Greek-speaking Jewish philosopher Philo Judaeus of Alexandria, writing between the 1st century B.C. and the 1st century A.D., stressed the difference between the diviner, who drew his own conclusions from omens and signs, and the true prophet, who received revelations from God and uttered them or acted upon them. The true prophet scorned the paraphernalia of the diviner's art. When he prophesied he became possessed by the word of God. He was under a compulsion. As Isaiah explains in Chapter 8 of his book of prophesy: "The Lord spake thus to me with a strong hand." The prophets were literally men possessed, and the very consistence of the message they communicated to successive generations throughout centuries of Jewish history suggests that whatever possessed them was quite independent of any of their individual minds. Indeed, on occasion the prophets did not always understand their message. The prophet Daniel recounts in Chapter 8 of his book of prophesy how even after he had been given the explanation of the vision of the ram and the goat, he remained astonished at the vision, "but none understood it."

According to scholars, the earliest records of the prophetic movement date from the 9th century B.C. Moses' sister Mary is a prophetess, and according to Chapter 12 of the Book of Numbers, God spoke through her; but the first outstanding figure is Samuel of Ramah. The story of Saul and Samuel as told in Chapters 9 and 10 of the First Book of Samuel gives a fascinating insight into the period. When Saul, the future king of Israel, was a young man he was sent by Kish, his father, to search for some asses that were missing. Accompanied by a servant, he traveled for three days on his quest, and they eventually came to Ramah, where they learned that there was a seer who they could consult. There is an explanation in the text that "Beforetime in Israel, when a man went to inquire of God thus he spake, Come, let us go to the seer: for he that is now called a Prophet was beforetime called a seer." Samuel knew all about the missing asses before Saul mentioned them, and was able to tell him that they had been found; and he was also able to tell him something far more important, for God had told him that Saul was destined to become king of Israel. Samuel welcomed the future king in his home, and before he left the following day he told him of three meetings he would have on his journey home. The third would be with "a company of prophets coming down from the high place with a psaltery [a kind of lute] and a tabret [a small drum] and a pipe and a harp before them; and they shall prophesy." And Saul, Samuel said, would experience the spirit of the Lord come mightily upon him and would prophesy with them and

Seers and Oracles

Above: a red figured Greek vase showing the god Apollo, left of center, and a fleeing pythia.

Left: a 19th-century engraving of the meeting between Saul and Samuel the prophet at Ramah. Saul, the son of Kish, of the small and warlike tribe of Benjamin, has an almost chance meeting while searching for some missing asses with Samuel, who is also searching, mentally, for the nation's future leader. Samuel promises Saul three signs as confirmation that he is to be Israel's king: the lost asses would be found; he would meet men from Tabor who would offer him part of their sacrificial meal; the spirit of prophesy would come upon him. The first sign was to convince him he was king by God's will, the second that he was king partly as God's representative, thirdly he must be king with the help of God's spirit.

Above: King Saul of Israel, a detail from a window in Chartres Cathedral, France, and dating from the 13th century. From the same man that anointed him king, Saul also heard his doom, when the witch of Endor conjured up the spirit of the prophet Samuel to advise the worried and careworn king.

Right: a company of Hebrew prophets with their musical instruments, from a 13th-century French manuscript. Music was both an aid to recollection and an accompaniment to the singing of praises to Yahweh. The music may also have excited the senses to a state of frenzy, producing psychic manifestations interpreted as prophecies.

would be turned into another man. Everything happened as Samuel predicted, and witnesses to the scene asked, "What is this that has come unto the son of Kish? Is Saul also among the prophets?"

What is particularly interesting in the passage is that it gives not only examples of Samuel's clairvoyant and precognitive powers, but also a vivid picture of a band of prophets with their musical instruments. Such groups, which began to appear in the country in the 9th century, would dance themselves into a frenzy and go into ecstacy or a trance—in much the same way as the later Moslem mystics known as dancing dervishes. Other Middle Eastern nations of the time also experienced the phenomenon of these "ecstatic" prophets. Canaan, Babylonia, Assyria, and Egypt all had men who believed the spirit of a god had entered into them. But in Israel the wandering prophets who appeared to imitate their pagan counterparts were not publicly regarded with much respect. The question, "Is Saul also among the prophets?" is scathing, and later we read that it was a habit of the wandering bands of musician-prophets to strip off their clothes and lie about naked while they prophesied. But to put these extra-ordinary prophets into their context, they were really part of a new wave of nationalist feeling that arose at a time when the Jews were suffering under Philistine oppression. They were therefore of some importance, for it was to the popular Yahwist-nationalist feeling that the later prophets addressed their urgent warnings and appeals.

Music and Dance, Ecstasy and Trance

Below: part of an Oriental manuscript showing Moslems dancing frenziedly. About five percent of all Moslems belong to a religious order known as Sufism. To become a Sufi (meaning "to don the woollen garment") is to put away everything that might direct the mind from Allah and divine things. The Sufis are divided into a large number of fraternities and orders some of which come under the heading of dervishes. They are known to howl, scream, and dance in wild ecstasies, and it is while in this state that they approach close to Allah to communicate with him.

The True Prophets

Another illuminating tale of this period, from the First Book of Kings, is told of King Jehoshaphat of Judah who proposed to Ahab the king of Israel a joint offensive against Syria. The kings gathered together 400 prophets and consulted them. The prophets, all fervent nationalists, assured the kings that they would triumph, but Jehoshaphat wanted the opinion also of the renowned prophet Micaiah. Ahab said, "I hate him; for he doth not prophesy good concerning me." Nevertheless he sent for Micaiah. The messenger urged the prophet to fall in with the others and tell the king what he wanted to hear, but Micaiah said, "As the Lord lives, what the Lord says to me, that I will speak," and when he confronted the kings he told them that he had a vision of "all Israel scattered upon the mountains, as sheep

Right: King Jehoshaphat of Judah, from a 14th-century stained glass window in Winchester College Chapel, England. Because his country was constantly threatened by powerful neighbors, he settled traditional differences with the northern kingdom of Israel and preserved his kingdom intact.

Above: a 19th-century engraving showing the kings of Israel and Judah, Ahab and Jehoshaphat, seated before the prophet Micaiah, with a gathering of prophets behind him. The kings conferred together to take back land that the Syrians had captured from them. They consulted with the prophets of Israel who said they would win the battle with the Syrians. But Jehoshaphat was suspicious; he knew that Ahab's pagan wife had persecuted Yahweh's prophets and that these survivors, though claiming to speak for Yahweh, were probably Baal worshipers. He asks for another prophet and Micaiah is sent for. He tells Ahab that he will die on the battlefield, and that the other prophets will one day have to flee for their lives.

that have no shepherd." Moreover, he described a gathering in heaven from which Yahweh had sent a lying spirit to deceive the 400 prophets in order to bring about Ahab's downfall. "Did I not tell thee that he would prophesy no good concerning me?" said Ahab, and he had Micaiah thrown into prison and ignored his advice—foolishly, for the battle against the Syrians went as the prophet had foretold and Ahab was killed in it, leaving his army scattered upon the mountains.

Ahab really ought to have known better than to scorn a true prophet's word, for earlier in his reign he had tangled with the formidable Elijah, who had told him that as a punishment for taking a heathen wife, Jezebel, and adopting her religion, God would send years of drought upon Israel, and the prophecy had been fulfilled. Elijah had later to flee from the hatred of Queen Jezebel and hid in a cave on Mount Horeb. There, preceded by a storm, earthquake, and fire, he received a communication from God telling him to anoint new kings of Syria and Israel, and naming Elisha as his own successor in the prophetic office. Elijah then traveled up the Jordan valley, where he met Elisha plowing his father's fields. He cast his own cloak upon Elisha to confirm him in his office of prophet, and Elisha followed him. A number of miraculous acts of Elijah are reported in the scriptures,

Below: a 19th-century artist's impression of King Ahab of Israel with his pagan wife Jezebel and the prophet Elijah. The king wanted the vineyard of Naboth, which adjoined the palace, but the owner, Naboth, refused him. Jezebel plotted Naboth's death and handed the vineyard to her husband. Elijah was commanded by God to go to the vineyard and pronounce judgment against Jezebel.

Right: the prophet Elijah in a chariot drawn by four winged horses casts down his distinctive hairy cloak—symbolizing his prophetic office—upon his successor, Elisha (below, from an icon in a museum at Sofia, Bulgaria). Apart from Enoch, a descendant of Adam, Elijah is the only person in the Old Testament to have been lifted into heaven by Yahweh.

and it is really impossible to separate historical fact from pious fantasy in his story. He stands as a mighty and solitary figure through whom God expresses his wrath and pronounces his terrible judgment upon all those who turn from their religion or break its laws.

Elisha stands in sharp contrast to his predecessor. He is a gentler and less austere figure, the agent not of God's vengeance but of his mercy. He became a power in the land and, because of his prophetic gifts, an invaluable aid to the kings of Israel as a political and military adviser. The truth of the many miracles attributed to him can never be known but what is clear is that with Elisha the idea of the prophet as the intermediary between

Yahweh and his chosen people became firmly established.

The major theme of the 8th-century literary prophets Hosea and Amos is the castigation of the people of Israel for neglecting their obligations under their covenant with Yahweh. Both were solitary men, unconnected with the groups of wandering prophets or established professional guilds connected with the priesthood and specific holy places, and both declare that they had been forced by Yahweh to speak his word. In Chapter 7 of the Book of Amos the prophet writes how prophesying got him into trouble at the royal shrine at Bethel. The chief priest eventually complained to the king, Jeroboam, who forbade Amos to continue his activities there, advising him instead to flee to the land of Judah. Amos's reply was: "I was no prophet, neither was I a prophet's son; but I was an herdsman, and a gatherer of sycamore fruit; and the Lord took me as I followed the flock, and the Lord said unto me, Go, prophesy unto my people Israel." What Amos is implying by this disclaimer is that the enthusiastic nationalist prophets were not revealing God's true message, which is why he had to be forced to take on the job. He had to dissuade the

Solitary Men of Supernatural Power

Left: the prophet Amos, from a stained glass window of 1557 in St. Mary's church, Shrewsbury, England. The office of prophet was not hereditary nor belonging to any class of person. Neither could it be claimed by any man, however religious or holy. It was a call from God alone as it consisted in the revelation of God's will, a purely supernatural office that could only come from God. Amos was called while with his flocks of sheep. Elisha was plowing with a team of oxen when God called him, through Elijah. Jeremiah was a priest.

Men of Visions

people from the naive view that Yahweh would always be on Israel's side. The prophecy that annoyed the high priest at the royal shrine was that the king would "die by the sword, and Israel shall surely be led away captive out of their own land." As the reign of Jeroboam was a period of prosperity and military strength and security, this prophecy, which was eventually fulfilled, was quite remarkable. Does it prove Amos's direct access to Yahweh's plans or his shrewd political foresight? As far as Amos was concerned Yahweh did nothing without revealing his secrets to his prophets. Nevertheless, the threat of the growing power of Assyria to the east would have been obvious to a man detached from the widespread euphoria of prosperity and power.

Amos spoke out firmly in the name of God against the reckless extravagance and injustice rife in the Israel of his day, attacking usury, dishonesty in business dealings, temple prostitution, taxation of the poor, and the practice of selling people into slavery, as well as the worship of false gods and the adoption of heathen rites in the worship of Yahweh. Sacrifices, burnt offerings, music and songs, and all the many ways of trying to appease him, were as a curse to the God of Amos, for he cared only that justice and righteousness should flow throughout the land. Through Amos, Yahweh reveals himself for the first time as not merely the god of a place and people, but as one who rules over all nature and all nations. His special relationship with the people of Israel is not denied, but it is regarded as involving special responsibilities and any backsliding would bring extremely severe punishment.

The God who speaks through Hosea tends to be gentler and more forgiving than the God of Amos, and he stresses his unfailing love for his people. The prophet's own constancy in love for his erring wife is presented in Hosea's story as a comparison of Yahweh's relation to Israel, but despite this the prophetic message is not an optimistic one. Yahweh's judgment upon the people is as severe as that communicated through Amos. They will suffer military defeat and exile, but if then they understand and acknowledge the cause of their downfall and mend their ways they will have a second chance, a new covenant, and Yahweh will await their change of heart as patiently as the prophet awaited his wife's. But whether Hosea's constancy toward his wife was ultimately rewarded is a question that his text leaves unanswered.

The greatest of the prophets, Isaiah, was a younger contemporary of Hosea and Amos. According to his writings he was married and had at least two children, whom he gave symbolic names, as Hosea did, on instructions from Yahweh. He lived in Jerusalem and was of high enough rank to be able to address the king directly and to say unpleasant things without fear. He dressed and behaved as a prophet and lectured and taught a group of disciples. He exercised considerable influence at the royal court for some time, but his political advice was not generally followed. His own vocation was revealed to him in the form of a vision he had one day in the temple, when he saw God enthroned in splendor and was touched on the mouth with a burning coal from the altar by a seraph, a six-winged angelic

Above: an illustration from a Latin psalter showing worshipers kneeling before two idols in the form of men on pillars. The Hebrews were constantly being reprimanded for worshiping the idols of the pagan nations around them: "Thou hatest those who pay regard to vain idols," declares the psalm that the picture above illustrates. Some of the prophets stressed Yahweh's vengeance, others his forgiveness to those who turned away from evil.

Above: a relief from the Palace of Nimrod, god of war and hunting, showing mounted Assyrian archers engaged in battle. The prophet Hosea lived and prophesied in a time of internal political decadence and general moral corruption. Yahweh, their God, was seen by the Hebrews as one god among many, who demanded sacrifices but had no interest in their moral conduct. Their religion became a system of performances of religious rites rather than the following of religious truths and moral concepts. Hosea announces that the people will be exiled to Assyria or Egypt for their wickedness.

being, in token of forgiveness. He was then called by God to be his spokesman.

Isaiah turned out to be as crushing in his denunciations of Israel's evils as Amos, but at the same time he was as certain of God's forgiveness as Hosea, and he was confident that in the end God would save his people. His many prophesies and his poetical use of language make him supreme among the prophets, and through his utterances Yahweh was revealed to the Hebrews as a universal God, the Creator and Lord of the entire world, whose wisdom is supreme if sometimes unfathomable and whose judgment is inescapable, although tempered with mercy for the repentant. It is doubtful whether the people of Israel would have been able to survive the Babylonian exile without Isaiah's high moral and far-seeing view of their God and their destiny.

The Exile was from 598 to 538 B.C., and it was the prophet

Above left: a 19th-century engraving of sorrowing Hebrews in Babylon. Heedless of their prophets, who tried to keep the religion of Yahweh untainted by pagan practices, the Hebrews pursued a foreign policy that excluded Yahweh—and his prophets—as it came more and more to exclude him from the religious life. Yahweh's punishment was that Israel, the northern kingdom, was to disappear—the people's faith was so weak it did not survive their exile. The people of the southern kingdom of Judah, with its capital of Jerusalem, survived with renewed faith their 60-year exile.

Jeremiah Ignored

Below: the prophet Jeremiah, painted
around 1440. Jeremiah, a priest of Judah,
was called by God to reveal the coming
destruction of Jerusalem. To avert their fate,
Jeremiah explained to king and people, they
must repent of their sins and submit to the
overwhelming power of Babylon. If they
obeyed these entreaties they would have
merciful treatment and ultimately the nation
would be restored. Jeremiah, like other
prophets, was not believed. He had to watch
the very evils he had prophesied come to
pass. When the Jews fled to Egypt they
forced Jeremiah and his secretary, Baruch,
to accompany them. There is a tradition
that he was stoned to death by the Jews in
Egypt.

Jeremiah's lot to be Yahweh's spokesman to his people in the
years leading up to their captivity. Jeremiah, the son of a priest
received his call as a young man and needed some persuading of
its genuineness. His first prophetic vision was of an attack upon
Jerusalem from the north. The idea of foreign conquest as
Yahweh's way of punishing his people's iniquities is a recurrent
theme throughout Jeremiah's work. As conquest and exile were
always possibilities to the small nations of the time, defeat need
not necessarily be God-sent. It could just as well be an intelligent
reading of the signs of the times. The northern kingdom of Israel
had fallen to the Assyrians in 721 B.C., and the little kingdom of
Judah was surrounded by warring powers. The mighty nations
of Assyria and Egypt were at war, and Judah lay between them.
To the east, in Babylon, a new and aggressive kingdom had been
established by an upstart prince, Nabopolassar who ruled from
625 to 605 B.C., and to the north the Scythians were taking over
Samaria. So in the circumstances, it would perhaps have been a
bolder prophecy to have guaranteed the inviolability of Judah.

Jeremiah, like Amos, Hosea, and Isaiah before him, spoke out
strongly against lax morality and the corruption of the true
religion with the worship of images and borrowed pagan rites.
However, early in his career sweeping reforms were carried out
by king Josiah, which made Jeremiah's raging against such evils
obsolete. One day the 18-year-old king had sent a servant to the
high priest, Hilkiah, on business concerning repair work on the
Temple, and the servant had come back with the news that
Hilkiah had found in the Temple the original Book of the Law as
written down by Moses. Josiah sent for the book and was so
alarmed by the divine appeals and the threats of what would
happen if the covenant and the law were disregarded that he
ordered the book to be read aloud to all the citizens of Jerusalem.
They, too, were cowed and frightened into righteousness by it,
and Josiah was able to bring off probably the speediest and most
thorough reforms of religion and law in history. Jeremiah was at
first an enthusiastic supporter of the new order, but he soon began
to see its drawbacks: how complacent it made people; how it
reduced worship to a mere formality. There was the danger, too,
that people would believe that Yahweh was now "bound by
contract" to help and protect the kingdom. Jeremiah was com-
pelled to speak out against those who kept strictly to the letter
of the Book of the Law, instead of reforming their attitudes to
life and their fellows. But he was ignored, and some 10 years
after the reformation, Josiah was killed in battle at Megiddo
and Jerusalem fell virtually under Egyptian rule through the
puppet king Jehoiakim, a son of Josiah but a cruel and exacting
despot.

Jeremiah, as Yahweh's spokesman, rebuked Jehoiakim for his
crimes and so put himself in great personal danger. Another
prophet who had spoken out against Jehoiakim, Uriah, was
murdered, and Jeremiah would no doubt have suffered the same
fate if he had not been watchful and had influential friends. He
did not lie low, however. He even spoke up in the Temple against
the tendency to concentrate on rites and ceremonies in the
religion practiced there—and got himself put in the stocks
overnight for his insolence. Undaunted, when released by

Pashur, the Temple governor, he uttered the famous prophesy (in Chapter 20 of the Book of Jeremiah) that was to be fulfilled to the letter: "I will give all Judah into the hand of the king of Babylon; he shall carry them captive to Babylon, and shall slay them with the sword. Moreover, I will deliver all the strength of this city, and all the labours thereof, and all the precious things thereof, and all the treasures of the kings of Judah will I give into the hand of their enemies, who shall spoil them, and take them, and carry them to Babylon. And thou, Pashur, and all that dwell in thine house, shall go into captivity; and thou shalt come to Babylon and there thou shalt die, and shalt be buried there, thou and all thy friends, to whom thou hast prophesied lies."

This prophecy must have seemed a wild one when Jeremiah made it, for Babylon was not at that time strong enough to challenge Egypt. But the Babylonian power grew, and eventually Egypt and Babylon were fighting a war on several fronts, with Judah a pawn between them. Jeremiah advised the kingdom to submit to Babylonian rule, and even went about with a wooden yoke on his neck as a symbol of submission for now he saw Babylon as the agent of Yahweh's chastisement.

His advice went unheeded and eventually the city and the country fell to the Babylonians. Nebuchadnezzar, the Babylonian king, who had heard of the prophet's pro-Babylonian recommendations, ordered that he should be given his freedom and a choice between remaining in Judah or going to Babylon, where he would be received with honor. Jeremiah chose to remain, which was the most dangerous course for him to take,

Above: Josiah, King of Judah, from the Tree of Jesse stained glass window in Canterbury Cathedral, England. It was during his reign that the Book of the Law was rediscovered during the repair of the temple. The threats of exile for king and people in the book moved everybody deeply. Thoroughgoing reforms were carried out by order of the king, and the Passover was kept as it had not been kept since the days of Samuel the prophet. Eventually Josiah died fighting against the Egyptians and everyone, including Jeremiah, mourned him.

Left: Moses and the Book of the Law from a 15th-century French manuscript. The horns coming from Moses' head are an artistic misconception of the "horns of radiance," that is, the prophet's face shone with beams or rays of light when he came from his conversations with Yahweh. Moses commanded the priests to read the words of this law "before the people every seven years in the year of remission" at the Feast of Tabernacles (Chapter 31 of the Book of Deuteronomy).

for he eventually fell into Egyptian hands and was deported. There was a tradition that he was stoned to death by his own people in Egypt. True or not, before his death he was able to send a letter to his compatriots who had been uprooted from Jerusalem and exiled to Babylon, telling them that Yahweh said they had better settle down and make the most of life in Babylon because they were going to be there 70 years, after which they would be restored to their homeland. Actually there were 60 years between the first deportations and the restoration, but despite the 10-year difference this must surely count as another prophecy that came true.

Jeremiah's greatness as a prophet was due not only to the truth of his predictions or the courage and fortitude he displayed in his life, but also to his insistent teaching that God was not to be identified with any object or any place, even the Temple, but that he could be found everywhere, was all-seeing and all-powerful. So after Jerusalem had fallen and the Temple had been first desecrated then destroyed, and the people herded off into exile— all of which Yahweh had foretold through his prophets—the dispersed nation still had a God who could be worshiped any- where, and whose promises they could believe and find hope in, not least because all the warnings and threats that they had ignored had been so precisely fulfilled.

Two prophets arose to keep up the morale and the hopes of Yahweh's people during their exile in Babylon: Ezekiel and the Second Isaiah. There was a tradition that Ezekiel was among the first batch of people to be deported, but this does not agree with the prophet's own account of his call in Chapter 3 of the Book of Ezekiel: "He said to me . . . go, get thee to them of the captivity, unto the children of thy people, and speak unto them and tell them, Thus saith the Lord God." Whether he was a deportee or a voluntary exile, Ezekiel seems to have settled in Babylon and to have had a home and family there. Like Jeremiah he was pro- Babylonian, saw Nebuchadrezzar as the instrument of Yahweh's just punishment, and believed that a purified remnant of his race would eventually be restored to Jerusalem. Facts about the private life of Ezekiel are hard to discover in his book, which is full of strange scenes, actions, and visions. It begins with a majestic visitation by God in a bright, fiery chariot-throne, which modern UFO enthusiasts have claimed was a "flying saucer," and its most memorable passage is the vision of the valley of dry bones that come together and put on flesh and stand up, to make a great army. The dry bones vision was probably meant as an allegory of the resurrection of Israel. Ezekiel has been described as the first great writer of Israel, which perhaps he was, but he was not a man like Jeremiah, who spoke directly and movingly of his personal life and anguish. Even when Ezekiel reports the sudden death of his wife he presents it as an act of God who, he says, told him not to show grief or go into mourning so that the exiles should understand that they too were not to mourn the fall of Judah. A remote, rather inhuman figure perhaps, but Ezekiel's visions, his encouragements to persevere in doing good, his denunciations of evil, and his prophecies are expressed in such vivid and imaginative language that no one could possibly doubt that he was inspired.

Ezekiel, God's Prophet in Exile

Opposite: Nebuchadnezzar, King of Babylon, orders the slaying of the sons of King Zedekiah of Judah. Zedekiah was Judah's last king. A weak character, he disregarded Jeremiah's warnings and pursued a pro-Egyptian policy, which hastened the conflict with Babylon. Eventually he revolted and the Babylonians laid siege to Jerusalem, capturing it and destroying it. Zedekiah had to watch while his sons were killed then his eyes were put out and he was taken in chains to Babylon. Jeremiah had warned him that he would be taken to Babylon—and that he would never see it.

Above: Ezekiel, Yahweh's prophet to his people in the exile in Babylon, depicted here in a French manuscript miniature shaving his head (a sign of mourning) with a sword.

Right: an engraving by the 19th-century
French artist Gustave Doré showing
Ezekiel's vision of the valley of dry bones.
This vision symbolizes the revival of the
nation by the return of the exiles from
Babylon.

Above: the prophet Isaiah as depicted in a
15th-century mural in the Church of the
Savior at Paleochorio, Cyprus. The prophet
known as the Second Isaiah has as his theme
the deliverance of the Jewish exiles from
Babylonian oppression through Yahweh's
chosen instrument, Cyrus, monarch of the
Persians and the Medes. Included also in
his writings are the four poems on the
Servant of Yahweh, that depict the Messiah,
not as a king and conqueror, but as worker
and sufferer.

The other great prophet of the Exile is known as the Second
Isaiah, author of chapters 40 to 55 in the biblical Book of
Isaiah, and is considered by the devout—and by the Church—to
have been a reincarnation of the First Isaiah. As an individual
personality he is even more obscure than Ezekiel. He appears to
have lived among the exiles in Babylon during the period when
the Persian king Cyrus, who reigned from 559 to 530 B.C., was
embarked upon his career of conquest and he correctly foresaw
that Cyrus's defeat of Babylon would give the exiles the opportunity to return to their homeland. His message is that by the
exile the Jews have paid the penalty for their sins, and that
Yahweh, whose love has been unfailing despite the distress his
people have caused him and the punishment he has had to
measure out to them, now wishes to restore them to their home.
Warnings, harsh words, and condemnations of sin and idol
worship are not lacking in the Second Isaiah, but the overall
message is of hope and reconciliation.

The God that is shown in the writings of the Second Isaiah is a God of the universe. Everything that happens everywhere is according to his plan, as in Chapter 46 he says: "I am God, and there is none like me, declaring the end from the beginning, and from ancient times the things that are not yet done." In Chapter 48 he declares that even the conquering Cyrus is only doing his will: "I, even I, have spoken; yea I have called him: I have brought him, and he shall make his way prosperous." In Chapter 45 God predicts through Isaiah that his universality will eventually be acknowledged: "Unto me every knee shall bow, every tongue shall swear."

The most intriguing and controversial passages in the Second Isaiah are those that speak of the Suffering Servant of the Lord, who will be the means by which the God of Israel will become the God of the whole world. It is hardly surprising that theologians have regarded the Suffering Servant passages as predictions of the coming of Jesus, particularly in view of the statements that appear in Chapter 53: "He was despised and rejected of men; a man of sorrows, and acquainted with grief;" "He was oppressed and was afflicted . . . And he made his grave with the wicked;" "he

The Sufferings of Christ Foretold!

Left: Christ crowned with thorns in a painting by the late-15th-century Flemish artist Hieronymus Bosch. Interspersed among the prophecies of the Second Isaiah are four poetic interludes about the Servant of Yahweh. The fourth interlude refers to the Passion, Death, and Triumph of the Servant of Yahweh. The Redeemer is to expiate by his sufferings and death the sins of mankind. Though sent to the Gentiles he lives, suffers, labors, and dies among his own people—only after his death will his teaching reach those others for whom it is also intended.

hath poured out his soul unto death: and he was numbered with the transgressors; and he bore the sin of many, and made intercession for the transgressors." Judaism, on the other hand, maintains that the Suffering Servant was not an individual but the Hebrew race as a whole. Whether it was through Jesus or through the Jews that Yehweh intended the worldwide dominion that was eventually all but established in his name remains a matter of debate, but certainly the Suffering Servant prophecies of the Second Isaiah are among the most remarkable and intriguing in all the literature of prophecy.

After the restoration of the Jewish people to their lands in 538 B.C. the prophetic tradition was carried on by Haggai, who urged the rebuilding of the Temple; by Zechariah, whose difficult and enigmatic visions deal with the restoration of Temple worship and of a future Redeemer; by Malachi, who forecast the arising of a messenger to prepare the way for the coming of the Messiah, and by such prophets as Joel and Daniel, whose apocalyptic prophecies—revelations of things to come—take on

Below: Daniel, the prophet of Judah, in a lion's den as depicted in an 11th-century mosaic from the Hoslos Lukeas monastery, Greece. Daniel was led away captive to Babylon in 605 B.C. and according to the Jewish historian Josephus he belonged to the royal family of Zedekiah, last king of Judah. With other Jewish youths he was educated at the Babylonian court. His extraordinary skill at interpreting dreams led him to high position in the empire. When he and three companions refused to worship a golden idol they were cast into a furnace but were miraculously rescued.

a different character to other prophetic writings. Whereas the other prophets deal with the reality of a community unfaithful to its God, Joel, and more especially Daniel write in terms of dreams and visions, monstrous beasts and angels. Future events are predicted in rich detail. Indeed the apocalytic prophets abound in the Hebrew literature of the period after the Exile. Some of their predictions of future events, particularly in Zechariah and Daniel, correspond so exactly to what happened later that they must either be genuine (and perhaps God-given) visions of the future or else those future events must have been modeled upon them.

The consistency of the message of the Hebrew prophets down the centuries, and the fact that their predictions were so often and so exactly fulfilled, raises an intriguing question. Is the reader witnessing a self-perpetuating and self-fulfilling tradition, or the direct utterances of God through his chosen spokesmen— men who were what we would today call trance mediums? The question whether God speaks through particular human beings is one on which opinion has long been divided. It is an area in the mysteries of the gods perhaps best left to the followers of reason or faith to answer after their own beliefs.

One man who had no doubt that God spoke through him and who regarded himself as the last of the prophets and the final seal of the prophetic tradition, was Muhammad, the founder of Islam. The word Islam means "submission," and Muhammad made the immense impact that he did upon history by a curious blend of manifesting and enforcing that virtue.

He was born in Mecca in the year 570 A.D., into the powerful tribe of Koreish, who were guardians of an ancient shrine that contained the Ka'aba, a black stone regarded as sacred, and probably a meteor. He was orphaned early and the young Muhammad was brought up by an uncle, Abu Taleb, a prosperous merchant. From an early age Muhammad traveled with his uncle's caravans, even as far as Syria, where he came into contact with Christians and Jews and learned something of their beliefs. The religion of his own people at that time involved the worship of a large number of different tribal gods. At about the age of 25 he became the business adviser to a rich widow 15 years his senior. He eventually married her and she had six children by him. It might have been the death of two of them that caused him to cut himself off from family and friends and seek solitude in a cave on Mount Hira, some miles north of Mecca. There he spent his time meditating and praying, and would remain there for days at a time without food. It is hardly surprising that he began to see visions and hear voices. One night a shining figure appeared before him, held out a silken scroll covered with writing and told him to read it. Muhammad protested that he had not been taught to read, but when the angel repeated the command he looked at the scroll again and found that he could understand it. It became the first revelation of the Word of God to Muhammad. According to tradition he had to wait another three years before the next revelation, but after that time his visions followed one another regularly. The angel had announced itself as Gabriel and had told Muhammad, "You are the prophet of God; arise, preach, and magnify the Lord."

Muhammad, the Prophet of Allah

Above: the newly born Muhammad, founder of Islam, in his mother's arms, is shown to his grandfather and to the wandering Meccans. Both Muhammad and his mother are shown veiled as a sign of reverence. Moslem holy figures are often represented with flaming halos. From a Turkish book painting in the Topkapi Museum, Istanbul, Turkey.

From Prophet to Champion of God

Above: Muhammad's vision of the archangel Gabriel. Muhammad had his vision while meditating on Mount Hira. There during the month of Ramadan "One came to me with a written scroll while I was asleep and said 'Read!' " Although the prophet protested that he could not read he looked on it and when he awoke it was as if the scripture was written on his heart. Months went by before the divine spirit appeared again. The next time Gabriel appeared sitting cross-legged on a throne between heaven and earth and said to him, "O Muhammad, thou really art the Apostle of God."

The prophet began his ministry in a modest way, gathering a few faithful disciples around him, preaching the unity of Allah (the name means "the mighty One"), and the virtue of submission to the divine will, and attacking the worship of idols, while he continued to receive, in trance, direct communications from heaven through Gabriel, which when written down made up the text of the Koran, the sacred book of the followers of Muhammad. The time came when he had to publicly announce his mission as Allah's prophet and try to reform the pagan rites practiced at the Ka'aba, where no less than 360 idols were worshiped. Challenged to prove he was a prophet by performing miracles, as Moses, Elisha, and Jesus had, he replied that there could be no greater miracle than the Koran itself, the divine Word miraculously revealed to an unlettered man. But the opposition was not convinced and eventually Muhammad and some of his followers had to flee for their lives to the northern city of Medina. Here he made many converts, especially among the warlike desert tribes, and eventually found himself virtually in command of an army.

It was at this stage that Muhammad had one of several communications from Allah that seemed to accord conveniently with the prophet's wishes. It was revealed to him that different prophets had been sent by God to illustrate his various attributes: Moses his clemency and providence, Solomon his wisdom and majesty, Jesus his righteousness, infinite knowledge, and power; but none of these revealed attributes had established the true religion of the One God throughout the world. "I, therefore, the last of the prophets," said Muhammad, "am sent with the sword." Muhammad became transformed from a preacher of patience, forebearance, and conversion by means of argument and persuasion, into the leader of a holy army by whose swords the unbelievers would be brought to acknowledge Allah by force. In future centuries the holy war, the *Jihad*, was to carry the Moslems into Europe as far as the Pyrenees in the west and nearly to Vienna in the east.

Muhammad's military adventures began with raids on caravans traveling to and from Mecca. A decisive victory over Meccan forces at the battle of Beder came next and then the successful repulse of a confederacy of enemies that attacked Medina. Eventually Mecca itself was taken and Muhammad was acknowledged ruler of all Arabia. If the motive of the prophet in calling a holy war was a desire for worldly power, he was remarkably unostentatious in wielding it. He went about in modest dress, held himself aloof from no one, performed menial tasks himself, and generally distributed his share of the spoils of war to the needy. His one weakness was in the consolations of the couch, and although his Koran limited the faithful to four wives he obtained a special dispensation from Allah to have nine, and in addition enjoyed the pick of the female captives of his campaigns. In his relations with his wives and concubines, however, no less than in those with his friends and disciples, Muhammad seems to have shown constant affection, generosity, and compassion. Those who sought to call into question the motives of the self-styled last prophet of God by criticizing his conduct were called on to remember that he never claimed to be anything but

Left: an 18th-century Turkish miniature
showing the prophet Muhammad with his
troops at the siege of Mecca. Once the
prophet had settled at Medina he set about
converting the rest of pagan Arabia. He
himself led some 20 battles and skirmishes
during the first 10 years. By 630 Muhammad
had conquered the holy city of Mecca.
Within 100 years of the prophet's death all
the land from Saragossa, Spain, to the
Caucasus was in Moslem hands. The green
flag of the prophet waved over all lands
from Gibraltar to the Himalayas. In 1453
Byzantium and the Balkans fell, and in 1529
the victorious armies of Islam stood before
the gates of Vienna—not to be turned back
until 1685.

an ordinary fallible and sinful man, distinguished from others
only by being God's chosen spokesman, and that as far as he was
concerned the deification of Jesus by the Christians was a far
more heinous offense than any sin of the flesh.

His militarism and multiple marriages apart, Muhammad
undoubtedly was a man cast in the mold of the great prophets of
antiquity, and his message is basically the same as theirs. As the
Koran says: "We follow the religion of Abraham the orthodox,
who was no idolater. We believe in God and that which hath
been sent down to us, and that which hath been sent down unto
Abraham and Ishmael, and Isaac, and Jacob, and the tribes,
and that which was delivered unto Moses and Jesus, and that
which was delivered unto the prophets from the Lord: we make
no distinction between any of them, and to God we are resigned."
Considering the worldwide distribution of Christianity, Islam,
and Judaism, it must be admitted that the prophets did rather
well for the desert god who pressed them into his service, and
even the skeptical may passingly wonder whether their God
might not have been precisely what he claimed to be: the first
and the last, the one and the only, the universal Lord.

Chapter 7
Who Was Jesus?

Albert Schweitzer's *The Quest for the Historical Jesus*, published in 1910, posed a question that scholars have been answering with greater accuracy ever since: What is the historical evidence for the life of Jesus Christ? The first step in this intriguing detective story is the so-called "synoptic problem"—that is, who really wrote the gospels and when? What is the truth? What do we know for certain about the original historical Jesus? How can we find out more, or must the problem be left, to some extent, to the faith of the believer? This chapter tackles the evidence that lies in what was written by the four Apostles; Matthew, Mark, Luke, and John.

What is the truth about Jesus of Nazareth, or the Christ (the Greek form of the Hebrew "Messiah," the Anointed One of God), or the Son of God, as he is variously called in the scriptures? What can we know about his life, personality, mission, and death? These questions are more important with regard to Jesus than with any other founder of a religion, for Christianity is based on the life and teaching of a man whose very existence has given rise to speculation and controversy.

It is an article of the Nicene Creed, which was formulated in A.D. 325 and expresses the basic elements of the Christian faith, that Jesus Christ "suffered under Pontius Pilate, was crucified, dead, and buried," and after three days rose from the dead. Christians have to believe that these events actually took place in Jerusalem in the third decade of the 1st century, and that they were preceded by a ministry in Galilee and Jerusalem in the course of which many marvelous, even miraculous, events occurred. Some Christians are unconcerned about the historical reality of the events as they are recorded in the gospels, and are content to say, along with the 2nd-century Christian writer Tertullian, "I believe because it is impossible." But others want to know what really happened during those momentous years in Palestine in the third decade; who Jesus of Nazareth really was and what he actually did.

The French missionary-scholar-musician Albert Schweitzer went on a literary search for the historical Jesus and published

Opposite: *The Head of Christ*, painted by the French painter Georges Rouault around the turn of the century. Rouault has tried to convey all the sorrow that Jesus bore and all the yearning, compassion, and love that he felt. No genuine portrait of Jesus is known to exist, nor even a description of his physical appearance. Artists have only the Gospel portraits in words of him as a man who, despite his humanity, was equally at home in the world of the spirit. He could be tired and hungry, rejoice with his friends, and weep with them in sorrow, he could speak out vehemently against his enemies and be prostrated with anguish at the thought of the torments he was to undergo. His effect on his contemporaries was of worshiping admiration or passionate hatred.

Above: *The Agony in the Garden*, by the late-15th-century Italian artist Ambrogio Bergognone. The mood of devotional calm that pervades Bergognone's portrait of Christ coincides with an all-too-familiar image that many people have of the Jesus of the Gospels as a gentle and unworldly dreamer. Close study of the Gospels, however, shows that he was no apparition from some higher realm clothed in human flesh, but a man of his age, a Jew, with all the ardor and ingenuity of his race. Even so, the wonders he performed and the mastery with which he performed them seem to have come from a source greater than human.

the result in his book *The Quest for the Historical Jesus*, in 1910. It remains to this day one of the most intriguing adventures in scholarship. Although, according to Schweitzer, some 60,000 books were written on the subject in the 19th century, and although there must have been at least as many published in the present century, the subject is inexhaustible and scholars keep coming up with new angles on, theories about, and sometimes evidence of, the life of the historical Jesus.

The result of modern historical research has been to establish that Jesus actually lived, whereas Schweitzer in his book, which surveyed the work of 18th- and 19th-century historians, came to the conclusion that "The Jesus of Nazareth who came forward publicly as the Messiah, who preached the ethic of the Kingdom of God, who founded the Kingdom of Heaven upon earth and died to give his work its final consecration, never had any existence."

Taking Schweitzer's researches first, what were some of the arguments that led him to this conclusion? Hermann Reimarus, the 18th-century German classical scholar and philosopher, was the first man to attempt to form a historical conception of the life of Jesus. He argued that Jesus was a political activist who tried to bring about the fulfillment of ancient Jewish prophecies about the Messiah but whose plans failed because of lack of support at the crucial moment. Heinrich Paulus, a German theologian writing in the 1800s, displayed a great deal of ingenuity in giving rational explanations to all the miracles in the New Testament accounts of his life, the *gospels* (good news).

The 19th-century German theologian David Friedrich Strauss concluded that it was not through the supernatural or the rationalist approach that the gospels could be correctly interpreted. He believed that they should be examined with an understanding of the process of myth-making, and with the realization that the Jesus of the gospels had been overlaid with "Old Testament Messianic ideas and primitive Christian expectations." Another 19th-century German theologian, Bruno Bauer, maintained that the history of Jesus was invented by one of the evangelists, Mark, and that the others took their accounts from his and expanded them with some inventions of their own. The French philosopher Joseph Ernest Renan's *Life of Jesus*, published in 1863, portrayed Jesus as a Galilean Romantic, a gentle and unworldly dreamer, while the great 19th-century Russian novelist Leo Tolstoy saw in him a forerunner of socialism and of the ideal of nonviolence. It is hardly surprising that with all these and many other ideas in literature, a man might conclude that it was quite impossible to find out whether there ever was a historical Jesus, and that even if he had lived there was no hope of ever knowing what he had actually done and said.

Since Schweitzer's day, however, scholars have improved their techniques for studying the New Testament, and have turned up other sources of information about Jesus' life and times, and today few doubt that Jesus actually existed and many claim that it is now possible to extract from the gospels a coherent picture of his life, character, and teaching. Indeed, the German theologian Rudolf Bultmann, described as the leading New Testament scholar of the 20th century, wrote in 1951 that "The

Gentle Dreamer or Revolutionary?

Left: a mosaic from Ravenna, Italy, depicting the evangelist Saint Mark. Above his head is his symbol, the lion, one of the four animals that appear in the prophecy of Ezekiel and which have been seen as symbolizing the four evangelists Matthew, Mark, Luke, and John. The lion, long thought of as the king of beasts, is the symbol of Saint Mark because his Gospel emphasizes the royal dignity of Christ. Mark's purpose in writing his Gospel was to provide the Christians of Rome with a faithful record of the teachings of Saint Peter, with whom he traveled.

The Evidence of the Gospels

Below: a 19th-century German engraving showing Christians being torn to pieces by wild beasts in the Roman arena during the 1st century A.D. It was the Christians' refusal to worship the emperor that first brought them to the notice of the Roman authorities—who tolerated many different religions. Nero, who was emperor from A.D. 54 to 68, blamed Christians for the burning of Rome in 64, and this led to savage persecution of those who declared themselves followers of Jesus.

Right: this relief from the inside of the arch of Titus in Rome shows part of a Roman procession bearing some of the sacred instruments from the great Temple in Jerusalem. After a period of misgovernment by Roman procurators and native rulers, the Jews revolted against Rome and those who collaborated with the Romans. The Romans conquered Jerusalem after a four-year siege, sacked the Temple, and removed most of the population in A.D. 70. The infant Christian Church there disappeared; but by that time Christianity had been preached to the Gentiles in other parts of the empire, and so survived.

basis of doubting whether Jesus really existed lacks foundation and doesn't deserve to be refuted."

Since in the Christian religion Jesus is worshiped, petitioned, and praised in the same way as a god—and indeed is believed to be God Incarnate—and as of all God-figures he is the one most familiar to us and the one whose earthly existence is most fully documented in our literature, the evidence that throws light on the mystery of the historical Jesus will be taken, in this chapter, from the gospels, and in the next chapter evidence that can be gleaned from other sources.

There are four gospels, named for the men who it was believed wrote them: Matthew, Mark, Luke, and John. The first questions that must be asked are: Who were these writers? When did they live? How did they relate to each other? Where did they obtain their information? What particular biases did they have?

The gospel of Saint Mark, most scholars agree, was the first of the gospels to be written. Tradition maintains that it was written in Rome for the Christian community there, which had been savagely persecuted by the Emperor Nero in the year 64 A.D. A great fire had devastated the city and Nero had made the Christians the scapegoats for it. Six years later the city of Jerusalem was sacked by the Romans, the temple was razed and the Christian community there disappeared. As Mark makes no reference to this disaster, it is most likely that his gospel was written between A.D. 65 and 70.

Mark himself is usually identified with the John Mark to whose house the apostle Peter went after his miraculous escape from prison, which is recounted in Chapter 12 of The Acts of the Apostles, and who accompanied Paul on his first missionary journey, described later in the same chapter. The First Epistle [Letter] of Peter ends with a greeting from "my son Mark," and this, together with the testimony of the 2nd-century writers Papias and Irenaeus, has led to the tradition that the gospel is based on the recollections of the apostle Peter. Papias, writing soon after A.D. 100, stated: "Mark, having been the interpreter of Peter, wrote accurately, though not in order, all that he remembered of the things said or done by the Lord." And later Irenaeus wrote: "after their death [Peter's and Paul's], Mark, the

disciple and interpreter of Peter, transmitted to us in writing what was preached by Peter." Evidence within the gospel supports this tradition, because in Mark's narrative the events at which Peter was present are related with all the vividness and detail of an eyewitness account. Also, in Mark's gospel, much is made of the disciples', and particularly Peter's, lack of understanding and weakness, which would be consistent with its being based on Peter's recollections of his own experiences.

Mark's is the shortest of the gospels and the language, in the original Greek, is often harsh. It is also significant that it is the only one that begins by declaring itself a gospel—and therefore that the "good news" was written for an evangelical purpose. As Mark takes pains to explain Jewish customs and Aramaic words, and to emphasize the significance of his gospel for the Gentile (non-Jewish) nations, it appears that his purpose was to spread

Left: part of an altarpiece painted by the 15th-century Italian artist Carlo Crivelli. It depicts the two greatest saints of the Christian church: Saint Paul, whom artists usually depict with a sword (he was beheaded) or book of his letters, and Saint Peter, depicted with the keys of the Kingdom of Heaven (a reference to Chapter 15 of Matthew's Gospel). Saint Peter was a fisherman of Galilee. It was Peter who answered Christ's question "whom say ye that I am," with the declaration "Thou art Christ, the Son of the living God." Christ's reply was to declare that "Thou art Peter and upon this rock I will build my Church, and the gates of hell shall not prevail against it." After traveling throughout Asia after the death of Jesus, Peter eventually went to Rome and founded the first Christian community there. Saint Paul was a well-educated Jew and a Roman citizen. At first a persecutor of the Christians, he later became converted and is considered to be the greatest missionary of the Christian faith.

Below: the mother of Jesus and three of his friends watch at the foot of Christ's Cross until the moment of his death. It is a Gentile, the centurion in charge of the execution party, who, impressed by the bearing of Jesus during the Passion, the rapid death, the darkness and earthquake (all mentioned in Mark's Gospel), declares that "Truly this man was the Son of God!"

the good news to people not of Jewish origin. He was not attempting to write a biography of Jesus, in fact we learn nothing from him about Jesus' early life, and he gives us very little of the content of Jesus' teaching.

Mark begins his story by emphasizing the divine Sonship and the Messiahship of Jesus, and gradually throughout his narrative he reveals the mystery of Jesus' identity, which is made plain in his passion and death. It is in fact a Roman centurion, present when Jesus breathes his last on the cross, who declared, "Truly, this man was the Son of God." It is a detail consistent with Mark's purpose of proselytizing the Gentile nations. Furthermore, by devoting one third of his text to the passion story (the events of the last week of Jesus' life), Mark is at pains to explain to the Gentiles—for whom the fact that Jesus was executed by the Romans for rebellious activities was an embarrassment that demanded some explanation—what the Jews, whose ancient scriptures predicted the death of the Messiah, already knew.

Saint Mark and Saint Matthew

Left: this detail from a 15th-century Italian manuscript shows Saint Matthew writing his Gospel. Matthew is said to have written his account of the life and teachings of Jesus in Aramaic, the language of the Jews of the time, for Jewish converts to the new Christianity. His Gospel is traditionally held to be the oldest of the four written accounts of the "good news," though many modern scholars hold that Matthew drew heavily on Mark's work. It contains the fullest account of the teachings of Jesus and records the post-Resurrection appearances of Jesus in Galilee.

Saint Matthew's gospel must have been written after Mark's, for it incorporates most of Mark's material, often word for word. It was probably written between A.D. 75 and 90. Although the version that has come down to us is in Greek, Papias wrote that "Matthew compiled the *Sayings* in the Aramaic language, and everyone translated them as well as he could," which has led some scholars to suppose that there must have been a collection of *Sayings of Jesus*, recorded perhaps by the disciple Matthew, on which his later gospel was based. This is guesswork, however, and the only thing that can be said with any certainty is that Matthew's gospel was written for Jewish Christians living in Palestine. The 3rd-century Greek Christian writer Origen maintained that it was written "for believers who had come from Judaism," and this is borne out by evidence from within the gospel, such as the vocabulary, the taking for granted a familiarity with Jewish customs, and particularly the concern the author shows to relate events in Jesus' career to prophecies contained in the ancient scriptures of Judaism.

Although he derived a lot of his material from Mark, Matthew sometimes altered it to improve the blunt style, and he also made some significant omissions, particularly Mark's references to emotions of indignation, anxiety, or tenderness manifested by

Right: the Prodigal Son. Having asked his father for his share of the inheritance he went away to another country and spent all of the money on riotous living. He is eventually reduced to eating with the pigs at their trough, when he realizes that the lowest servant in his father's house has a better existence than he does. When he returns home to beg for a lowly position in his father's household he is welcomed with open arms and a special feast is prepared. When his dutiful brother, who has remained at home, hears of the reception given to the wastrel he is angry, but his father replies everyone should rejoice, for his brother was dead and is now alive again, he was lost and is found. The story is one of the parables—the fictitious but lifelike stories composed to illustrate a fact or truth—that are a feature of Christ's teaching.

Below: shepherds with sheep and goats at the foot of the Mount of Temptation, near the Dead Sea. Jesus drew his parables from such everyday scenes as this.

Jesus, and four references to his inability to accomplish what he wished. Only twice in his gospel does Jesus ask a question just for information rather than as a means of delivering a reproach. Matthew is concerned to maintain the dignity of Jesus, to stress his divinity rather than his humanity. His book contains five long sermons that represent the main source of our knowledge of Jesus' teaching. When Matthew relates one of Jesus' parables or tells one of the miracle stories, he always takes care to interpret and explain and to point out the relevance of the story to the life of the Christian community.

Matthew's writing is solemn, skillfully constructed, and composed as if for recitation. It is not only a life of Jesus, but also a meditation upon his life and commentary on its significance for mankind. Although Matthew appears to address himself primarily to the Jews, the religious nature of his concern is to show how Jesus came to fulfill the prophecies and to accomplish God's plan as revealed in the Old Testament. This was a plan ultimately to make salvation from sin and membership of the Kingdom of God accessible to men of all nations. This plan has always to be borne in mind when seeking the historical Jesus in Matthew's gospel.

Saint Luke, a physician from Antioch in Syria, and a traveling companion of Paul, was the author of both the gospel credited to him and of The Acts of the Apostles. According to scholars the styles of the two books point to a common author. Acts begins with a reference to the author's "first book" and a brief summary of the contents of Luke's gospel. Several times in Acts the author uses the first person plural, in Chapter 20, for instance, he says, "we sailed away from Philippi . . . and in five days we came to them at Troas, where we stayed for seven days." In Chapter 4 of his Epistle to the Colossians, written from prison in Rome, Paul wrote: "Luke the beloved physician and Demas greet you."

It is clear from his books, too, that Luke was a man of culture, capable of writing literary Greek with elegance and poetry, and capable, too, of telling a story that was both memorable and to the point. The story of the crowded inn at Bethlehem, the birth of Jesus in the stable, the visit of an angel to shepherds to inform them of the birth of the Savior and their going to pay homage to him—the entire Christmas story, in fact—appears only in Luke's gospel. His is the most artistic of the four gospels. Addressing his work to Theophilus, identified as a wealthy Roman convert from Antioch, his declared aim was to write an accurate biography of Jesus using all the sources available to him.

According to advanced scholarly research, Luke's gospel might well be the most historically reliable of the four. It was also probably the first attempt to write a biography of Jesus. The author claims to have consulted both the many written accounts of the gospel history, and people who were "eyewitnesses and ministers of the word," and to have compiled from them "an orderly account" of Jesus' life and teaching. His expressed intentions should not be interpreted quite as a modern historian would mean them, however. His account follows that of the classical historical models of the time. It was not a stringing

Saint Luke the Biographer

Below: the town of Bethlehem with Joseph holding a donkey, and Mary, mother of Jesus, seated on the ground. Perhaps the most famous of all the stories from the New Testament is the Nativity or Christmas story. The longest and fullest account of it is in Saint Luke's Gospel where it takes up more than a tenth of the whole Gospel. Luke, a physician from Antioch, was a disciple or follower of the Apostle Paul who took as his sources the many written accounts of the Gospel history and the many eyewitnesses of the events he described, such as Joanna, wife of Herod's steward Chusa, and Susanna and many other women who helped Jesus. A clue to the source material for the infancy story, scholars have suggested, may lie in the reference in Chapter 2: "But Mary kept all these things and pondered them in her heart." It might be that the mother of Jesus herself was the direct or indirect source of his material.

together of unrelated facts in strict chronological order about the life of the historical Jesus, but an account of the teaching of the young Church concerning his life.

Luke verified his facts before setting them down, and was scrupulous in keeping as much as possible to the wording of his sources. His principal source was the material of Mark's gospel, which he neither tampered with as much as Matthew did, nor break it up to incorporate it piecemeal to the requirements of his own composition. When he used Mark's material he used it in blocks and almost word for word.

Like Matthew, however, Luke tended to omit or tone down some of Mark's references to Jesus especially where he considered them unbecoming to the dignity of Christ. But what he sometimes added to Mark's account is significant, too, particularly when in his passion narrative he made a point of specifying the precise charges against Jesus—which neither Mark nor Matthew did. Luke regarded himself as a historian as well as a believer and begins his gospel "It seemed good to me also having followed all things closely for some time past to write an orderly account . . . that you may know the truth concerning the things of which you have been informed."

The claim that Mark's gospel was the first to be written is helped by the fact that both Matthew and Luke incorporated most of his material. However, both Matthew and Luke also have a great deal of material in common with each other that is not found in Mark, which suggests that Matthew and Luke both had access to another source, not available when Mark wrote, and which contained mainly an account of Jesus' teachings. Scholars sometimes called this source the Teaching Document, or simply "Q" (from the German, *Quelle*, meaning "source"). Some hoped that it might one day be found, but today it is generally agreed that "Q" was not a single separate document, just a convenient symbol for the materials not found in Mark, and that were probably passed down by oral tradition.

The gospels of Mark, Matthew, and Luke are known as the synoptic gospels, from the Greek *synopsis*, "seeing at a glance." The fourth gospel, of Saint John, is quite different from the other three. It is more spiritual and philosophical than the others and strikes a characteristic note at the opening of the gospel: "In the beginning was the Word, and the Word was with God, and the Word was God . . . And the Word became flesh and dwelt among us, full of grace and truth."

From the early years of the 2nd century onward, tradition held that the author of the fourth gospel was John, the son of Zebedee, one of the 12 apostles. Toward the end of the final chapter of the gospel is written: "This is the disciple who is bearing witness to these things, and who has written these things; and we know that his testimony is true." The "we," here, are taken by scholars to be John's disciples who wrote down the gospel at his dictation and published it after his death. The author writes with authority, particularly when dealing with events in or near Jerusalem, which has led some modern scholars to suggest that John was a Jerusalem disciple of Jesus. It is also generally agreed that the gospel was probably written about A.D. 90, probably for the instruction of Christians who were familiar with Greek philosophic thought

Saint John the Philosophical

Opposite: the Nativity of Jesus, seen through the eyes of the 15th-century Flemish painter Hans Memling. The wealth of detail given in the Nativity narrative by Saint Luke, coupled with his strong sense of the supernatural which he shows in references to the working of the Holy Spirit and the ministry of angels, has made his Gospel a source of inspiration for many artists. Luke, a Gentile, inherited the tradition of Greek historical and biographical writing. He sets his Gospel within a framework of world history, with his references to imperial officials, vassal kings, and Roman emperors. His biographical interest in Jesus can be seen in the long infancy narrative, and he is the only Evangelist to refer to Jesus' boyhood.

Below: Saint John the Evangelist writing The Revelation to John, or The Apocalypse. Before John was exiled to the isle of Patmos, where he wrote the Revelation, he wrote the fourth of the Gospels of the New Testament. His writing has been regarded as touching the highest peak of Christian revelation—one of the reasons he is given the symbol of the eagle that soars to the heavens in Christian art.

Whose Version is Most Accurate?

Below: *Christ Driving the Money-changers out of the Temple*, by the 17th-century Italian painter Bernardo Cavallino. John places the cleansing of the Temple at the beginning of Christ's ministry whereas the other evangelists place this incident near the end (possibly a logical grouping of Jerusalem incidents under the last Jerusalem visit, rather than a concern for chronology). When the uneasy authorities demand a sign to authenticate Jesus' personal authority for driving out the traders and bankers, he answers "Destroy this temple and in three days I will raise it up." John adds: But he spoke of the temple of his body.

but not so familiar with the Jewish background of their faith.

The problem of disentangling the history from the theology in John's gospel is more difficult than in any of the synoptic gospels. John appears to choose the events he relates chiefly for their symbolic significance, and the dialogues he records are obviously worded so that the questions put to Jesus either cue him for an important statement or serve to emphasize man's lack of understanding of the mystery of his Incarnation. Also, the statements of John's Jesus are often so puzzling that they have to be explained. For example, when Jesus has cleared the traders out of the temple and the authorities ask him, "What sign have you for doing this?" Jesus answers, "Destroy this temple and in three days I will raise it up." The Jews are puzzled by his statement and point out that the temple took 46 years to build. Then, in Chapter 2, John explains: "But he spoke of the temple of his body," and refers to Jesus' resurrection three days after his crucifixion, saying that then the disciples remembered what he had said about the temple, and "they believed the scripture and the word which Jesus had spoken."

This passage is typical of John, and as Jesus' statement is not

Left: when Christ washes his disciples' feet at the Last Supper, seen in this painting by the 19th-century British artist Ford Madox Brown, John contrasts his behavior with the baseness of Judas, who, the reader is told, has already made up his mind to betray Jesus. This incident occurs only in the Gospel of John, and has all the details of an eyewitness account.

paralleled in any of the other gospels we cannot tell whether John knew of it because he had been present at the time, or whether he invented it in order to explain the divine plan behind the Resurrection. This is the basic problem posed by John's gospel. It contains a good deal of material not found in the other gospels and omits or only passingly refers to facts and events that the other three make much of.

Some of John's sources, as well as his style and bias, appear to have been different from the others', and some critics have suspected that the unique parts of his gospel are invented in order to put across particular moral lessons. This theory, however, does not account for the fact that many of the details found only in John, particularly about the events of the last week of Jesus' life, have no theological significance at all but are details such as somebody who had been present would note.

While the differences between the four gospels make the problem of finding the historical Jesus in them extremely difficult, they do not suggest that Jesus never existed in the flesh. On the contrary, if we had only one gospel, without any internal inconsistencies, this would be suspect, but that four men of different abilities, experience, and purpose should react differently to a particular historical person or event is quite to be expected. The very muddle of the composite picture of Jesus and his life presented by the four gospels is a virtual guarantee that they were based upon reality. The question is: what reality? How can we sort out from the muddle the portrait of the authentic Jesus and the story of his life?

Here are some of the points to be looked at in order to clear the way through the material. The problem may not be as insurmountable as it looks at first. Each of the evangelists' biasses must be taken into consideration; all material that seems to be derived from the later Christian Church and its theology should be rejected; events that seem to fulfill Old Testament prophecies

Jesus' Birth and Boyhood

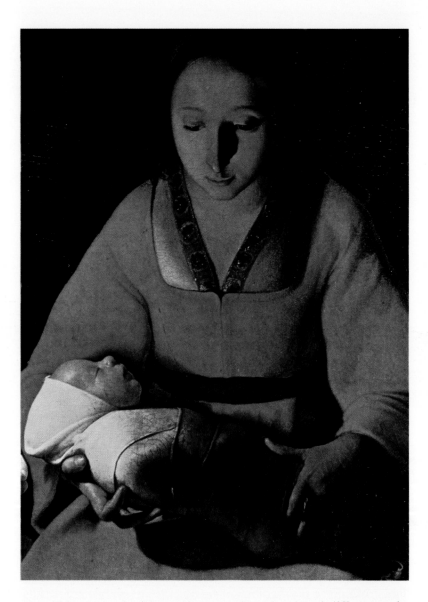

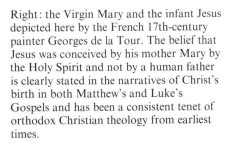

Right: the Virgin Mary and the infant Jesus depicted here by the French 17th-century painter Georges de la Tour. The belief that Jesus was conceived by his mother Mary by the Holy Spirit and not by a human father is clearly stated in the narratives of Christ's birth in both Matthew's and Luke's Gospels and has been a consistent tenet of orthodox Christian theology from earliest times.

should be treated with caution; on the other hand differences in the way Matthew, Mark, and Luke report events and sayings should be taken into account. Material that serves no theological purpose and that might have been an embarrassment for the evangelists to include in their gospels—but that presumably could not be excluded because it was part of the known tradition—should also be carefully noted. In this way it should be possible to extract a picture of the life, mission, and character of the authentic historical Jesus from the gospels.

The accounts of Jesus' conception, birth, and early years constitute a gospel all of their own. Luke positively states that he was born in Bethlehem, while Matthew states that he was born there to fulfill a prophecy of Micah, and John says that he was born in Galilee. The belief that he was born of a virgin is a disputed point to this day.

Only Matthew and Luke tell the story of the virgin birth, and again Matthew says that "this took place to fulfill what the Lord had spoken," and quotes a passage from Isaiah. It was customary for historians of the ancient world to deify men of extraordinary

achievement and attribute their birth to divine intervention. Matthew's and Luke's stories of the Virgin Birth have a superficial resemblance to such a presentation but we know that Luke checked his sources.

The story, found only in Luke, of the 12-year-old Jesus amazing the teachers in the temple at Jerusalem with his knowledge, and of his responding to his parents' reproach for causing them anxiety with a reference to his "Father's house" should be seen in the context of later Christian teaching, which saw Jesus as the fulfillment of the law and the prophets from his earliest years. Mark has nothing to say on the subject of Jesus' childhood and youth except that Jesus was a carpenter from Nazareth and that he had four brothers and an unspecified number of sisters, and Matthew significantly amends this to the statement that he was a carpenter's *son*, probably because he felt it inappropriate that the Son of God in his earthly incarnation should be an ordinary workman.

A point that all four evangelists are agreed upon is that Jesus was baptized in the river Jordan by John the Baptist and that his ministry in Galilee began soon after this event. They agree, too, that John the Baptist was something of a wild man, a severe ascetic with a formidable line in verbal lashing and exhortation, who preached the wrath to come and the necessity of uncompromising self-sacrifice.

John's teaching, in fact, apparently has much in common with that of the Essene community at Qumran, which was near where he was baptizing, and it is probable that he was associated with the community. They and he also believed that the time of the long awaited setting-up of the Kingdom of God on earth was to take place, and according to the gospels John also taught the coming of the Messiah, the Anointed One of God.

Above: the child Jesus is found in the Temple at Jerusalem—a detail from his childhood found only in Saint Luke's Gospel. Neither women nor children were bound by the rule that required attendance at the three annual feasts of the Temple. Boys, however, fell under the obligation when they became "sons of the law" at 13, but it was customary to anticipate this age by a year or two, which is why Jesus is in Jerusalem. Luke records the incident to show that at the age of 12 Jesus is conscious of his divine sonship—"Did you not know that I must be in my Father's house?" The painter of the scene, the British artist William Holman Hunt, went to very great lengths to give his pictures an authentic air. In the 1850s he traveled to Palestine in search of background information for his religious pictures.

All four evangelists record John as recognizing Jesus as the Messiah and treating him with due reverence, saying that he himself is not worthy to untie the thong of Jesus' sandals. The gospels are unanimous on this point, and all attribute the same expression of deference to John, but in Chapter 3 of John's gospel there is a hint—though not in the context of the baptism story—that the disciples of John and Jesus were rivals, and both Matthew (in Chapter 11) and Luke (in Chapter 7) state that when John the Baptist was in prison he sent messengers to ask Jesus, "Are you he who is to come, or shall we look for another?"

There seems little reason for thinking that the question was sincere but it seems scarcely consistent with John's having recognized Jesus as the Messiah from the start and having seen (in Chapter 1), when he baptized him, "the spirit descend as a dove from heaven" and settle upon him. Must the explanation be sought in the lack of reference to the final days in Jesus' preaching which caused doubts to be sown in John's mind?

That Jesus was baptized by John and that it was a turning point for him are very likely propositions. In fact, the baptism

Above: a 5th-century ivory panel from Rome showing Jesus being baptized by John the Baptist. Above Jesus' head descends a dove from heaven, held by the hand of God.

Right: John the Baptist from the Church of the Holy Cross, Patanistasa, Cyprus. After hundreds of years, Israel had once again had a prophet sent to it. John was wearing the official clothing of a prophet, the camel-hair garment that perhaps no one then alive had seen before. The Gospels (and the Jewish historian Josephus) tell of the immense stir his baptizing and preaching caused. He demanded what the prophets before him had demanded—a change of heart on the part of the people.

is one event the evangelists might have preferred to leave out if it hadn't been an indispensable part of the tradition, for John was baptizing "in token of repentence for the forgiveness of sins," and surely the Son of God could not have any sins to forgive.

Matthew faces the problem, and in his account John says that Jesus ought to be baptizing him and Jesus replies in effect that the baptism is a formal religious observance that a devout Jew should conform to. So we can put some confidence in the historical fact that Jesus, the carpenter from Nazareth, was baptized by John, and that this would mark the beginning of his public life and work.

The evidence also points to the fact that Jesus was influenced by the Baptist, and the fundamentals of their teaching about the coming Kingdom of God and the need for a change of heart came from the prophets before them. Luke gives this away in Chapter 16 of his gospel when he reports Jesus as saying: "The law and the prophets were until John; since then the good news of the Kingdom of God is preached." John was the last of the prophets before Jesus of Nazareth.

It was in Galilee, all the evangelists agree, that Jesus began his mission, though they are not unanimous as to where exactly he began. Luke says at his home town, Nazareth, where he was given short shrift, whereas Mark and Matthew say he began at Capernaum, and John mentions the miracle he performed at Cana as "the first of his signs" and the beginning of his ministry. Again, all agree that in Galilee Jesus recruited his disciples, though there are differences in their accounts of how he did so and of who the 12 were. John, in fact, though he speaks of the 12, names only six of the disciples, and Mark, Matthew, and Luke

The Baptism of Jesus

Left: a 12th-century Swiss painting of the marriage at Cana. This is the occasion of the first of the miracles of Jesus and is mentioned in Saint John's Gospel. Although apparently reluctant, Jesus performs a miracle at the suggestion of his mother during a marriage feast to which they have been invited: "Son, they have no wine." Jesus replies "What to me and to thee?" which is a Hebrew idiom used at that time to decline a request or resist an interference. He adds, "My hour is not yet come." Mary is undismayed at the apparent rebuff and tells the waiters: "Whatsoever he shall say to you, do ye." Jesus told the waiters to fill six stone jars with water then to draw it out and serve it. They do so and find the water has been turned to wine.

"Fishers of Men"

Right: Mary, the mother of Jesus, and the Twelve Apostles receive the Holy Spirit in the form of tongues of fire at Pentecost. Of the many disciples that gathered around Jesus, 12 were to hold a special place, chosen by Jesus to represent a totality of Israel with the 12 tribes. When Judas, who betrayed Jesus, is considered to be irretrievably lost to salvation the Apostles hold an election to make up the number again. Saint Peter puts forward the qualifications by which one of the two candidates could be chosen as the new Apostle: he had to be one "who has companied with us, all the time that the Lord Jesus came in and out amongst us, beginning from the baptism of John, until the day wherein he was taken up from us . . . a witness with us of his resurrection."

agree on the names of only eight of them. They agree, too, that the first recruits were fishermen and that Jesus summoned them into service by promising to make them "fishers of men," though the story of the miraculous catch of fish that persuaded Simon, James, and John to follow Jesus is found only in Luke, who generally tends to be prodigal in his accounts of miracles.

Several spectacular successes by Jesus as preacher, healer, and miracle-worker are recorded in the gospels for this period, but the inescapable fact emerges that, overall, the mission in Galilee was a failure. The unpalatable fact of his rejection at Nazareth is recorded by all three synoptics. In Chapter 6 of his gospel Mark says that Jesus marveled at the unbelief of this fellow townsmen and that because of it "he could do no mighty work there." Matthew (Chapter 13), loath to admit total failure, changes this to: "he did not do many mighty works there, because of their unbelief." Luke doesn't mention his failure to perform miracles at all, but he tells in Chapter 4 how Jesus' preaching in the synagogue incited his townsmen to throw him out of Nazareth and

Above: like a set from a religious opera, an artist has sought to depict Jesus choosing his first disciples. Most of the Apostles, the special inner circle of disciples, were fishermen of little or no education and often did not grasp the high principles that Jesus sought to teach. The lake of Galilee, a $12\frac{1}{2}$-mile-long by $7\frac{1}{2}$-mile-wide freshwater lake, is rich in fish—some 22 species have been found there. It is not as important as a source of food as it was in poorer biblical times when Jesus called Peter, Andrew, and the sons of Zebedee to leave their boats and follow him. Broken columns and capitals and mounds of dressed stone on the beaches and in the water of the lake point to there having been many pleasant towns clustered around its clear waters.

Left: a view of present-day Galilee. In Jesus' time it was one of the four Roman divisions of Palestine and occupied a favored position on the main trade routes between Egypt and Syria. It must therefore have been a cosmopolitan province. It includes such famous biblical names as Nazareth, Capernaum, Bethsaida, and Magdala and was the scene of a considerable portion of Jesus' early life.

The Problem of the Miracles

how he narrowly escaped being hurled from the top of a cliff for his presumption.

Mark tells how (in Chapter 3) apparently even Jesus' own kinsmen rejected him, and considered that he was out of his mind. This must have caused Jesus considerable anguish, for Matthew and Mark record that he says "Who are my mother and brothers?" when they turned up where he was preaching and sent a message to him, and Luke, who gives us the charming Bethlehem nativity story and is therefore creator of the Holy Family image, records in Chapter 14 that harshest of Jesus' sayings: "If any one comes to me and does not hate his own father and mother and wife and children and brothers and sisters . . . he cannot be my disciple." Matthew repeats the saying but omits the word "wife."

Here, surely, we hear the authentic voice of Jesus, for the evangelists would not have invented something so demanding, and outrageous, as this claim to absolute loyalty even over the love of family. The way the emotion dovetails with his teaching also has an authentic ring, as in Chapter 12 of Luke's gospel: "Do you think I have come to give peace on earth? No, I tell you, but rather division, for henceforth in one house there will be five divided . . . father against son and son against father, mother against daughter and daughter against her mother, mother-in-law against her daughter-in-law and daughter-in-law against her mother-in-law."

John (Chapter 6) records that many of Jesus' followers left him during the mission in Galilee, dismayed by his harsh precepts and his unacceptable teachings. The nucleus remained loyal, but

Below: *Christ in the House of his Parents*, by the 19th-century British painter Sir John Millais. Saint Luke makes the only reference to the hidden years of Jesus' life before he starts his public ministry. In Chapter 2 of his Gospel he notices, like a good physician, the child "grew and waxed strong," and that his mental and physical development won him approval with both God and man. It seems he passed through the normal stages of boyhood and youth. He would learn the carpenter's trade from Joseph and the Law from the synagogue school at Nazareth— since the Jews' return from exile, every town of any size had a school in which all male children were taught the Law.

their understanding of the message was far from clear, as can be seen by the human and realistic touch in Chapter 10 of Mark, when James and John clamor for favored places in the coming Kingdom. And although the evangelists tell us that when the disciples went out alone or in pairs on teaching and healing missions they had some notable successes, they are vague about what they actually achieved; which they surely would not have been if the achievements had been impressive. All in all, the Galilee mission was obviously, from the testimony of the gospels themselves, a failure.

We read of many miracles performed by Jesus during the Galilee mission, and these pose perhaps the biggest problem of all for the seeker after historical truth. The literal mind demands whether things like the stilling of the storm, the feeding of the 5000, the walking on water and the raising of Lazarus from the dead really happened, and considers that if they did not, then the gospel writers were either deliberate liars or naive reporters of superstitious hearsay. This view does not take account of the fact that in the tradition in which they were writing, and in Eastern literature generally, the miracle story, like the parable, was a teaching device, a means of conveying a spiritual truth that could not be communicated in straightforward language.

Luke relates a parable about a man who had a fig tree in his vineyard and ordered it to be cut down because it had not produced any fruit. In Mark and Matthew, too, there is a story about a barren fig tree that Jesus rather unreasonably curses because he is hungry and hoped to find fruit on it, and which subsequently withers. What was a parable in Luke is related as a miracle in

Above: Gustave Doré's engraving shows Peter and John healing a lame man. It illustrates one of the miracles wrought by the Apostles in Jesus' name. A 40-year-old beggar born lame in his feet and ankles was sitting at one of the Temple gates at the time of the evening sacrifice when Peter and John pass him. They have no silver or gold, they tell him, but bid him rise up in the name of Jesus of Nazareth. The lame beggar leaps up and walks into the temple.

Left: illustration from a manuscript showing the incident described in Chapter 14 of Matthew's Gospel when Jesus walks over the waters to join the Apostles in their boat. When the Apostles saw him approaching they cried out that it was a ghost. As soon as they heard his familiar voice, however, Peter too tried to walk on the water toward his beloved master. After a while he lost confidence and began to sink. The artist here shows the moment Jesus reaches forward to rescue Peter.

Right: a 19th-century engraving of Jesus healing the sick. Nowhere in the Gospels does Jesus appear to cultivate the role of wonder-worker, or thaumaturge. On the contrary, he goes to great lengths not to parade his miracles. He saw them as useful in the last resort in persuading the incredulous that he did indeed come from God: "though you will not believe me, believe the works." Nor are the miracles of Jesus and his disciples (who achieved them in Jesus' name) shown to be arbitrary interferences with the course of nature; there is always a reason over and above the obvious one of God's love and concern for man's human condition, and that is a demonstration of the claim that God had given all power to his Son, the Messiah.

Mark and Matthew, and this change makes many wonder if there are other miracles attributed to Jesus that were originally parables.

Jesus' cursing of the fig tree symbolized the divine anger with Israel, whose religion flourished outwardly, yet was barren of fruit. His walking on water symbolized God's triumph over evil, for in the Old Testament, particularly the Psalms of David, the sea represents the forces hostile to God, but many Christians accept that this actually took place. His feeding the multitude with five loaves and two fishes was also a reenactment of a miracle attributed to the prophet Elisha, and it symbolized the New Covenant that God was making with Israel as he had approved the Old Covenant through Moses by sending down manna from heaven. In the story of the raising of Lazarus, which John alone relates, Jesus tells his disciples that he is glad for their sake he was not present when Lazarus was ailing, because to raise him from the dead is a more convincing demonstration of the power of God. The miracle was performed, then, according to Chapter 11 of John's gospel, "so that the Son of God may be glorified by it."

In John's gospel only seven miracles are related, and they are all of a kind, stupendous reversals of the laws of nature that manifest the all-embracing power of God and his Son the Messiah. Such miracles are to be found in the other gospels, too, but in them the majority of the miracles are healings or exorcisms. These are not so incredible as the nature-reversal miracles, for psychic healing and exorcism are not unknown in our day and age, and the reality of the former has been scientifically demonstrated.

No doubt Jesus was a great healer, but it is important to note that his miracles of healing and exorcism were not generally performed for humanitarian reasons alone, but as a means of teaching belief and demonstrating that the New Age had begun. "If it is by the finger of God that I cast out demons," he says in Chapter 11 of Luke's gospel, "then the Kingdom of God has come upon you." Furthermore, the presentation of the healing miracles in the gospels sometimes has a symbolic meaning, as for instance when Matthew begins his Chapter 8 with accounts of three successive healings, of a Jewish leper, of the servant of a Roman centurion, and of the disciple Peter's mother-in-law, thus illustrating that Jesus has come to take upon himself and alleviate the sufferings of Jew, Gentile, and Christian alike.

After the failure of the mission in Galilee, Jesus went to Jerusalem. There can be little doubt that his manner of entering the city and some of the things he did while he was there were conscious and deliberate actions performed in order to fulfill scriptural prophecies. Zechariah had written: "Lo, your king comes to you; triumphant and victorious is he, humble and riding on an ass." And Jesus organized his entry into Jerusalem in the manner suggested by the prophecy. There was a point to his doing this, apart from demonstrating his belief that his mission would fulfill the scriptures, for the triumphant king in Zechariah was a man of peace and humility, and by emulating

Messiah-or Miracle-worker?

Below: Jesus heals Peter's mother-in-law, from a 15th-century mural in the church of St. Mammas, at Louvaras, Cyprus. Peter and his brother Andrew had invited Jesus to their home where Peter's mother-in-law was (according to the physician Luke) at the height of a fever. Jesus cures her—and to show that the cure was instantaneous and complete the Gospels state that she prepared a meal for Jesus.

Above: Christ's entry into Jerusalem—a fresco from the great basilica at Assisi, Italy. Jesus finally allowed, at the end of his career, a public acknowledgment of himself as the Messiah-King making a fitting entry into his royal city. It is for Jesus the last sign of his dignity before the glory of his resurrection—which as Luke repeatedly warns can only be reached by the humiliation and degradation of the Passion and crucifixion.

him Jesus was making the point that those who expected a militant Messiah who would lead them in the overthrow of the Romans were mistaken. But his first recorded action in Jerusalem, the expulsion of the traders from the temple precincts, was not exactly that of a peaceable man, although again it fulfilled a prophecy of Zechariah.

By clearing the temple precincts Jesus in effect challenged the authority of the powerful Jewish ruling priesthood, the Sadducees, and set in motion the sequence of events that was to lead to his death. Now, according to Luke (Chapter 19), the disciples "supposed that the kingdom of God was to appear immediately" as soon as they arrived in Jerusalem.

The main theme of Jesus' teaching had been that the Kingdom of God was imminent and that he had come to inaugurate it, and by acting out the Zechariah prophecies he indicated that the day of fulfillment had arrived. Chapter 14 of Zechariah begins: "Behold, the day of the Lord cometh," and it ends with the statement, "and in that day there shall be no more the Canaanite [traders] in the house of the Lord of hosts." So Jesus did not clear the traders out of the temple because he was indignant about their sacrilegious activity, but in order to assert that the day of the Lord had come and he was the Messiah. But then nothing happened, except that the Jewish authorities started planning reprisals.

It is difficult to pinpoint when Jesus began to mention his death. The gospels refer to "the hour of the Son of Man" and we are told that before coming to Jerusalem he began to talk to his disciples about his passion and death. According to Chapter 10 of John, he had gone to Jerusalem some six months before, "not publicly but in private," at the time of the Feast of the Tabernacles, and had preached and had a mixed reception. "Many of the people believed in him," but some thought him mad and said, "You have a demon," and "some of them wanted to arrest him."

If John's testimony on this point is reliable (and, remember, he was probably a Jerusalem-based disciple of Jesus), then, when Jesus made his final visit to Jerusalem he must have been well aware of the danger he was courting. So the hints of possible martyrdom that he dropped and that so distressed his disciples could have been his reading of one possible outcome of the desperate gamble he had decided to embark upon after he had failed in Galilee and had been warned to get away because Herod wanted to kill him. At this point, it was only in Jerusalem that he could present his message in the form of a challenge that would get a decisive response one way or the other. Significantly, he timed his arrival for the festival of Passover, which commemorated the liberation of Israel from Egypt and the birth of the nation, as well as the moment of the great sacrifice.

By the time when he ate the ritual Passover meal with his disciples, Jesus knew that his death was imminent, and Judas that his master had failed again. The events as recorded in the gospels from the last supper to the resurrection are written to emphasize their theological meaning, but the basic facts stand out and we can be confident of their historical accuracy both because the crucifixion of Jesus was an outcome so shocking and so unjust that nobody would have invented it, and because there are a number of details in the story that ring true for they must have been decidedly unpalatable for the evangelists who recorded them.

For a start, it was shocking that one of the trusted inner group of 12 disciples should have betrayed Jesus as we can gather from the list of apostles ". . . and Judas who betrayed him." John establishes Judas Iscariot's hypocrisy by reporting him caviling about Mary using expensive ointment on Jesus' feet, and says that he was a thief and embezzled money from the communal fund that he was entrusted with.

Various theories about Judas' motivation have been proposed,

Jesus Betrayed

Below: Judas betrays Jesus, from a 15th-century manuscript. Judas led the representatives of the Sanhedrin—the Jewish supreme court of justice—armed with clubs and swords to the garden where he knew that Jesus frequently went to pray. Because in the darkness it might be difficult to identify Jesus from the other Apostles, Judas arranged that the customary form of respectful greeting, a kiss, would identify the right man.

Below: this 15th-century mural from a church in Cyprus depicts the three denials of Peter, as given in all four Gospels: Matthew (Chapter 26), Mark (14), Luke (22), and John (18). Peter is waiting in an open-air courtyard around which the palace is built, while the trial of Jesus is going on in an upper chamber (top center). At the bottom right of the picture Peter is sitting by the fire when a maid recognizes him. He denies knowing anything. A little later another maid asks him if he is one of Jesus' disciples; he denies again. When a third person accuses him of being a follower of Jesus, he again vigorously denies it. At that moment the cock crows and Peter goes out and weeps bitterly (left).

such as that he was disappointed in Jesus or that he knew his scriptures and expected the martyrdom of the Messiah to usher in the Kingdom of God, but these are guesses and the only fairly certain historical fact we have is that Jesus was betrayed by his disciple Judas.

The way the betrayal occurred also appears to be true historically. At the time of the festival, the Mount of Olives, just outside the city walls, would have been crammed with bivouacking pilgrims and therefore a convenient place for Jesus and his party to get lost in the crowd. The Sanhedrin (supreme council of the Jewish authorities) had decided to move against Jesus, but they wanted to do so cautiously and without risking an uprising of popular support for his cause. When Judas went to them with his offer it must have seemed an act of Providence. The arrest

Peter's Denial, Jesus' Trial

Left: *Christ before the High Priest*, by the 17th-century Dutch artist Gerrit van Honthorst. Although the Talmud declares night-trials to be illegal, this is only one irregularity in the Sanhedrin's efforts to bring a capital charge against Jesus. The court meets under the presidency of the High Priest Caiaphas. Two witnesses are found to bring in evidence of blasphemy, which carries the death penalty. Neither of the witnesses is in complete agreement. Dissatisfied with their testimony, the High Priest tells Jesus directly, "Tell us if thou be the Christ, the Son of God!" When Jesus agrees that he is, Caiaphas tears his garments from the neck downward for a palm's length in the manner prescribed for the hearing of blasphemous speech.

was made under cover of darkness, and if Jesus' followers offered any resistance it was only superficial. They were apparently so appalled by the way things had turned out that they disbanded and proceeded to deny any association with Jesus when challenged: shameful conduct that the evangelists would surely not have recorded if it were not true especially with regard to Peter himself who three times denied Jesus.

The way the trial of Jesus was conducted, and the way the High Priest, Caiaphas, contrived to charge him for a political offense that would carry the death penalty according to Roman law, is reported in the gospels in a manner consistent with what is known about the political and religious situation in Palestine at the time; and consistent, too, with the slyness, expedience, and legalistic shifts and stratagems that have been characteristic of disreputable political trials at all times.

The distaste of the Roman Prefect, Pontius Pilate, for the whole business, and his willingness to acquit and discharge the prisoner, have no doubt been correctly reported in the gospels. Jesus had no armed following and was no threat to the Roman power, and Caiaphas' translation of "Messiah" into "King of the Jews" was a transparently slanted interpretation of the word whose proper meaning was well understood in Judaism. But the priestly establishment managed to assemble a well-briefed crowd

Right: in Judaea only the Roman governor could order an execution. Pontius Pilate is impressed with Jesus' bearing when he is brought before him and offers to set him free as a Roman gesture for the festival. The crowd calls for someone else to be set free instead, and Pilate washes his hands of any share in Jesus' death.

Below: the 15th-century Flemish painter Jan van Eyck's *Crucifixion* shows one of the soldiers offering Jesus a sponge dipped in vinegar (the sour wine and water, known as *posca*, that the troops carried).

to clamor for Jesus' death, Pilate washed his hands of the matter and Jesus was duly condemned and escorted off to Golgotha to undergo the barbarous punishment that the Romans imposed for political crimes.

This much seems historically certain. So does the curious detail that it was Joseph of Arimathea, a member of the despised Sanhedrin, and not one of the disciples, who obtained permission to take down Jesus' body from the cross and inter it. It is the sequel to this, the disappearance of the body from the tomb, the resurrection, the appearance of the risen Jesus to certain of his followers, that has always been at the center of the Christian message.

There have been many alternative opinions, of course, and in a book published in 1965 entitled *The Passover Plot*, the biblical historian Hugh Schonfield put forward a theory that Jesus did not die on the cross but planned his "resurrection" in a last desperate attempt to inaugurate the Kingdom through his martyrdom in line with prophecies of Isaiah. According to this theory Jesus deliberately provoked the authorities by his conduct in the temple, exploited a weakness in Judas to get him to betray him, and, after making himself elusive until the night of the Passover, then gave Judas the opportunity to perform the act of betrayal. Timing, and the cooperation of friends in Jerusalem unknown to the disciples, were essential to the success of the plan.

By having himself crucified on the Friday, Jesus managed things so that he would be left on the cross for only a few hours instead of for days as was usual, for it was customary not to leave victims on the cross over the Sabbath and to take them down before sunset on the Friday. It was also customary to despatch them if they were not already dead, and Jesus avoided this fate by having an accomplice administer a drug that would make him appear dead. For, as Mark reports in Chapter 15, "one ran and, filling a sponge full of vinegar, put it on a reed and gave it to him to drink."

Jesus had another accomplice, Joseph of Arimathea, influentially enough placed to be able to secure the release of his corpse for interment. Pilate was surprised at the request and "wondered if he were already dead," but when one of his soldiers confirmed that he was, the Prefect granted Joseph's request. Perhaps, Schonfield speculated in his book, it was in this manner that Jesus fulfilled Isaiah's prophecy of the Suffering Just One and his Resurrection and at the same time unwittingly laid the foundations of a faith that was to sweep the world.

Perhaps. The theory is consistent with Jesus' habit of teaching through doing, of being a living parable. It is, however, as Schonfield admits, speculation, a theory based upon an interpretation of the available literature. But what the gospels give us beyond doubt is the person of Christ who, as the temple police stated, "spoke like no other man" (Chapter 7 of John's gospel). Christianity has always claimed that Christ was the Son of God and that is why even today he is understandably regarded by millions as no mere man but God himself Incarnate.

No Mere Mortal

Below: *The Resurrection*, by Andrea Mantegna. It is fundamental to Christian belief that Jesus Christ, after his death and burial, rose again in the body on the third day. It was the Resurrection that gave the Apostles a renewal of faith and enabled and inspired them to preach the Gospel—the good news, of which the Resurrection itself was a basic part.

Chapter 8
The Non-Biblical Evidence

Apart from the Gospels, what other documentary or archaeological evidence is there for the life of Jesus? This chapter assesses it all, from references to Jesus and his followers by contemporary historians and commentators to recent finds such as the Dead Sea Scrolls. It looks at the claim that Jesus the man may even have survived the crucifixion to die at Masada at the age of 80. Finally, there is the amazing Shroud of Turin, belief in the authenticity of which seems to grow the more scientists examine and test it. The findings are fascinating, but the tantalizing mystery remains: Did the most loved and revered of all historical figures really live after all?

In December, 1964, Donovan Joyce, an Australian writer, was offered $5000 by a man who called himself Professor Max Grosset (who said he was a professor of Semitic Studies at an American university) if he would smuggle out of Israel an ancient parchment scroll. According to his own account, Joyce demanded to know more before he would consider the proposition, and the professor took him into the men's lavatory at Tel Aviv's Lod airport, where he took the scroll from a black cabin bag, telling Joyce, "Compared with this, the best of the Dead Sea Scrolls is an unimportant scribble." Joyce handled the parchment and, turning back a corner of it, saw neat rows of legible writing in a language he was told was Aramaic. Grosset divulged some details about the text of the scroll, though not many. The writer, he said, identified himself as "Yeshua ben Ya'akob ben Gennesareth" and said that he was 80 years of age and the last rightful heir to the Hasmonean throne of Israel. He wrote his testament, the scroll, during the night before the Romans launched their final assault upon Masada after spending years building an earthwork ramp to reach the top, which was on April 15, A.D. 73. The professor, writes Joyce, then proceeded to tell him the most fantastic story, the conclusion of which was that the scroll had been written by none other than Jesus himself.

Donovan Joyce tells this story of his meeting with the professor, who, he believed, may have defected to the Soviet Union with the scroll, in the preface to his book, *The Jesus Scroll*. It is

Opposite: an aerial view of the ruins of the wilderness fortress of Masada, near the Dead Sea. It was the last refuge of a fiery group of nationalist Jewish men and women known as Zealots. Their hatred of Roman rule and of those who collaborated with the Romans led them in the spring of A.D. 66 to break into the Temple and kill the High Priest, a known Roman sympathizer, and to spearhead an open rebellion against the Romans. If there had been a member of the former Hasmonaean royal house still alive, he would have found a loyal following here among the Zealots at Masada.

QVOD VATES BELLVM CREVIT NON ESSE DVELLVM
CODIT & MVLTIS·VOBISQVI CERNERE VVLTIS·
EST IOSEPHVS DICTVS FERT LIBRVM CORPORE PICTVS·

Above: the historian Josephus Flavius
presenting his first literary work *The Jewish
War* to the Emperor Vespasian—an
illustration from an 11th-century Latin
edition of his book. Josephus was a
Palestinian Jew of priestly family who went
to Rome after the fall of Jerusalem in A.D.
70 to enter the service of the Caesars. His
account of the Jewish War was therefore a
work of contemporary history.

Right: in this painting by the 15th-century
Italian artist Fra Angelico, Joseph, Mary,
and the infant Jesus take flight for Egypt to
escape the massacre of all children under
the age of two in Bethlehem, where Jesus'
birth occurred. The journey would have
taken some five or six days. When they
returned they went to Mary's birthplace,
Nazareth, an insignificant village not
mentioned in either the Talmud or in
Josephus.

not, however, the professor and the mythical scroll that is so
fascinating, but the report of subsequent researches Joyce conducted over a period of eight years along lines suggested by the
slender facts divulged to him by "Professor Grosset" (who could
not be traced to any American university) that night at Lod
airport, researches that led him to the conclusion that the scroll
could be just what the mystery professor claimed it was: the
last testament of Jesus.

The signature, "Yeshua ben Ya'akob ben Gennesareth" trans-
lates as: Jesus son of Jacob of Gennesareth. Which seems very
different from Jesus of Nazareth, whose father's name anyway
was Joseph. Gennesareth, however, is another name for Galilee,
and in fact is used as such in the gospels. A curious thing that
Joyce discovered was that there was no mention of the name
Nazareth, except in the gospels and writings derived from them,
until the 2nd century. The 1st-century historian Josephus Flavius,
who was also Jewish military commander in the Galilee area
during the Roman war of A.D. 66–70, never mentions the town,
although he names all the towns in Galilee that he fortified, and
the site of present-day Nazareth is certainly a strategic one.
Furthermore, some historians have suggested that there was no
settlement at Nazareth until the 2nd or 3rd century, and if they
are right the name "Jesus of Gennesareth" clearly could have
belonged to the man known to history as Jesus of Nazareth, for
if the prefix "Gen" (Hebrew for "garden") is dropped, the words
"nesareth" and "Nazareth" are almost identical.

But what about the problem of the father's name being Jacob instead of Joseph? Well, Joyce believed that Joseph did divorce Mary and she married a man named Cleophas, or Alpheus. Oddly enough, the word "Alpheus" in Greek means "successor," and the Hebrew word with this meaning is Ya'akob—or Jacob. Now, it was customary for male Jews to keep their Hebrew name for family use and adopt a Greek name for public use. Joyce suggests that Alpheus, or sometimes Cleophas, was the public name adopted by Mary's second husband, Jacob.

According to gospel traditions, Jesus was a man of humble origin, whereas the man who was supposed to have signed the Masada scroll claimed to be the heir to the Hasmonean throne of Israel. This seemed to Joyce a major objection to the theory of the identity of the two until he got down to researching Jewish dynastic history. The gospels claim that Jesus was born of King David's line, but David had lived 1000 years before Jesus. During that period the Hebrew aristocracy had been broken up and exiled to Babylon, so the royal line of descent had been hopelessly lost. In the previous 200 years B.C. the undisputed Jewish ruling family was that of the Hasmoneans, or Maccabees, who had driven the Syrians out of Israel. As a result, the Messianic expectations had largely been transferred to them. Interestingly, the Hasmoneans had arisen in central Galilee and had acquired as their own estate the fertile Plain of Gennesareth. But after their triumphs over the invaders they had fallen to quarreling among themselves—which gave Rome the opportunity to take over Israel.

The Romans at first tried to sort out the Hasmoneans' family quarrels, but eventually gave up, abolished the monarchy, and appointed Herod I ("the Great") King of Judea. He in turn appointed his son Herod Antipas as governor of Galilee. Herod I then embarked on a campaign to liquidate all Hasmoneans including his Hasmonean wife Mariamne, as Josephus said, "not so much because they claimed the throne, but because they were entitled to it."

What, then, was Jesus' connection with the Hasmoneans? The gospels tell us that Jesus and John the Baptist were cousins, and that John's father, Zacharias, was a priest in the temple. Donovan Joyce argues that Zacharias was in fact a Hasmonean, and that after his death and the liquidation of everyone with a claim to the throne of Israel his son John became the heir apparent. John in turn was killed by Herod Antipas, because he accused Herod of adultery. Joyce suggests that Herod Antipas didn't care in the slightest for John's ravings, and that he had him arrested because he was the Hasmonean heir. After John's death, the gospels record, Jesus made haste to get out of Herod Antipas' territory, although they do not explain why. Could it be because, with John gone, Jesus was now the heir to the Hasmonean kingship?

To explain how Jesus came to be at Masada in A.D. 73, Joyce suggests that the charge leveled against Jesus—that he was claiming to be "King of the Jews"—was literally true, and that he survived crucifixion and achieved his "resurrection" by the schemes put forward in Hugh Schonfield's *The Passover Plot*. After his escape from the tomb, Joyce further suggests, Jesus might have taken refuge with the Essene community at Qumran

"King David's Line"

Below: the "Tree of Jesse" according to a 15th-century Italian manuscript. It is a genealogical tree showing the descent of Jesus from the royal line of David. The tree springs from Jesse, the father of King David, and ends in Jesus and his Mother.

Jesus the King?

Right: after the archangel Gabriel had announced to Mary that she was to conceive the long-awaited Messiah, God's Son, she paid a visit to her pregnant cousin Elizabeth, who was herself, although quite old, carrying the future John the Baptist. Elizabeth's husband was Zachary, a Levitical priest of the Temple. As there were some 20,000 priests they fulfilled their functions by drawing lots. Zachary had drawn the lot of offering incense in the sanctuary and had just completed the ritual when an angel appeared to him and told him his prayer had been answered. The official prayer of priest and prophet at incense offering was a set form of prayer for the coming of the Messiah and the redemption of Israel, but Zachary seems also to have desired offspring in spite of the advanced age of his wife. The birth of John was to answer both prayers.

and remained there until A.D. 68 when the Romans attacked the monastery-city, and after that he might have escaped to Masada, 30 miles to the south. Why the Romans should have attacked the Essene community in the first place, and why they should have put the enormous efforts they did into the conquest of Masada, are questions that have puzzled historians. So, too, have the questions as to why the Zealots should have retreated upon Masada as soon as the war with Rome began in A.D. 66, and why they should have taken their own lives on the night of April 14–15. These facts all become more understandable on the theory that the last claimant to the Hasmonean throne lived at Qumran and when the Romans discovered the fact he moved on to Masada, which had been occupied in anticipation of just such an eventuality. As April 15 was a Sabbath, when Jews were forbidden to fight, the Romans could be expected to swarm onto the mountain fortress, so they might well have chosen to die by their own hands the night before. During that night the 80-year-old last royal Hasmonean, Jesus of Gennasereth, might have written before he died a scroll to tell the world of the fate that had overcome the Hasmonean line and the long-guarded secret of its last uncrowned king.

This leads to the question: How could Jesus have been 80 years old in A.D. 73? Matthew's gospel tells how Herod sought the death of Jesus when he was a child, and according to Josephus Herod died in 4 B.C. so Jesus could not have been born in the year A.D. 1. The traditional dating was the result of a miscalcula-

Above: King Herod sent his soldiers to Bethlehem to massacre all the children under two years old when he heard of the prophecy that a King would be born there. The murder of a few children in a remote village would hardly worry Herod, who came to his throne through a sea of blood, murdering even his own family. The emperor Augustus said of him "I'd rather be Herod's sow, than his son." (Herod, a Jew, was forbidden to eat pork, so pigs were not butchered, but he put his three sons to death.)

Left: the head of John the Baptist being placed on a plate held by Salome, Herod's stepdaughter.

Above right: the ruins of the Essene community's monastery-city of Qumran, near the Dead Sea. The Essenes, both men and women, lived strictly disciplined lives. They ate their meals together, owned no individual property, wore a simple white linen robe, and practiced ritual bathing as part of their code of purity. They believed that they were following Isaiah's command to "make straight in the desert a highway for our God," and that a Messiah would come who would overthrow the Romans and establish the Kingdom of God on earth so that all nations would worship the one true God in his Temple in Jerusalem.

Above: the ruins of Masada. For three years after the fall of Jerusalem in A.D. 70, Jewish resistance to the hated Romans continued from three desert citadels. Two, Machaerus and Herodium, surrendered, but Masada held on until A.D. 73, when the remaining 953 Zealot defenders—men, women, and children—took their own lives rather than surrender to the Romans. The Australian writer Donovan Joyce has suggested that it was during that fatal last assault on Masada that Jesus of Nazareth took his own life. He suggests that, indeed, the Romans went to such great lengths to overcome the fortress because this same Jesus was the last rightful heir to the Hasmonaean throne and High Priesthood of the Jews.

tion made by a 6th-century monk, Dionysus Exiguus. Some biblical scholars give the date of Jesus' birth as not later than the early months of 4 B.C., but in an article on the Chronology of the New Testament in Hastings' *Dictionary of the Bible* the date of Jesus' birth is given as between 7 and 6 B.C., which would indeed have made him 80 when Masada fell.

Donovan Joyce's speculations on the basis of his researches are certainly wilder than any academic historian would permit himself. But then his incentive for undertaking the research in the first place was rather unusual. The tale told him by the mysterious "Professor Max Grosset" appeared to contradict the orthodox version of Jesus' life and background but his own subsequent researches were enough at least to diminish the improbability of the "professor's" story even if it didn't prove it true. If the "Jesus Scroll" really exists and comes to light one day, it will certainly be the most sensational archaeological find of all time so far as the history of Christian origins is concerned. Until such time, however, Joyce's theories must be considered as fascinating conjecture.

By far the most important find likely to have any bearing on the search for the Jesus of the Bible must remain the Dead Sea Scrolls found at Qumran in the Judean desert in 1948. They were discovered by Bedouin tribesmen, who at first had no idea of their value. When they found that there was a keen market for them they tore them up and sold them bit by bit. The scrolls themselves are a veritable treasure trove for biblical scholars. They contained copies of Old Testament books 1000 years older than any previously known, which allowed scholars the opportunity to compare translations in those books accepted by the Church as "Holy Scripture" with the Hebrew originals and to prepare new translations based on the older sources. But for New Testament studies the most significant discoveries at Qumran were the nonbiblical texts on ceremony, belief, and community rules written by the Essenes. Until the scrolls were found little was known about the Essenes except that they constituted a school of Jewish doctrine that rivaled the Pharisees and the Sadducees. The Jewish historian Josephus had written in the 1st century that there were 6000 Pharisees in Israel and 4000 Essenes, so the Essenes were a sizeable minority, but nobody knew what they had believed and taught until their settlement and library at Qumran were discovered. Then it was found that there were remarkable similarities between Christian and Essene beliefs.

The Essenes had considered the Jerusalem priestly aristocracy to be corrupt and unworthy, and, believing themselves to be the children of the New Covenant with Yahweh, had retired to the Judean wilderness to await the coming of the New Age, the Kingdom of God. They revered the founder of their sect, the "Teacher of Righteousness," who had received from God the revelation of secrets about the "last days," but had been persecuted by the "Wicked Priest." They believed that during the "last days" there would arise from within their community two Messiahs, one priestly and the other royal, and that after a 40-

Did Jesus Die at Masada?

Left: the caves at Qumran, on the west side of the Dead Sea. It was near here that the Essenes established their monastery-city, some miles north of the fortress of Masada. The caves were used as storehouses for the library at Aumran, and when the Romans overran the monastery and drove away the Essenes, the community buildings lay forgotten in the wilderness for 19 centuries. Below: a copper scroll found in the caves at Qumran. It contained an inventory of the Essene's most treasured possessions buried at various locations. Other caves contained the famous *Manual of Discipline*, listing the rules of the community, psalms of praise, and many old Bible texts.

Jesus and the Essene Sect

Right: with the aid of special equipment at the Manchester College of Technology, England, the copper scrolls were cut apart so that they could be read.

Above: infrared photography used on the leather scrolls that in the course of 2000 years became black (top). The leather reflected the infrared, the carbon ink absorbed it, and the result was a reasonably legible text (lower).

year war between the Sons of Light and the Sons of Darkness the two Messiahs would occupy the temporal and spiritual thrones of Israel and thus establish the Kingdom of God.

There are obvious correspondences with Christianity in these doctrines of the Essenes, and certain sayings attributed to Jesus in the gospels have an unmistakable Essene stamp. When the Qumran manuscripts were first published, some people suggested that the Jesus of the gospel stories had been modeled on the Teacher of Righteousness and that the origins of Christianity were traceable to Qumran and the Essenes. This view has been altered in the light of later studies of the Essene material, and particularly with the discovery of what a fanatically exclusive community the Essenes were, believing themselves to be the elect of God and destined to be the sole survivors of the "last days," whereas Christianity taught that salvation was available to all, Jew or Gentile. But if Christianity did not entirely derive from Essene teachings there are enough similarities between them and the teachings of Jesus recorded in the gospels to indicate that the historical Jesus might well have been familiar with the sect and its doctrines, and probably also with the community living at Qumran. In any case, the similarities help substantiate the existence of the historical Jesus, for they indicate that his teaching and his belief in himself as the Messiah were characteristic of the place and the time in which he lived.

Neither archaeology nor ancient non-Christian literature has supplied any direct evidence of the life story of Jesus or any extra information about him not already found in Christian sources; that is, if we rule out the "Jesus scroll." Archaeology has, however, helped to confirm the view that John, the author of the

fourth gospel, was a Jerusalem-based early Christian who was thoroughly familiar with Palestine, which is significant in view of the fact that John's gospel is more theological than biographical and the authenticity of its information has often been doubted. There are nine Palestinian place names in John that are not found in the other three gospels, and archaeologists have located all of them, showing that John knew Palestine, particularly the southern part, like a native.

Considering that Christianity sprang up within the Roman empire and spread throughout it, non-Christian literary sources of information about Jesus are surprisingly few and poor. There are references to him in the Talmud, the collection of Jewish law and tradition, by rabbis of the 1st and 2nd centuries. They claimed he practiced magic, ridiculed the wise, stirred the people to rebellion and was hanged (crucified) on the eve of Passover. Josephus, both a Jew and a Galilean, makes only two references in all his work, one an obvious introduction into his text of Christian piety totally uncharacteristic of the author, who was pro-Roman and despised Jewish preoccupation with Messiahs and "New World" theories, and an earlier passing reference in a passage about the murder by the High Priest Ananas in A.D. 62 of James the brother of "Jesus, the so-called Christ." The sneer implied in this reference is enough to prove that the later pious reference was an editorial insertion from a later date.

Three Roman writers (two served as officials in the Levant and all three were hostile to Christianity) put on record references to Christianity that, while of interest to the historian, tell us nothing about Jesus himself. All three wrote between 80 and 100 years after the crucifixion. Pliny the Younger, writing to the emperor

Above: early Christian signs and symbols written on the walls of the Catacombs of Rome. On the left is the Chi-Rho sign, the first two letters of Christ in Greek (three in English "Chr"). As here, they are often interwoven as a monogram. The Greek Christos is translated as Messiah. The dove symbolizes the soul, the laurel branch victory.
Below: the faces of an early Roman Christian family look out from a 4th-century glass miniature.

The Holy Shroud

Opposite: Saint Veronica, who offered her head-cloth to Jesus to wipe the sweat and blood from his face as he was dragging his cross to his crucifixion. He returned it to her with his portrait impressed on it.

Below: the Crown of Thorns, worn by Jesus at his crucifixion, is brought to France from Constantinople in 1239 and housed in the Sainte-Chapelle by Louis IX of France. There is a long history of belief in the power of relics. That God himself approves of their use because of the power he invests in them is shown by such biblical references as that in Chapter 13 of the second book of Kings "some that were burying a man . . . cast the body into the sepulchre of Elisha. And when it had touched the bones of Elisha, the man came to life, and stood on his feet." In Chapter 19 of the Acts, people came with faith and humility to touch Saint Paul with handkerchiefs and aprons and took them away to the sick so that they were cured. In the Middle Ages, however, the cult of the veneration of relics became extreme and abuses inevitably occurred.

Trajan, said that the Christians sang a hymn "to Christ as to a god;" a statement that implies that Pliny knew that Christ was a historical human being. Then the Roman historian Suetonius, the author of the *Lives of the Caesars*, wrote that the emperor Claudius (A.D. 41 to 54) "expelled from Rome the Jews who were constantly rioting at the instigation of Chrestus." Suetonius appears to have received his information in a garbled form, almost certainly the Jewish community was in turmoil because of the intrusion of Christian ideas in their midst. But the longest reference in ancient literature comes from the *Annals* written around A.D. 100 by another Roman historian, Tacitus, who, in a passage about the persecution of the Christians in Rome after the great fire of A.D. 64, explains that: "The founder of this sect, Christus, was given the death penalty in the reign of Tiberius by the procurator Pontius Pilate; suppressed for the moment, the detestable superstition broke out again, not only in Judea where the evil originated, but also in the city of Rome to which everything horrible and shameful flows and where it grows." Although this adds nothing to our knowledge of Jesus, it is a valuable independent testimony of the strength of the religion that arose based upon him in the years soon after the crucifixion.

Throughout the Middle Ages religious relics allegedly associated with Jesus, the Virgin Mary, or the Apostles were revered by pious but gullible men and women throughout Christendom and exploited by such unscrupulous rogues as the Pardoner in the *Canterbury Tales* by the 14th-century English poet Geoffrey Chaucer. Among these relics there were several shrouds that were claimed by their devotees or owners to be the original burial cloth in which Jesus' body had lain in Joseph of Arimathea's tomb after being taken down from the cross. But unique among these shrouds was the one in the possession of the Dukes of Savoy (later, Kings of Italy), for it had upon it faint shadowy stains merging into one another which, from a distance, took on the outlines of a human figure lying with hands crossed. The stains were held to be the imprints of Jesus' physical body miraculously preserved on the Savior's burial cloth. The legend surrounding the shroud states that it was taken from Jerusalem to Constantinople, where it was seen in 1204. In 1353 Robert de Charny built an abbey for it at Chambery. Then in 1578 it was taken to Italy so that the aged Archbishop of Milan should be spared the journey across the Alps to see it. It has remained there ever since safely stored in a silver casket in the Cathedral of Turin. It is still unique, for it is the only alleged religious relic that, instead of having been proved bogus by scientific investigation has on the contrary convinced many scientists that it must be genuine.

The question whether the "Holy Shroud of Turin" is an authentic artifact directly associated with the historical Jesus is one of the most intriguing of all religious mysteries; the more so because the full mystery has only emerged in the present century.

It was in 1898 that a Turin photographer named Secondo Pia was commissioned by King Humbert I of Italy, the "guardian" of the Shroud, to take the first-ever photographs of the holy burial cloth. When he developed his photographic plates, Pia

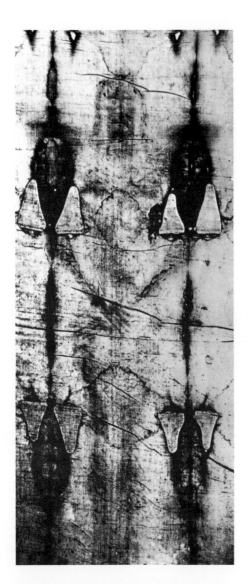

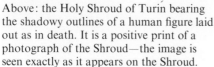

Above: the Holy Shroud of Turin bearing the shadowy outlines of a human figure laid out as in death. It is a positive print of a photograph of the Shroud—the image is seen exactly as it appears on the Shroud.

Above right: the face from the Shroud seen as a photographic negative. As the image imprinted on the Shroud is itself a reversed image, the negative is in effect a "positive" print of the face. This face, many Christians and non-Christians believe, is that of Jesus.

was astonished and at first thought that he must have made some mistake, for on his negative plate he saw not a reversed image of the brown stains but a picture of a bearded face wearing an expression of great serenity and nobility. Whereas the face visible on the Shroud was rather blurred and the features were ill-defined, the one on the plate was perfectly clear. When he recovered from his initial astonishment, the photographer realized what must have happened. As the picture on his negative plate was a positive, he must have photographed a negative. Incredibly, the shadowy markings on the cloth were the opposite way round in terms of light and shade, like a photographic negative. Others were to puzzle over the problem of how this could be and propose various explanations, but it seemed to Secondo Pia when he looked at his first negative plate that he had witnessed a miracle. It was as if the Holy Shroud had been waiting 19 centuries for man's discovery of the art of photography to unlock its secret.

When Secondo Pia's discovery was announced and his photographs were made available for study, there were naturally people who suggested that a clever fake must have been perpetrated. More photographs were taken with the same results, which exonerated Pia, but it was now suggested that the shroud had been faked by a Medieval artist who had painted the markings on it. But when this possibility was examined the mystery deepened. Microscopic examination showed that there were no deposits of paint on the fabric, every individual thread was distinctly visible, those that were stained were stained right through, and there were no outlines or shadings such as would be found on work done by human hand. Furthermore, not only was it technically impossible for an artist to have faked the image on the Shroud, but also nobody in the Middle Ages, when of course the principles of photography were unknown, could have conceived or executed the idea of reversing the light and shade and so imprinting a negative image on the Shroud.

The testimony of medical men also ruled out the possibility of Medieval forgery. In those days knowledge of anatomy was rudimentary and nothing was known of the circulation of the blood, but the markings on the Shroud are exact in anatomical detail and proportion and the authenticity of marks made by blood flowing from the wounds is confirmed by forensic medicine, which has shown those marks to be consistent with the known behavior of shed blood. Forensic examination has, moreover, confirmed the gospel accounts of the execution of Jesus. The dark stains on the Shroud that come up white on the photograph clearly show wounds on the left wrist (the right one is covered by the left hand), on the soles of the feet, on the right breast, on the brow and all over the back, which respectively bear out the story that Jesus was crucified, pierced by a Roman soldier's lance, crowned with a crown of thorns, and scourged. Medical men have also noted that the expanded rib cage and the drawn-in hollow below it indicate that the man of the Shroud died while hanging by the arms.

In the many paintings of the crucifixion, Christ is shown nailed to the cross through the palms of his hands, but the wound markings on the Shroud suggest that the nails penetrated the wrists.

The Shroud Discovered

Left: Leo Vala, a photographer working in Britain, with a picture of the Shroud (left) and his profile photograph of the face from the Shroud, produced as a result of a unique process he has developed. "The development of this picture," Vala has stated, "has given me a vehicle upon which to produce a corresponding three-dimensional picture of the whole shroud. There are no bounds to what information this could reveal."

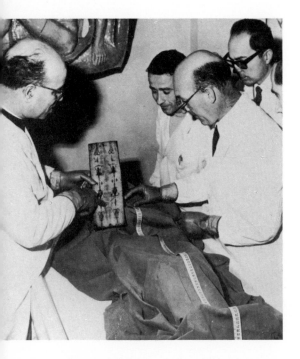

Above: using a piece of material of the same dimensions as the Holy Shroud an anatomy expert and a Vatican archivist carry out a practical experiment to determine how tall Jesus was at his death. They also measured the length of an uninterrupted print of a forearm bone on the Shroud and concluded that Jesus was five feet four inches tall—about the average stature of a Palestinian of his time. The Holy Shroud has proved to be one of the most fascinating religious relics to come to the notice of scientists in recent times. The Shroud itself has been called the Fifth Gospel.

A French doctor, Pierre Barbet, conducted what must have been the most macabre scientific experiment ever when he crucified the body of a deceased patient with nails through the palms of the hands, only to find that the nails tore through the hands as soon as the cross was raised. At a second attempt Dr. Barbet hammered the nails through the wrists and found that the bony structure there could support the weight of the body. And he noticed another thing: that when a nail penetrated the wrist the thumb bent inward into the palm. The absence of thumbs from the hands of the man of the Shroud had until then been an unexplained puzzle for the students of the relic.

Scientists have also tried to explain how the negative image might have become imprinted on the Shroud. John's gospel states that Joseph and Nicodemus bound Jesus' body into the Shroud with a mixture of powdered myrhh and aloes. These spices, it has been suggested by Dr. Paul Vignon, a professor of biology, could act like the sensitized plate of a film in a camera, and a chemical reaction upon them produced by ammonia vapors rising from the body could account for the photographic effect on the linen. An alternative theory, which is supported by Dr. Barbet, is that the cloth is stained with a component of aloes known as aloentine which was produced by moisture given off by the body. Both theories have been put to the test with a degree of success sufficient to establish the point that markings like those on the Shroud could have been caused by a chemical action upon the spices with which the Shroud and Jesus' body were liberally covered (according to John, Nicodemus brought about "a hundred pounds' weight" for the purpose) before being put in the tomb. Another theory that has been proposed but which cannot be tested experimentally is that the image on the Shroud was produced by chemical action at the moment of Jesus' resurrection, caused by a radiation of energies particular to that unique event.

As science becomes more sophisticated and more tests are devised in the hope of finally authenticating the Shroud or proving it a fake, the relic continues to baffle those who hope to discredit it. At a conference on the Shroud held in the United States in March, 1977, some recent developments were reported. Physicists from the Jet Propulsion Laboratory in Pasadena, California, used the computer techniques employed to enhance or magnify photographs sent back from Mars on a photograph of the Shroud, and they made two significant discoveries. First, the lack of what they call "linear directionality" in the shading of the image indicates that it was not painted on the fabric; and second, the enhancement technique enabled them to produce a three-dimensional version of the images on the Shroud, and it was found that the intensity of the image varied according to the distance the sheet would have been from the body at each point.

Textile experts long ago confirmed that the linen of the Shroud is identical in material and weave pattern to many fabrics from the eastern Mediterranean that have been reliably dated from the 1st to the 3rd centuries. Now a Swiss professor named Max Frei has come up with more evidence that supports the tradition that the Shroud was taken from Jerusalem to Constantinople and then brought to Europe at the time of the

Crusades. Frei is a pollen analysis expert. Pollen, which does not deteriorate with time, indicates where things have been, and Frei has discovered that some of the pollen on the Shroud is identical with that from 2000-year-old sediments from Lake Galilee, and that other pollen traces show that the Shroud moved through Palestine, Asia Minor, and Savoy.

Up to now the custodians of the Shroud have refused to sacrifice a portion of it for a carbon dating test, which could determine its age to within 100 years. But recently a Chicago microanalyst, Dr. Walter McCrone, has improved carbon dating technique so that now only half a square inch, instead of two square feet, of the material need be destroyed for the test. Even so, it is doubtful whether even this small amount will be made available for the test. If it is, and if the Shroud is proved to be 2000 years old, then the very least that could be said for it is that its association with the Jesus of the gospels and of the Christian faith will not have been disproved. Yet the mystery of the Shroud will remain, as will the mystery of its supposed one-time occupant, the most loved and revered as well as most enigmatic and elusive of historical figures.

A Fascinating Religious Relic

Below: Fra Angelico, the 15th-century Italian painter, depicts Jesus rising from the tomb with the shroud in which he was bound. Matthew, Mark, and Luke all agree that Joseph of Arimathea brought a winding sheet and wrapped the body of Jesus in it. As there was little time left before the Sabbath only the minimum arrangements were carried out and, indeed, the Shroud shows that the body was clearly unwashed—contrary to Jewish practice. It seems that the women intended to perform this rite and the proper anointing with spices when they visited the tomb early Sunday morning.

Chapter 9
What is Sacred?

Men and women of all times and cultures have accepted a startling variety of objects, places, animals, and individuals as possessing strange and uncanny power. These powerful symbols inevitably become invested with mystery and supernatural significance—they are accepted as the divinity communicating its will to men. In a word, they have come to be regarded as sacred. What exactly are these media, through which man in his turn tries to achieve communion, as it were, with the God or gods of his belief? What in fact is the symbolism—for that is largely what the sacred is all about—of the sacred? This chapter sets out to answer the question: What is the sacred?

When Abraham's grandson, Jacob, was on his way to Haran to choose a wife from his cousins, "he lighted upon a certain place, and he tarried there all night, because the sun was set." He used as a pillow a large stone, and in his sleep he dreamed that there was "a ladder set up on the earth, and the top of it reached to heaven; and behold the angels of God ascending and descending on it." He had a vision of God himself, who repeated the promise he had made to Abraham, to make his descendants as numerous and widespread as the dust of the earth. When Jacob awoke after his dream he said, "Surely the Lord is in this place; and I knew it not. And he was afraid and said, How dreadful is this place! this is none other but the house of God, and this is the gate of heaven." Taking the stone he had used as a pillow, he set it up and poured oil on it to consecrate it, and he named the place "Bethel," which means "House of God."

This story from Chapter 28 of the Book of Genesis throws light on several aspects of the question, What is sacred? In the first place, Jacob arrived, apparently by chance, at a place he came to believe was naturally sacred. He did not consecrate, or sanctify, the place because of the experience he had undergone there. He believed that he had had the experience because he had happened to stop at this particular place. When he realized that the place was special, that the Lord was in it, his first reaction was of mixed fear and awe. Then he performed a simple ritual, setting up a special stone to mark the holy ground. The place was, he

Opposite: this 16th-century stained glass window from an English church illustrates Jacob's dream. Fleeing from the anger of his brother, Esau, Jacob rested in the desert. He made pillows out of stones and lay down to sleep. While asleep he dreamed of a ladder that reached from earth to heaven and angels were ascending and descending on it. God stood above the ladder and spoke to Jacob telling him that he would give the land on which he was lying to him and to his descendants for ever. When Jacob awoke he was filled with awe and realized that he had by chance stepped on holy ground. He immediately set up one of the stones he had used as a pillow, poured oil on it, and consecrated the spot as a house of God.

Above: Mount Fuji, the sacred mountain venerated by the followers of the Shinto religion—Japan's national religion.

Below: a priest breaks the host over the chalice at a celebration of the Christian Eucharist. To Christians of many denominations the Eucharist is at the heart of their worship. Most Christians agree that Christ himself is in some way present in the Communion.

believed, "the gate of heaven," in order words it was one of those rare places where heaven and earth were connected, where that which is above and beyond human experience could be felt or seen by humans: a point emphasized by Jacob's dream image of the ladder with the angels ascending and descending.

The sense of sacredness, or holiness, is the one basic common factor in all religions, primitive or advanced, and it consists precisely in the conviction that the divine reveals itself in the physical world. This manifestation may be through any object; a stone, a tree, a plant; or through a special person or a person acting in a special way, such as performing a ritual act or gesture, for instance; or it may be in a particular place or at a particular time, such as a religious festival; or again, it may be in a physiological act, in sex or eating. As the Romanian religious historian Mircea Eliade wrote: "we cannot be sure that there is *anything*— object, movement, physiological function, being or even game— that has not at some time in human history been somewhere transformed into a hierophany." The term *hierophany* is Eliade's invention, meaning "a revelation or manifestation of the sacred." He continues: "it is quite certain that anything man has ever handled, felt, come in contact with or loved *can* become a hierophany."

When religious feeling transforms a thing into a hierophany, it can either become for the believer something quite different, as the wafer and the wine become the flesh and blood of Christ in the ritual of the Eucharist; or it may be recognized as at the same time itself and an embodiment of the divine; or thirdly it may be recognized as simply a sign or symbol of divinity. These three forms of the sacred have given rise to much theological controversy, for instance over the question whether Christ was

Sacred Objects, Acts and Places

Left: an illustration from a French history of the Crusades up to Louis IX, showing the Crusaders' assault on Jerusalem in 1099. The Crusader conquest of Palestine was ruthless and bitter. As with all conquering religions, the Christians desecrated the holy places of the non-Christians. In a letter from the leader of the first Crusade, Godfrey of Bouillon, to the pope he tells of his men riding "in the corridors and in the temple of Solomon . . . the blood of Saracens as high as the fetlocks of their coursers." When the battle was over, the Jews, according to one refugee, "were assembled inside their synagogue which was then put to the fire."

God incarnate, or was both God and a man, or was a man who was sent or inspired by God as a sign and representative of his concern for the world. Religions that teach belief in a single god have always had to be on guard against the human tendency to take the part for the whole, the sign for substance, the image for the god. According to Chapter 26 of Leviticus, God laid down the law that the Israelites should make for themselves "no idols nor graven image . . . neither shall ye set up any image of stone in your land, to bow down unto it." And he ordered Moses (in Chapter 33 of Numbers), on entering Canaan, to destroy the stones of worship, break up the statues, and lay waste the sacred high places of the Canaanites, so urging what conquering religions have always done: the destruction and profanation of all that the conquered held sacred. Battles over the question of what is sacred—theological battles as well as physical ones—have only served to emphasize the fact, for those not involved, that virtually anything can be experienced as an appearance of the divine in the world. This fact may, however, lead to two very different conclusions: that sacredness is something that can be projected upon things quite at random by the human mind, or that it is a natural, inborn property of things themselves; in other words, that nothing is sacred or that everything is. These beliefs are characteristic, respectively, of the man who lives by reason alone, and the poet; "everything that lives is Holy" proclaimed the poet William Blake. But the religious man does not normally take such a universal view of the matter. He regards only certain things as sacred; he sharply divides the sacred from the profane; and the more his faith tends toward believing that the divine comes from a single source, the more he limits the number of things or places he regards as sacred.

Objects of Awe

Above: from the center of an Egyptian celestial tree a goddess distributes the food and drink of immortality. Among many religions, not only is the god (or gods) holy, but the dwelling place of the god—tree, mountain, cave, spring, temple, altar—is also holy. Those who serve the gods, whether priest or prophet, magician or shaman, are holy too.

Right: a principal place of Jewish pilgrimage is the Wailing Wall, depicted here in a picture painted in 1922 by the British artist Isaac Snowman. The Wailing Wall is what is left of the western wall of Herod's Temple in Jerusalem. According to tradition it is also part of the original wall of Solomon's Temple. Jews have been accustomed to pray and lament there on the anniversary of the downfall of the Temple and also on the Sabbath.

To regard a thing as sacred does not necessarily always involve experiencing it as such. Often as religions become more institutional, they tend to get away from the sacred experiences that were usually present at their foundation. Sacred objects become revered, but the sacred is no longer experienced—the divine ceases to be revealed through them. To experience a thing or place as sacred is to experience a presence within it that inspires a feeling of awe. The experience was well expressed by the early 19th-century English poet William Wordsworth. In his reflection on nature in the poem *Tintern Abbey* he mentions how he felt a presence that "disturbs me with the joy of elevated thoughts," a presence whose "dwelling is the light of setting suns, and the round ocean, and the living air . . . and the mind of man." The poet eloquently expresses the sense of the divine presence that is a part of the experience of the sacred. The other aspect of the experience, the fear and sense of awe, such as Jacob felt when he awoke from his dream, was also memorably expressed by Wordsworth in his autobiographical poem *The Prelude*, where he tells how one night he took a rowing boat out on a lake and as the boat moved it seemed that the surrounding mountains moved in relation to the sky and the stars and became like living things—"huge and mighty forms, that do not live like living men, moved slowly through the mind . . ." This experience would have been described by the German theologian Rudolf Otto as "numinous" (from the Latin *numen*, the power of the gods, the divine will). In his book *The Idea of the Holy*, published in 1917, Otto found that terror, dread, and awe were the chief characteristics of the experience of the numinous, and described manifestations of it as mysteries at once awe-inspiring, fascinating, and conveying an overwhelming sense of power.

As man becomes more knowledgeable and sophisticated there

Left: meteorite showers have long been a phenomenon of awe—and, wherever they land, often a symbol of divine wrath. Often meteoritic stones were revered as having come from the gods.

Below: a Siberian tribal shaman (a priest-magician) dressed as a woman, because women were thought to be more receptive to the inspiration of spirits.

is less and less in the world that fills his mind with blank wonder and astonishment. For instance, before astronomers discovered what meteorites were, the phenomenon of stones falling from the sky seemed to men a manifestation of the awful power and unpredictability of God. The sacred stone at Mecca, the Ka'aba, is in fact a meteorite, an immense rock that hurtled out of the heavens and made a great crater in the earth. Today we can explain the phenomenon scientifically and so take the mystery out of it, but only 200 years ago the great French astronomer and mathematician Pierre Laplace solemnly announced that stones could not fall from the sky because there were no stones in the sky; so it is not difficult to imagine the astonishment, the terror, and the awe with which prescientific man regarded the phenomenon. The meteorite was not of this world, it belonged to another sphere of reality and yet there it was, substantially and immovably on the earth, a visible and touchable sign of the divine power; no wonder it was regarded as sacred.

Anything in any way remarkable, anything exceptionally monstrous, beautiful, perfect, bizarre, may be regarded as displaying some aspect of the divine. In many primitive societies people with physical deformities, such as dwarfs or albinos, were considered as natural candidates for the priesthood, and shamans and medicine men were often chosen from among the neurotic or the epileptic. Writing in the early 1900s the Scottish anthropologist Sir James Frazer recorded that among the Konde of East Africa: "Anything great of its kind, such as a great ox or even a great he-goat, or any other impressive object, is called Kyala, by which it may be meant that God takes up his abode temporarily in these things. When a great storm lashes the lake into fury, God is walking on the face of the waters; when the roar of the waterfall is louder than usual, it is the voice of God. The earthquake is caused by his mighty footstep, and the lightning is

Mana and "Taboo"

lesa, God coming down in anger. God sometimes comes also in the body of a lion or a snake, and it is in that form he walks among men to observe their doings.

The Melanesians have a similar idea, and use the term *mana* for the mysterious power with which any exceptional person or thing is permeated. *Mana* is a god-given property of things or persons, it is what makes a warrior unbeatable, a boat swift, a sow prolific, an arrow accurate and deadly. *Mana* may reside in talismans, in a bone, a stone, or a stick, but it is not a permanent property of these things, or even of people who have it. It is a property they might lose as mysteriously as they came into posession of it. It is often believed to be controlled by spirits or higher beings, and, in order to ensure that these entities maintain the supply of it, sacrifices and ceremonies are performed to please them. *Mana* is power not under human control, and therefore although it is extremely desirable it is also greatly to be feared.

When the predominant feeling inspired by an object, a place, or a person, is the feeling of fear, then it may be regarded as taboo. "Taboo" is a Polynesian word meaning "forbidden" and 19th-century anthropologists adopted it to describe anything believed to be dangerous because it deviated from a familiar standard. Frazer wrote that "taboos act, so to say, as electrical insulators to preserve the spiritual force with which these per-

Below: an African sunset. Spectacular natural phenomena arouse feelings of wonder, pleasure, awe, apprehension, or fear in all but the most unfeeling spectators. In many primitive religions it was, and is, a belief that God manifests himself in the forces of nature, and particularly in any unusual weather conditions.

sons are charged from suffering or inflicting harm by contact with the outer world." Here he was referring to such persons as kings, priests, murderers, girls at puberty, and women in childbed: people who are either dangerous, or in danger, or who manifest supernormal power. To minimize the danger or to keep the power in check it is believed to be necessary to deal with such people in particular ritual ways, or to make them behave in certain ways, and to set them apart from normal society. It may be taboo, for example, to turn one's back to a king, to look directly at him, speak to him or touch him, and among certain African tribes it used to be an offense punishable by death to speak aloud the name of the king. In the same way it was taboo for the Hebrew to speak the name of God. The secret of how to pronounce correctly the Tetragrammaton, Y H V H, was a secret jealously guarded by the priesthood, and the sacred name was only pronounced once a year by the High Priest. (The modern renderings, Yahweh and Jehovah, had to be guessed at, for Hebrew had no vowels.)

So man's attitude to the sacred is ambivalent because he feels that the sacred can either elevate him or destroy him, can put him in touch with what is ultimately real, or utterly and finally sever him from it. Man's attitude can also express itself in the fear of being annulled, of completely losing one's reality, through

Above: an engraving of a New Zealand warrior at the time of Captain Cook's first voyage of discovery in 1769. In common with many religions the Maoris of New Zealand believed in a power underlying all magic that resided in their kings, their *tohungas* (priests), and in objects and places. It was Mana, a power that, according to the way it was handled, could be dangerous or beneficial.

Left: an Aborigine headsman is being fed by one of his wives because a close relative has died and the law of taboo forbids him to touch any food for a certain period afterward. Many taboos are bound up with cleanliness, both physical and spiritual. Enactment of the taboos leaves a deep impression on participant and onlooker and helps bind the tribe together as a unit.

Above: the interior of St. Peter's Cathedral in Rome. It was commissioned by Pope Julius II (1503–13) and took 120 years to complete. The lofty grandeur of the huge building dwarfs man to insignificance and induces in him a "creature feeling." Appropriately, the mass for the dedication of a church opens with the words, "Terrible is this place: it is the House of God, and the gate of Heaven; and it shall be called the Court of God."

the encounter with the sacred. Rudolph Otto called it "creature-feeling" and explained: "it is the emotion of a creature, abased and overwhelmed by its own nothingness in contrast to that which is supreme above all creatures."

Man's greatest religious artifacts, his cathedrals, temples, and mosques, serve admirably to bring about this "creature-feeling," for their immensity and permanence make man feel how insignificant, frail, and short-lived he is by contrast. At the same time the sense of being in a place set apart from the world, and possibly contemplating the art displayed there or hearing the music played, may make a man experience a feeling of belonging to that immensity, of being a part of something infinitely greater than himself, and of being transported above the level of the worldly and the profane; which is the positive aspect of the experience of the sacred.

Mircea Eliade makes the point that *sacred* and *profane* are "two modes of being in the world," and that there is a distinction between two distinct human psychological types (which has nothing to do with their degree of sophistication or intellectual attainment) into those who seek and prefer to live in a world in which sacred rites and observances are not looked upon as either unusual or unnecessary, and those who prefer a world where the extraordinary or supernatural is scientifically explainable and therefore stripped of mystery or holiness. The latter, Eliade points out, have been predominant in our world for centuries, and he questions whether the inverse ratio law—whereby the sense of the sacred decreases as science advances—is really a thing that has benefited man's life and the modern world. This question of the value of the sense of the sacred, and its importance psychologically and socially, is worthwhile returning to after first looking at pre-scientific man and the extent to which he lived in a "sacralized" world. This can be done by taking one type of hierophany and examining it in some detail—for example, sacred stones.

The Ka'aba at Mecca and the stone Jacob set up as a pillar of the "House of God" are examples of stone hierophanies already considered. There was also the divine injunction not to set up any image of stone or to adore it. The warning, from the Book of Leviticus, was from regarding stones as divine objects in themselves, as having an indwelling spirit that could be gratified or appeased by certain human actions, rather than as a sign, or manifestation of God. It was no doubt a necessary prohibition, for to preserve the true sense of the sacred, of using something seen and felt as a window opening upon the infinite and the spiritual, it required a sustained effort on the part of the worshipers involving feeling, understanding, and inspiration. Often, they found it easier to turn the sacred sign into a cult object and worship it in and for itself.

The tendency among primitive peoples to consider stones as receptacles for spirits has been vouched for by many anthropologists. Among the tribes of central India it was customary to erect a tall standing stone near a person's burial place, and if a man met a violent death the stone was erected where he died so

The Meaning of Sanctity

Below: the Black Stone of Mecca was blessed by Muhammad and carried by four tribal chieftains (at the four corners of the carpet) into the Ka'aba, the holy sanctuary, in order to integrate it into the Islamic religion. Before that time it had been an object of worship by the pagan tribes that Muhammad eventually overcame when he captured the city in A.D. 630.

Europe's Great Stone Structures

that his soul should be imprisoned in it and not go roaming about giving vent to his resentment at his premature end. The belief that, in the words of one anthropologist, "stones are the petrified spirits of ancestors," is found all over the world, which probably accounts for the worldwide distribution of huge stones such as *menhirs* (tall standing stones) and *cromlechs* (structures consisting of a flat stone laid horizontally on standing ones). The thinking behind the erection of these huge stones is indicated by the fact that the Khasis of Assam believe that the Great Father of the clan dwells in the menhir and the Great Mother in the Cromlech. In southern India it is customary for women who want children to rub themselves against the stones of cromlechs and sometimes to place in them offerings of food for the spirits that dwell in them.

The belief that certain stones can make women fertile occurs all over the world, and in some places a quite literal understanding of the idea is found. In Brittany women who wished to conceive used to squat on a cromlech with their skirts drawn up, and in many places it was a belief that fertility could be so ensured by a woman sleeping for several nights on a particular stone. The sacred stone of Lia Fail in Ireland was credited with prophetic as well as fertilizing powers, and it was believed that it would start singing when a man worthy to be king sat upon it, would make a man accused of a crime turn white if he was innocent, would exude blood for a woman destined to remain sterile and milk for one who would become a mother.

All these beliefs belong to a stage in the evolution of religion that has been called "animatism," in which inanimate objects and natural phenomena are held to possess consciousness. They are the sort of beliefs that the Levitical law sought to eradicate. Throughout the Christian centuries the Church has had to fight the same battle, for among the peasantry of Europe such beliefs died hard. The idea that animatism is the explanation for all ancient religious practices involving sacred stones is to take too limited a view of the matter, however. It is fairly certain that something else accounts for the existence of such elaborate megalithic structures as Stonehenge in England and the avenues of some 3000 menhirs at Carnac in Brittany, not to mention the hundreds of stone circles scattered all over northern Europe. Many visitors to these sites even today become aware of at least a general feeling of the uncanny, and some have a distinct sense of a numinous presence, and experience the awe, the wonder, and the sense of personal insignificance that are typical of the encounter with the sacred. These man-made structures are certainly evidence of a religion more sophisticated than a naive animatism.

There have been many theories about these giant stone structures but one fact that has emerged with certainty from recent studies of them is that the siting and arrangement of the stones are related to the movements of the sun, moon, stars, and planets, and to astronomical events and incorporate higher mathematical principles and calculations of faultless accuracy. Scientists have discovered that Stonehenge can be used as a gigantic astronomical clock and as a computer capable of predicting lunar eclipses, which suggests that Stone Age man was no mean engi-

Above: the Men-an-Tol ("stone of the hole") stone near Madron in Cornwall. This wheel-shaped stone stands upright between two standing stones. Its central hole is about two feet in diameter. In the British Isles holed stones were considered especially potent in curing children from a number of ailments, particularly those of a rheumatic nature. Infants were passed through the stone following a certain sequence of actions; adults had to crawl through the stone. All three stones were thought to have once been part of a Neolithic burial chamber.

neer. Arguments supported by a wealth of mathematical data have been put forward suggesting that the Stone Age men responsible for the erection of the megaliths had a science of "sacred engineering" that involved the creation on earth of structures that mirrored constellations in the heavens and the movements of heavenly bodies. There are several people who claim to have discovered "zodiacs" laid out on the landscape of Britain incorporating natural and man-made features. If they are right these features represent literally the bringing down to earth of the things of the heavens, and they suggest that "megalithic man" invested tremendous efforts in making sacred the space he lived in.

Below: Stonehenge, a Celtic shrine in southern England, was known as far away as ancient Crete. Archaeology has revealed that it was constructed in three stages over a period of 500 years, starting in about 1900 B.C. During the important second stage the entrance to the temple-structure was aligned with the position of sunrise at midsummer. Golden sun-disks were also found among the remains of the peoples who almost certainly used the structure as a temple of the sun.

Above: the white marble omphalos from the temple of Apollo at Delphi, Greece. It was the most famous of the navel-shaped stones to be worshiped throughout the Mediterranean area. Statues of two golden eagles were placed beside the stone because of the story that when Zeus wanted to find the center of the earth he caused two eagles to fly toward each other at the same speed from the western and eastern rims of the world. They met at the spot where the stone was kept.

Pyramidologists have made much of the fact that the greatest of man-made stone structures, the Great Pyramid of Gizeh, is located at the center of the habitable dry land of the earth, and this is a distinction claimed for several natural rock formations, especially the great rocks of the temples at Jerusalem and Delphi. The rock that lay at the center of the Temple at Jerusalem and which constituted the floor of the Holy of Holies, was known as an *omphalos* (Greek for "navel"), because, the ancients believed, just as the body of an embryo is built up in its mother's womb from its navel, so God built up the earth around this Stone, the Navel of the Earth. Similar beliefs were held with regard to the *omphalos* at Delphi.

The Ka'aba at Mecca is held in Islamic tradition to be the highest point on earth because the pole star shows it to be opposite the center of the sky. Great rocks such as these are venerated and made sites of pilgrimage because it is believed that they occupy a central location where heaven and earth make contact and where it is possible to pass from the level of the profane to that of the sacred; in fact, to be reborn. They are the

Right: a raked sand garden in a Zen Buddhist monastery in Japan. The activity of raking the garden and reflecting on the pattern of rocks and white sand is one of the aids to contemplation, an essential ingredient to most Eastern religions. Such techniques of physical and mental self-control were developed as a means of awakening higher states of consciousness.

Place for Prayer

Left: a 19th-century engraving of Moslems carrying out ritual ablutions before entering a mosque. The word mosque, from the Arabic word *masjid*, means "a place of prostration (in prayer)" and, like a Christian church, the inside is considered to be holy ground sanctified by the prayers of the devout and the sacred books. The ritual washing cleanses the worshiper from the contamination of the profane world outside—Catholic Christians similarly make the sign of the cross with holy water provided at the door of a church to cleanse themselves before coming into the presence of God.

equivalent, in Jacob's words, of "the gates of heaven."

These, then, are some examples of stone hierophanies. They have ministered to a wide range of human needs, from the need to be fertile to the need for a spiritual rebirth. Hierophanies involving sacred trees, plants, shells, animals, fish, or sacramental activities like dancing, love-making, eating, or cultivating the land, were all used to satisfy similar needs. Taking another lead from the story of Jacob, some consideration should be given to the idea of sacred space.

When, in Chapter 3 of Exodus, Moses drew near to the fabulous bush in the desert that was burning without being consumed (a vegetation hierophany), the voice of God spoke from the middle of it and told him not to come near. Then it told him to take his shoes off because the ground on which he was standing was holy ground. Jacob, too, found himself inadvertently on holy ground, and proceeded to lay the foundations for a Bethel, a "house of God." The houses of God, the cathedrals, churches, temples, and mosques of the world all constitute holy ground, sacred space, a special area, cut off from the profane world, where communication between the worldly and the unwordly is possible. Man's need to discover, enclose, or create sacred space is strong, and sometimes as in Medieval Europe, it becomes obsessive. The American historian Henry Adams observed that: "The twelfth and thirteenth centuries, studied in the pure light of political economy, are insane." Adams calculated that the French people of that period poured virtually all of their wealth into cathedral and church building. In this way they "expressed an intensity of conviction never again reached by any passion, whether of religion, of loyalty, of patriotism, or of wealth; perhaps never even paralleled by any single economic effort, except in war."

Churches and temples are often conceived as reproductions of Paradise or as built according to a God-ordained design. "Thou hast commanded me to build a temple upon thy holy mount," says Solomon to God, ". . . a resemblance of the holy tabernacle which thou hast prepared from the beginning." And God commands Moses in Chapter 29 of Exodus: "let them make me a sanctuary; that I may dwell among them." The Bethel, the house of God, becomes not only an island of sacred space in a profane world, but also a power center that continually resanctifies the profane world. As far as the space around it is organized in relation to it, that space too is made sacred, it becomes a cosmos as distinct from the chaos of the surrounding indeterminate space. The "zodiacs" and intricate patterns of "leys" (straight tracks linking churches, ancient sites, outstanding natural features, and man-made landmarks) of the countryside of Britain testify to early man's need to rescue his living space from chaos and make a cosmos of it. Though not directly connected, it is an interesting point that many of the legendary haunts of dragons in Britain stand in line with others. Also, on the same lines there are a remarkable number of churches and place-names associated with the legendary dragon-slayers Saint Michael and Saint George. Remember that in the ancient creation myths the primordial serpent of chaos is killed by the hero-god, the existence of these alignments and names suggests that early man created his local "cosmos" by imitating the actions of the gods. The slaying of the dragons symbolized the conquest and ordering of chaos, the creation of sanctified space.

The common belief that the world was created from a tiny center outward also influenced the design of buildings and human settlements. Josephus wrote of the Temple in Jerusalem that the central Holy of Holies represented heaven, the Holy Place repre-

Above: a carved bench-end from a church in Somerset, England. It shows two men killing a dragon. Stories of dragons abound in Britain and most of them on investigation are connected with ancient sites, stones, mounds, and sacred places that are themselves thought to contain an energy force known as an earth current, or ley.

Right: *The Tower of Babel*, by the 16th-century Flemish painter Pieter Brueghel. The biblical story of the tower of Babel was an attempt to explain how the nations of men —all descended from the sons of Noah— came to speak in a "confusion of tongues." Towers were a feature of Mesopotamian cities. They were temple towers—ziggurats —often constructed in seven stages representing the old seven-planetary system and regarded as a means of communication between gods and men. In Babylon the great ziggurat of Marduk, God of Babylon and King of the Gods, was said to have had a temple on top into which Marduk descended each night.

sented earth and the outer court represented the sea. Throughout the world the practice of constructing a town or village often involves elaborate symbolism, as in Bali, where the four sections of the village determined by the central intersection are thought of as corresponding to the four horizons of the universe, and a ceremonial house with a roof that represents heaven is built at the central point. According to the 1st–2nd century A.D. Greek biographer Plutarch, when Romulus founded Rome he dug a deep trench, filled it with fruit, covered this with earth, set up an altar over it, and then drew a rampart round it with his plow. The trench, significantly, was called a *mundus*—the Latin word for "world." The ancient Romans, then, obviously thought of their city as a microcosm, or little world. The Babylonian ziggurat, the pyramidlike terraced temple tower with a long flight of steps leading to its summit, is another example of the kind of thinking that has to give sacred space a form and structure. The seven terraces of the ziggurat represented the old seven planetary heavens (Sun, Moon, Mercury, Venus, Mars, Jupiter, and

Sacred Places, Holy Spaces

Left: Romulus fixes the site of Rome. According to the legend Romulus dug a deep trench, filled it with fruit, covered it with earth, and erected an altar over it (bottom right, a priest pours a libation onto the flaming altar). Romulus then marked with a plow the place where he wished to erect the walls. The rites carried out at the foundation of the city are thought to mean that the Romans saw their city as a world in miniature.

Mankind's Need for the Sacred

Below: the church of St. Mary, Warwick, England, closes up the end of a street. The tower, shown here, has a public footpath through its center. The church has in fact been built over a ley—one of the mysterious lines of force running beneath the earth's surface that have been "felt" by men since Stone Age times. At first, it is believed, the lines were marked by large and small stones or by mounds, and gradually they came to be revered; temples or shrines were built over some of them especially where leys crossed and the force was particularly strong. With the coming of Christianity, many marking stones, pagan altars, and temples became the sites of churches—many of the very old churches and wayside crosses are found to align on the leys.

Saturn—the celestial bodies that appeared to move against a background of "fixed" stars). By ascending the terraces the priests finally reached the summit of the universe. In man's buildings, his villages, towns, and cities, and in his landscaping, he has from an early time felt the need to create an earthly copy of the heavens or to imitate the gods' original act of creation, and so sanctify his dwelling space.

The question whether the places that men hold sacred have anything in common that sets them apart from other points on the earth's surface was investigated with some interesting results by a British amateur archaeologist and dowser, Guy Underwood, who in 1969 published his findings in a book, *The Pattern of the Past*. Underwood had long puzzled over the fact that many churches are built at a distance from the village they serve, and are often erected in ground unsuitable for heavy structures when there is much more suitable ground nearby. It also puzzled him that in many old churches and cathedrals there were structural inconsistencies, eccentric alignments that seemed to indicate that the builders hadn't known how to build straight walls or determine true right angles. His investigations led him to the discovery that both the siting and the structure of these buildings were determined by lines of force running beneath the earth's surface that he called "geodetic lines," which were related to underground water courses. In every sacred building he investigated, including Neolithic stone circles, Underwood found that the central or crucial spot, for instance the site of the altar or spire was located directly above what he called a "blind spring," which he defined as a point upon which a number of water lines converged and from which an energetic force was given out above the surface in a spiral pattern. "The blind spring," he wrote, "was the esoteric centre of the Old Religion, as well as being the actual centre of its monuments. In early biblical days such a site was venerated as a place where God dwelt, and a Beth-el or House of God was consecrated by marking it out and separating it from the profane space around it. It then became 'Holy Ground.' Since all prehistoric monuments are enclosed by the spirals produced by one or more springs, the reasonable assumption is that their positions were determined by these phenomena. The blind spring designated the spiritual centre of the site, while the spirals bestowed that 'divine protective sanctity' postulated by students of the Old Religion."

Other dowsers have confirmed Underwood's investigations, and their findings raise the interesting question whether, in the case of places, the concept of the sacred has now been rationalized and the mystery taken out of it. Jacob's thought when he awoke from his dream was that the Lord was in the place where he had slept, and he had not known it; but was it perhaps a case of there being a blind spring beneath him and Jacob's not knowing that he was endowed with the dowser's sensitivity? Maybe, but then why should the knowledge that the earth is constellated with blind springs and intricately veined with underground lines of force that influence events on the surface undermine man's sense of the sacred any more than does his knowledge of the awe-inspiring heavens with their unimaginably distant galaxies, or of the unseen and unfelt cosmic forces that subtly influence his life? Surely it should induce in him a realization that this is a matter of the awakening and transformation of consciousness that must be acted out in order to be experienced. Which is precisely the sense of the sacred.

We come back to the observation that sacred and profane are two ways of living in the world. The religious man wants and seeks always to live in the closest communion possible with the sacred, because for him the sacred alone is real. All things, all acts, all places stripped of the dimension of the sacred can give him only passing satisfaction without any deep meaning. The naturally religious man consecrates his living space and the objects or tools that he uses in his daily life, and he endeavors in all his activities to live his life as a sacrament. And to do that he needs ritual.

Below: a Burmese girl lights a candle in a Buddhist temple to celebrate the Buddha's Enlightenment. Originally Buddhism was a religion without a deity founded by a teacher who taught man how to break loose from the everlasting cycle of rebirth and reach Nirvana, eternal and blissful peace. Followers of the Buddha gradually transformed their religion into one that could give expression to their sense of the sacred with all the forms of a cult religion— incense, candles, vestments, and rituals.

Chapter 10
The Meaning of Ritual

The codes of behavior, customs, and beliefs that people use to keep themselves together in racial, social, or cultural groups often become encapsulated into what we know as ritual. But not only does ritual help people recognize each other's status or beliefs; it also serves as an outward form of worship. All man's important activities or stages of life—birth, puberty, marriage, death, sowing and reaping, hunting for game—all demand and receive special rituals in primitive and sophisticated societies alike. The nature of ritual provides the material for this chapter, with some fascinating insights into the need for ritual as well as its mere outward show.

Lemuel Gulliver, the much-traveled hero of *Gulliver's Travels*, relates that the six-inch high Lilliputians buried their dead with their heads downward. The reason for this was that they believed that the earth was flat and that on the day of the eventual resurrection of the dead it would turn over, and so the resurrected would find themselves conveniently standing on their feet.

Since the 18th century, when the English author Jonathan Swift wrote of his hero's fictitious travels, European and American travelers have been observing the quaint customs and rituals of primitive peoples the world over with a godlike Gulliverian mixture of amusement, indulgence, and superiority. For indeed, it has seemed to many that to undertake elaborate actions based upon misinformation, baseless hope, or crude superstition, is really one of the more absurd follies of mankind. But the rationalist attitude to primitive customs is often itself misinformed. Worse, it is disqualified from ever becoming informed, because the rationalist's world is profane, the sacred is a concept without meaning for him, and, in consequence, he finds religious ritual utterly incomprehensible.

Ritual has several different aspects and serves several different purposes, from laying down behavior in social situations and so saving the newcomer to them from embarrassment, to creating for the religious man a supreme experience that can change his life. Ritual may be regarded as the routine of worship, the mere observance of formalities according to rule, or as the very height

Opposite: the customs and rituals of other peoples are looked upon with fascination, horror, or amusement by peoples of an alien culture. Here Captain Cook is presented with a roast pig by South Sea Islanders during his voyages of discovery. The Maori chief's head, "the face curiously tattooed, or marked, according to their Manner," is shown above.

Worship Takes Dramatic Form

Opposite: Mexicans walk in procession during a Good Friday ceremony to mark the crucifixion of Jesus Christ. Nine out of ten people in Latin America are Roman Catholics and religious festivals play an important part in their lives. Many of the great ceremonies of the Church are looked upon as reenactments in time of an important, sacred event in the Church's history. The cycle of religious ceremonies and festivals became part of an eternal, sacred time, participation in which gives the religious man or woman a glimpse into truths that are not communicated in other ways.

Below: mummers acting out their roles during the Christmas revels in the 17th century. Saint George and the dragon played leading parts (far left of picture); behind the dragon is a Turkish knight and then the doctor with a box of pills guaranteed to restore the dead to life. Behind the mummers' playacting lies a very long tradition that goes back to pagan times and to the plays performed in temples that had as their themes death and lamentation, and resurrection and victory over death and decay.

of worship, the act in which the encounter with the divine is accomplished. Ritual may serve to maintain the beliefs, usages, and customs, that give a social or cultural group its identity. On the other hand it may be a way of passing on certain basic cosmic or psychological principles that transcend any group interest and are of universal relevance. Of course, ritual actions can also be a symptom of mental illness, especially when they are simply repetitious and divorced from meaning. It is the rituals that illustrate and elaborate a meaning that are a powerful means of working upon and elevating human emotions and thought. Rituals also serve to reconcile, to petition, or to initiate; they may be fertility rites, "rites of passage" from one stage of life to another, reenactments of actions of the gods; they may serve to bring about altered states of consciousness; they may release the basest urges of human nature or stimulate and aid its loftiest aspirations; they may be regarded as escapes from reality or as means of entering more deeply into it.

For the religious man ritual gives a dramatic form to his worship of the deity; it is the means by which the sacred "takes place" in time. For him time itself is sharply distinguished into the sacred and the profane. Sacred time is preeminently the time of the great festivals of a religion, such as Christianity's Passion Week (when the suffering and death of Jesus is commemorated), and Christmas (which commemorates his birth into the world). All religions have such festivals, which are considered not just commemorations of some past event but rather a reliving of it. There was a time when the gods were active on earth, and in the festival they become active again, coexistent with living man. It is by performing ritual actions that man enters sacred time.

In ancient Babylon, the Creation Epic, the *Enuma Elish*, was ritually recited at the end of the year, and the battle between the monster Tiamat and the god-hero Marduk was mimed by actors,

Snake Ritual of the Hopi Indians

Right: dancers in the Snake Ceremony, performed by members of the Hopi Indian Snake Society. The photograph was taken around the turn of the century. During the ceremony, snakes (representing lightning) are blessed by the priests and released to carry their prayers through the underworld and up to heaven. Because of their phallic shape, snakes are also seen as fertility symbols, as they are in many religions. In one famous rain-making ritual members of the Snake Society are joined by members of the Antelope Society. As the snake is connected with the fertility of the earth, so the antelope is connected with the spiritual world—because the antelope's horn is situated on the top of its head, where, in man, the Hopis consider the place of coming and going of life is situated.

and at the end of the ceremony the priest said: "May he continue to conquer Tiamat and shorten his days." This reenactment of the original act of creation in which order was imposed upon chaos was preceded by acts of abandon and destruction involving wild orgies, which were meant to symbolize the tendency of the world to fall back into chaos and its need of the continuing presence and activity of the gods. By engaging in the ritual a man entered into that cyclical time which is not really time at all but eternity, where the gods are ever-present and ever-active. Unlike profane time, which is a succession of moments each one of which drops irrecoverably into the past, sacred time revolves as invariably as the planets in their courses or the seasons of the year, and festivals and rituals are man's points of entry into it.

In *The Book of the Hopi*, the American anthropologist Frank Waters compiled a record of the Hopi Indians of Arizona, put together from information given him by 32 Hopi elders. It is an astounding book, for it shows that although the rituals of these simple people, eking out a bare existence from inhospitable country, appear at first sight to be the characteristic rituals of a localized vegetation religion, they in fact also contain buried within the rituals ideas of the creation of the universe, of man, and of their own race, as well as a philosophy on the nature and destiny of man.

Many tourists go to watch the great Hopi public ceremonies but few of them can understand their full significance. The biggest tourist attraction is the "Snake-Antelope Ceremony," which is held every other year in August, and which offers onlookers the spectacle of Indians dancing with live rattlesnakes in their mouths. The Snake Dance is in fact the concluding event in a 16-day rain-making ceremony. Its participants are members of the Snake and Antelope Societies, each of which has its own *kiva* (an underground ceremonial chamber) where it sets up its altar. One ritual involves the symbolic marriage of the Snake Maiden to the Antelope Youth. It is part of a fertility rite—the snake representing mother earth from which all life comes, and the antelope representing fertility, because it generally produces two offspring. But it has a further meaning, too. It is seen as the merging of two principles essential to mankind's spiritual fulfillment. Frank Waters explains: "as the bodies of man and the world are similar in structure, the deep bowels of the earth in which the snake makes it home are equated with the lowest of man's vibratory centers, which controls his generative organs. The antelope, conversely, is associated with the highest center in man, for its horn is located at the top or crown of the head, the *kopavi*, which in man is the place of coming in and going out of life, the 'open door' through which he spiritually communicates with his Creator." The snake and the antelope, then, are also seen as the two opposite yet balancing factors in man's make-up: the physical, animal part, and the spiritual, psychical part that controls the former.

Waters' interviews with the Hopi elders persuaded him that Hopi ceremonies always have this deeper level of meaning, which often has close ties with the ideas expressed in Indian mysticism. In one of the Indian Schools of Yoga, the Hindu goddess Kundalini, who represents a latent power in mankind, is represented as a snake coiled at the base of the spine. A tube runs through the spine past various centers of spiritual power until it reaches a position under the skull. This form of Yoga aims to awaken Kundalini and bring up the power to the highest point of man. There is a curious linking of ideas between this symbolism and that of the Hopi Snake and Antelope Races, which take place during the rain-making ceremony. Members of the two Societies start the race out in the desert and race along a trail that ascends to the top of the ridge where the village is situated, and which leads finally to the kiva where the Antelope or Snake chief has planted his ceremonial standard. Priests are stationed at inter-

Above: a Hopi Antelope priest, from a photograph taken in the late 1800s.

Left: the interior of a *kiva*, which is a combined men's club and center of religious ceremonial. Here, a screen has been set up for the purposes of a religious drama. It is decorated with symbolic pictures and serpents that can be manipulated from behind. At either side of the screen are men wearing the masks of "mud heads"—a special class of sacred beings. The third figure is masked to represent a Kachina, or ancestral spirit.

Prayer Through Dance or Mime

Below: an Indian painting of the Hopi Turtle Dance. In front of the line of dancers with rattles in their hands are two masked Kachina dancers as well as two sacred clowns with painted striped bodies. A third clown is seen on the roof of a kiva, and behind the figure in beaded leggings and shawl is the supervising priest. The dances are really dramatized prayers with every step and gesture carefully rehearsed.

vals along the race track, and at about the halfway mark the runner in the lead is given a bunch of prayer sticks and a jar of holy water, which in turn is given to any runner who overtakes him. The winner is allowed to take the prayer sticks and the holy water to his family's fields in order to ensure their fertility. According to Waters, the long, winding race track represents the central nerve of the human spinal column, the priests' stations along it become centers vitalized by the life force as it is called up.

The union of the two principles is symbolized in the final event of the ceremony, the Snake Dance, which takes place on the village square. A hole in the middle of the square, covered with a plank, represents the place of contact with the lower world. The plank serves as a sounding-board on which the Snake dancers stamp, making a sound that both imitates the thunder that will bring rain and serves as a summons to the slumbering life force in the lower centers of both earth and man to awaken and rise upward. The snake chief dances round the square, gripping a snake between his teeth, and the other Snake priests follow suit. Then the dancers put their snakes on the ground and repeat the dance with another one. The loose snakes are handed to the Antelopes, who take them in their arms and stroke them sooth-

Left: ruined remains of a Hopi settlement now in the Mesa Verde National Park, Colorado. The round buildings in the front are the various society kivas, now with their roofs fallen in. The houses were used mainly to sleep in and for storage. In fair weather all activity of the Hopi people was carried on in the open.

Below: a wooden Kachina doll painted with phallic symbols. At annual Kachina ceremonies dolls are given to children by masked adults impersonating legendary supernatural Kachinas, who bring the people's prayers to the gods. The dolls are sacred objects, presented to children as part of their education.

ingly. The controlling of the snakes by the antelopes symbolizes the uniting of the two opposites, female and male, sensual and spiritual, that create a whole. From this Union is meant to flow a force that will revitalize mankind's spiritual life and the outward sign of this revitalization will be the rain that makes the earth fruitful.

"The Snake-Antelope ceremony," Waters writes, "shows how the interplay of universal forces within man can be controlled and made manifest in the physical world." This is not really such a fanciful interpretation as it seems. Indeed it is entirely consistent with the Hopis' general views on religion and philosophy as expressed in their legends and their other great ceremonies. The Hopi creation myth, for instance, tells of the creation of four successive worlds. The first three worlds had to be destroyed because the people of the earth ignored the Creator and his plan. Only the few who kept the Creator's plan in their hearts were saved to begin a fourth and present world. But like the others it, too, will be destroyed if man again forgets his Creator and the plan of creation. The Hopis' ceremonies are their way of remembering the Creator and his law, and it is a tradition among them that their ancestors chose to settle where they did because the desert enforces a frugal and pure way of life and their dependence on rainfall keeps them mindful of their Creator and of the powers he endowed them with, powers that can be brought to life by means of ritual and prayer.

Another tradition that finds expression in Hopi ceremonies is that when the clans landed in the Fourth World and migrated in different directions to find their places of settlement, they were guided by the *kachina* people (ancestral spirits), who taught them many things: the history of the world and the universe, the structure and functions of the human body, the laws of nature and of the influence of cosmic events upon life on earth, and how

Rituals of Death

to open the door of the vibratory center in the crown of the head in order to contact the Creator.

This great creation myth is the background of the ceremonial cycle of the Hopi year, which comprises seven great ceremonies. The first of these takes place in November, and consists of a number of rituals symbolizing the beginnings of creation and the germination of all forms of life on earth. During it young men are initiated into Hopi lore and taught the significance of the sacred history of the four worlds.

The winter solstice ceremony sees the appearance of the first kachinas, wearing ritual masks and kilts of white cotton embroidered to suggest clouds and falling rain. The kachinas are to remain six months on earth, and during that time they will help men both practically, by bringing rain, and spiritually, by guiding them along the Road of Life. The masked men who impersonate them do so in observance of the instructions of the real kachina people, who before they last left for their "homes" in the San Francisco Mountains or the nearby Kisiwu spring told the Hopis: "You must remember us by wearing our masks and our costumes at the proper ceremonial times. Those who do so must be only those persons who have acquired the knowledge and the wisdom we have taught you."

The kachinas are also active in the next major ceremony of the year, which is held during the February moon and represents the final phase of creation. It begins with the ritual planting of beans, which actually sprout before the 16 days of the ceremony are completed. They are meant to simulate the real crops that will be planted a few weeks later.

The November, winter solstice, and February ceremonies bring to an end the winter ceremonies in which the drama of the original creation is reenacted and related to the themes of the annual cycle of planting, germination, and growth and of the initial stages of man's journey on the Road of Life. These three interrelated themes of the development of the worlds, the annual crops, and man himself are elaborated also through the summer and autumn ceremonies (the Snake-Antelope ceremony is the last of the summer ones), and so throughout the year the Hopis endeavor to live and grow according to the law and plan of the creator.

Below: Black Jack, the riderless horse with stirrups reversed that followed the gun carriage carrying the body of President Kennedy in 1963. It was an old Celtic belief that souls traveled on horseback to the land of the dead, an idea echoed in this rite enacted at the President's funeral.

Hopi ritual, then, which ranges in degrees of sophistication from simple imitative magic to a profound symbolism of spiritual growth, serves as a good example of the range of feelings and ideas expressed in rituals. It also shows that many widely held ideas about the naivety and ignorance of primitive cultures need to be revised, and as it is a living culture in our midst, indeed in the midst of the most powerful and most materialistic country in the world, it helps us understand how far we have come from really understanding the meaning of ritual and of life lived as a sacrament.

The need for ritual in certain circumstances is basic to man, even modern secular man. As the American historian of mythology Joseph Campbell has remarked, the assassination of President Kennedy in 1963 so shocked Americans that it "required a compensatory rite to reestablish the sense of solidarity of the nation." That rite was the solemn funeral ceremony, which virtually all Americans participated in through television.

Campbell saw significances in aspects of the Kennedy burial rites that few others could have appreciated. The gun carriage bearing the flag-draped coffin was drawn by seven clattering gray horses with blackened hoofs, and beside it slowly trotted another horse with an empty saddle and stirrups reversed. "I saw before me," Campbell said, "the seven ghostly steeds of the gray Lord Death, here come to conduct the fallen hero on his last celestial journey, passing symbolically upward through the seven celestial spheres to the seat of eternity, whence he had once descended . . . The steed with riderless saddle, stirrups reversed, prancing by the dead young warrior's side, would in the ancient days have been sacrificed, cremated along with the body of its master in a mighty pyre symbolic of the blazing, golden sun door through which the passing hero-soul would have gone to its seat in the everlasting hero-hall of the warrior dead. For, again symbolically, such a steed represents the body and its life, the rider, its guiding consciousness: they are one, as are body and mind."

Although these significances could not have been understood by the millions of television viewers of the ceremony, the symbolism, Campbell believed, was "recognized within by all—in the slow, solemn beat of the military drums and the clattering black hoofs of those horses of King Death through the absolutely silent city;" and the occasion caused him to reflect upon the "nature of the human mind, which can find the models for its consolation in such mystery games as this of imitating the passage of the soul from earth through the ranges of the seven spheres."

Joseph Campbell's reflections bring us to another aspect of the meaning of ritual. Human beings cannot let the great occa-

Above: the 19th-century French artist Gustave Doré's *The Rider of the Pale Horse.* The rider on the pale horse is, of course, Death, one of the four horsemen from the Apocalypse of Saint John.

Below: an artist's impression of a Viking funeral. The body of a dead king or warrior was wrapped in furs, his weapons by his side, then placed in a longship which was set alight and pushed out to sea—to travel to Valhalla in fiery splendor.

At Childbirth and Puberty

sion in their lives—birth, puberty, marriage, death—go by without some kind of ritual. These four "stages on life's way" are times of change from one way of existence to another, and with varying degrees of emphasis people of all cultures explore their significance and endeavor to bring supernatural influence to bear upon them through "rites of passage."

The seclusion of a woman in childbirth from society, and the requirement for her to undergo rituals of purification before returning to normal life, are customs found all over the world. Surprisingly widespread, too, is the custom of *couvade*, in which a father takes to his bed when his child is about to be born. He simulates the mother's movements and agonies of labor, and is solicitously cared for by the other women of the family. At first sight the custom seems preposterous, but it illustrates a very important point about ritual: that is a means of bringing about emotions and thoughts appropriate to an occasion. Couvade is to an extent a ritual of compensation. Through it a man affirms his paternity, asserts his rights, and takes on its responsibilities.

Birth rites may be a means of giving an appropriate reception to a soul believed to have newly arrived in this world. Sometimes, too, they are a means of signifying the purpose of life and dedicating the child to that purpose. A Hopi child is kept in darkness

Above: two women of Kondo, New Guinea, their faces smeared with mud as a sign of mourning. Death, in most societies, is always an occasion for ritual, sometimes simple, more often elaborate, especially where the belief occurs that there is some form of existence after death.

Right: carved wooden bed board from Zaire, Africa. It is used in a hut in which girls are kept in isolation during puberty rites. To prepare them for initiation into womanhood, they are surrounded by representations of their future role in life. Here, on the left, a naked woman gives birth, while her fully dressed husband lies by her side. All the important stages of human life are marked in some way in most societies at various levels of sophistication, but especially in primitive ones. By focusing attention on the initiate, everyone is aware of, and able to accept more readily, the initiate's new role in life.

for 20 days after birth before being introduced to his father, the sun. During this period an ear of perfect corn, representing the universal mother, earth, is kept beside him. On the 20th day the child is taken out before dawn by his mother and grandmother. They face east, pray, cast pinches of cornmeal toward the rising sun, and when the sun is fully risen the mother holds the child up to it and says, "Father Sun, this is your child." They then return to the village, where the crier announces the birth and a feast is held in the child's honor.

Childbearing involves a change of status and life for the mother as well as for the child, which is why in many societies women in and after childbirth are required to follow certain ritual observances. Ritual is a means of speeding up the process in which people mature and which is necessary for entry upon a new stage of life. When the change is a big one, as the change from boyhood to manhood in primitive societies, the rituals are correspondingly elaborate and impressive, for they have to bring about a complete reorientation of emotion and thought. The initiation rites of puberty often involve symbolism of death and rebirth, and in some societies a male child was put through quite harrowing experiences to signify his death as a child and rebirth as a man. The rights and responsibilities of the two distinct states of life were so utterly different that there was no question of a gradual passage from one to the other. In fact, the child had to be annihilated before the man could be born.

Elaborate puberty initiation rites occur among Australian aboriginal tribes. The rites, as observed by modern anthropologists begin with the separation of the children sometimes quite violently from their mother. They are taken by strangers, who are often masked, to an unfamiliar place far from home. This is the sacred ground prepared specially for the ceremony,

Above: a family group in Java. The whole family from the elderly to the very young gather around the newly born member of the family. The infant's umbilical cord is still attached. Childbirth is still one of the great mysteries of life. It is also a time of crisis, to be surrounded with spells, incantations, prohibitions, precautions, a mixture of magic and religion that will protect the mother and the child. In those parts of the world where astrology is a living belief one of the first duties of those attending a birth is to note the exact moment of delivery so that a horoscope may be cast for the child.

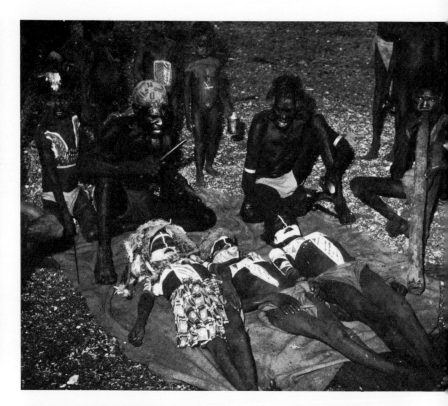

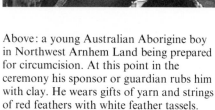

Above: a young Australian Aborigine boy in Northwest Arnhem Land being prepared for circumcision. At this point in the ceremony his sponsor or guardian rubs him with clay. He wears gifts of yarn and strings of red feathers with white feather tassels.

Above right: the same boy (lying on the left) with two others is about to undergo circumcision. They have been dressed and painted in ritual patterns.

Right: these circumcised boys have men's conical caps placed over their genitals as a mark of their new status. These rites are meant to bring the boys into manhood and into the tribe's collective identity. Circumcision is a symbolic sacrifice.

and here the boys are put through a series of ordeals. They may be covered with branches and leaves and made to lie as if dead while terrifying noises are made around them, or they may be placed in front of a great fire and made to stand and stare at it for a period of time. Physical ordeals continue for the first few days of the rituals, including deprivation of sleep, food and drink, and the boys are not allowed to speak. They are as if dead, or in the process of being born, for in fact they are being reborn into a world that had previously been around them but that they had not belonged to. It is at this time that they are circumcised, and in some tribes they also have to undergo another genital operation in which a wound resembling the female vulva is made. Thus they are introduced to the mysteries of blood and sexuality.

The initiations are accompanied by oral instruction, and the young male may spend months out in the bush with his elders, so that by the time he returns he is indeed quite a different person from the child who was snatched away from his mother. In some tribes a series of initiations, spread over a period of years, gradually introduce the young man into adulthood. The later ceremonies take on an increasingly religious perspective as the males are introduced into the traditions and knowledge of the tribe, and the revelation of what the tribe holds sacred.

Rites of initiation are not confined to primitive societies or to the age of adolescence. In ancient Greece, the mystery cults recruited many members through their ceremonies, and many great men were among the initiates. The 1st-century B.C. Roman philosopher Marcus Tullius Cicero was one, and he wrote that "among the many excellent and divine gifts of Athens to the life of men, nothing is better than those Mysteries by which we are drawn from savagery to civilization. They are rightly called intuition, because we have thus learned the first principles of life; and have not only received the method of living with joy, but also of dying with better hope."

Cicero was referring to the rites of the Eleusinian Mysteries, which were performed for over 1000 years at the temple of the earth-mother Demeter at Eleusis near Athens. No complete description of the Eleusinian ritual has come down to us, but by

From Boyhood into Manhood

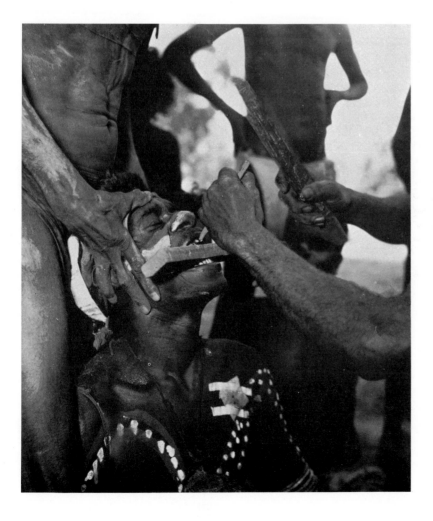

Left: a tooth-extraction ceremony is part of an initiation rite for older youths among the Aborigines of Northwest Arnhem Land, Australia. A bar of wood is inserted between the teeth of the initiate and another piece is used as a hammer. The blows are then directed onto a small piece of wood placed directly against the tooth. This passage from youth to maturity is marked by another symbolic death—just as circumcision marked his earlier passage from boyhood to youthful manhood. Although the token of his ordeal is fairly mild—knocking out a tooth is less painful than the earlier rite of circumcision—it is still necessary in order to be reborn into the new status.

combining testimonials from different sources scholars have been able to reconstruct the greater part of it. The basis of the rites was the myth of Demeter and Persephone. The story went that one day when Persephone, who was the daughter of the goddess Demeter by Zeus, was gathering flowers in a field, she was seized and carried off to the underworld, by its god, Hades. The distressed Demeter wandered all over the earth seeking her daughter, and in her distraction she allowed the crops of the earth to wither, and there was famine. On behalf of her pleading, Zeus interceded with Hades and prevailed upon him to release Persephone from the underworld to spend a part of each year with her mother. Eleusis was the place where they were reunited, and in celebration of the fact Demeter requested a temple to be built there in which she would give initiates the joy of a second birth into immortal life.

Initiates were known as *mystae*, and the rites they participated in took place in the autumn and were made up of four stages. There was a period of ritual preparation and purification, following which the *mystae* walked in procession from Athens to Eleusis. Then they spent some time roaming about the seashore in imitation of Demeter's wanderings in search of Persephone, before they entered the underground Hall of Initiation in the temple, where they underwent the experience that brought the rites to a climax and gave the initiate a mystical vision. Whatever happened during these final rites, it certainly worked powerfully on the senses of the participant. Music, dance, and lighting effects were apparently used, and possibly initiates were given

Above: the head of Demeter, the Greek corn-goddess and Earth Mother. Her daughter was Persephone who was carried off by Hades, god of the underworld, while she was gathering flowers (below). Her mother searched for her, while crops were left to wither on earth, and finally she was allowed to spend two-thirds of every year with her mother, the other time with Hades The myth was the basis of the Eleusinian Festival and Mysteries in Athens.

Fertility Rites

consciousness-altering drugs. Several ancient writers tell us that
a sexual act took place between the initiate and a priestess of
Demeter in ritual reenactment of the ravishing of Persephone by
Hades, but it is more probably that the rape was mimed or symbolically represented. Another highly dramatic moment was the
calling up of Persephone from the underworld, and then came
the actual culmination of the ceremonies, the presentation to the
mystae of "an ear of corn reaped in silence." Here, then, is the
significance of these rituals, and the realization they had for the
initiate: that it is through death that life comes about; without
dying, there is no fertility.

The moment the young goddess rises from the kingdom of the
dead to be reunited with the divine mother who sought her,
mourning and lamenting her, is the moment the divine mother,
in her joy causes the grain, to which men owe their civilization,
to rise again with her. The *mystae*, as witnesses of this event,
realize that what they are watching is not a play, but a divine
presence. As for the goddess, so for the initiates. They, too, would
pass from Hades to happiness. The Eleusinian Mysteries did for
their initiates what rites and ceremonies have always done for
mankind. For it is to reconcile man to his mortal state, to enable
him to step out of time into eternity, to assist at the Creation
and walk with the gods as familiars, and above all it is to keep a
man ever aware of and in contact with the sacred, that human
beings the world over have engaged so enthusiastically in rituals
and ceremonies.

Chapter 11
Heaven and Hell

What happens to the soul after death? The question is a timeless one, and each of the world's great religions provides its own answer. Each promises heaven for the virtuous, hell for the damned. The irony is that, while the heavenly vision ranges from the sensual to the plain banal, the prospect of horrific punishment seems to have inspired the ingenuity of the human imagination. Perhaps the reason is simply that, while pleasures pall, pain is infinitely variable. Perhaps the reason lies in the unbelievable cruelty of man himself, which he expects to be magnified in his God or gods. This chapter explores the variations on the themes of heaven and hell, and comes to some unexpected conclusions.

Dr. Samuel Johnson, the 18th-century writer, critic, noted conversationalist, and wit, was a man of robust intellect and strong, independent opinions. He once told a friend that he feared himself to be "one of those who shall be damned." His friend, a a rational man, asked him, "What do you mean by damned?", to which Dr. Johnson "passionately and loudly" replied: "Sent to Hell, Sir, and punished everlastingly." For the great man was also a good and orthodox Christian, and his sudden outburst was simply his expression of what millions of his contemporary fellow Christians firmly and vividly believed. They believed that, after death, those who lived virtuously would enter heaven, a place of joy and peace where God dwelt, while sinners would be damned to everlasting punishment in hell. Dr. Johnson did not suffer, as some have suggested, from a personal paranoia, but one that millions of Christians have suffered over the centuries, a fear not of psychological but of doctrinal origin.

This doctrine of eternal damnation might seem to fit awkwardly with the Christian teaching that God is love. Certainly the idea that God exacts the price of infinite torment for a finite offense is not consistent with the idea that he is just. But when we look at the teachings of the world's great religions we find that these ideas are not at all unusual, but on the contrary are common to all creeds. They all have their concepts of heaven and of hell, and without exception they have far more to say about hell than about heaven. Indeed the human mind may find it hard to

Opposite: the late 15th-century Italian artist Luca Signorelli's vision of *The Damned in Hell*. Everyone knows that they must die. The intriguing question that many ask is what happens afterward? For very many people the answer to that is some form of life after death and in some different kind of world than the one we know on earth. Very many ideas about that other world involve some kind of belief in reward and punishment to iron out the anomalies that were never solved during their lifetime on earth. The obvious way to do this is by the rewards of perfection in Heaven and the punishment of pain inflicted in Hell.

Above: a 17th-century Portuguese painting
of the tortures of Hell. Excruciating pain is
inflicted by all manner of tortures—some of
which were inflicted on criminals in real life,
others are the product of the artist's
imagination. The lurid details painted in
such pictures, many of which were hung in
churches, were meant as deterrents to crime
and sin in earthly life.

picture heavenly bliss, but when it comes to envisaging torment
it has a riotously fertile imagination.

The idea of reward or punishment after death appears comparatively late in the development of religious thinking. It has
proved the craftiest of priestcraft's inventions, facilitating
government by fear and exalting so-called spiritual authority
over the merely temporal. Primitive hells were simply abodes of
the dead, grim places to be sure but not gruesome, where the
shades simply wandered aimlessly about. Punishment carried
out by vindictive devils, intent on roasting, mutilating, dis-
membering, or otherwise torturing sinners is a concept we find
only in the higher later religions. Primitive man certainly
believed in and was terrified by spirits. But it did not occur to
him that the misdeeds of this life might be punished in the next.
In the Hades of Greek mythology a few unfortunates who have
incurred the personal wrath of the gods, like Tantalus, Sisyphus,
or Ixion, suffer punishment. But there is no general judgment of
the dead, no balancing up of their accounts of good and evil

deeds. Nor is there in early Assyrian or Egyptian mythology, preoccupied as those cultures were with man's fate after death, although in later Egyptian religion Osiris becomes the lord and judge of the dead. The early Hebrew afterworld, Sheol, is likewise a rather neutral, dull, bleak place where nothing much goes on. When Saul asked the witch of Endor to summon the spirit of Samuel, the dead Samuel's first words to Saul were, "Why hast thou disquieted me, to bring me up?" as if he was irritated at being disturbed from his eternal repose. It was not until after the Babylonian exile, when the Jews had been in contact with Eastern ideas, that the concept of a punitive hell entered their theology. And from there, of course, it went on to be elaborated with truly diabolical ingenuity in Christianity.

The Christian hell must take the prize for the most extravagant of all the hells conceived by mankind, and the one upon which the most unstinting investment of intellect and imagination has been lavished. But the Hindu and Buddhist hells do not lag very far behind. According to the Hindu scriptures, the *Puranas*, there exist 100,000 hells, each devoted to the punishment of a particular offense. It is notable that offenses against religion and the priesthood are the main category. People who have insulted

The Hades of the Ancient Greeks

Left: Ixion on the fiery wheel. He was the son of the King of Lapithae and treacherously murdered his father-in-law. Although pardoned by Zeus, Ixion then tried to seduce Hera. As a punishment for his crimes Ixion was bound to a fiery wheel, which turned for ever.
Below: the Witch of Endor, mentioned in Chapter 28 of the first book of Samuel. She was the woman with "a familiar spirit" consulted by King Saul when he had been forsaken by God and threatened by the Philistines. At his request she calls up the prophet Samuel, who told him that he would die and his army be destroyed.

Brahmins are condemned to be cut in pieces, those who have robbed them to be sawn in half, and those who have scorned religion to be cast upon knife-blades for as many years as they have hairs on their bodies. There are hells where the art of punishment is executed with rare craftsmanship and finesse, such as the one where a soul is ground between millstones until it is sufficiently attenuated to be twisted into a wick for a lamp, in which it is then gradually consumed. And when they have suffered their punishments in hell, sinners will be further victimized by being reincarnated in their next life on earth in lowlier life-forms. For instance, thieves of meat will become vultures; of fat, cormorants; of molasses, frogs; of water, cuckoos. A Brahmin who drinks alcohol will become an insect, and if he steals another Brahmin's money he will be reincarnated one thousand times as a snake or a spider. The Hindu equivalent of hell does not have the ultimate horror of everlasting punishment that so terrified poor Samuel Johnson. But it does have instead the variation of alternating torture in the world of the dead with humiliation in the world of the living through an innumerable series of deaths and reincarnations.

Buddhism developed numerous versions of hell as it spread throughout Asia and absorbed the ideas and traditions of various countries. Although Buddhism is the mildest, most merciful, and tolerant of the world's religions, its system of punishment after death is as terrifying as any. Indeed it seems out of place in its system of belief until one recalls that in Buddhism there is no god perpetually overseeing people's conduct and being gratified or grieved by it, and therefore the idea of reward or punishment after death is all the more necessary as a regulator of behavior.

The following story, for example, is from a Chinese source. One day the soul of a man named Chang was brought before the Lord of the Underworld for judgment. When the Lord looked up his record of good and evil deeds he found that a mistake had been made. His devils had brought the wrong man, so he ordered them to take Chang back and reunite his soul with his physical body. On the way back, Chang prevailed upon the devils escorting him to make up for their earlier mistake and the anxiety it had caused him by giving him a conducted tour of purgatory. He was shown many interesting things, such as the cliff from which sinners were hurled onto a mass of sharp spikes below, and a tree with branches of sharp blades that would hack at anyone who passed near. Then they came to a place where a Buddhist priest was hanging upside-down from a tree by a rope through a hole in his leg, screaming with agony and pleading for death. Chang was all the more aghast when he recognized the priest as his own brother. He asked the devils what had brought him to this pass. They said that the priest was being punished for embezzling money that he had collected for his order and squandering it on gambling and debauchery. So when Chang was back in the world he went to his brother's monastery, expecting to find him dead. He wasn't, but he was in great pain, suffering from an abcess in his leg, which was hoisted above him and bound to the wall. When Chang told him about his visit to purgatory and what he had seen there, the priest was so terrified that he vowed that he would in future live an ascetic life and

Below: a Hindu Brahmin, or priest, whose function is the performance of sacrifices and teaching. Hinduism does not teach belief in an afterlife that includes the body. Indeed, it teaches that it is an illusion that life in the body even in this world is desirable. Because men cling to their earthly bodies, they can never escape from this world and are constantly reincarnated in a succession of bodies, human or animal. Salvation comes through enlightenment, so that as a person realizes the truth he leaves the wheel of rebirth and becomes one with Brahma, the only true reality.

Buddhist and Hindu Concepts

Left: a Chinese Buddhist painting showing Yama, the king and judge of the dead, enthroned in his hall of judgment in the seventh hell. In the foreground, demons and dogs drive sinners into a river. It is Yama who sends souls to the appropriate paradise or hell. The good and evil actions of the dead are weighed before him; those judged as wicked are led off to punishment in the eight hot hells and the eight cold hells.

The Buddhists' Wheel of Life

Above: a late Ming pottery statue of a
judge of hell. There were 10 law courts in
the Chinese Buddhist hell, each equipped to
deal with a particular type of transgressor.
Before being passed to the judge for
assignment to a suitable new incarnation,
each soul had to pay for the crimes that
until then had not been atoned for.

Right: the death of the Buddha, surrounded
by his disciples, from an Indian stone
carving of the 2nd–3rd century. When
Buddha attained Nirvana he went to the
Land of Extreme Felicity in the West, where
souls above reproach are sent to join him.
It is impossible for Buddhist artists to depict
the Land of Extreme Felicity because it is a
state of liberation from all earthly and
human conditions.

dedicate himself to religious exercises. He recovered from his
abcess and thereafter his conduct as a priest was exemplary.

The story does not tell us how the priest eventually fared in the
afterworld, whether his later conduct absolved him from the consequences of his crimes, but it does make the point that fear of
punishment after death can indeed be a powerful regulator of
conduct in this world.

Purgatory, according to Chinese Buddhism, has 10 courts,
each presided over by a different Yama-King, or Infernal
Majesty, competent to judge particular types of offense. Attached
to each of these courts there are a number of hells in which the
prescribed punishments are administered to sinners. When a person dies, the soul is seized by two demons known as Ox-Head and
Horse-Face and taken to the first court, where its record of good
and evil is scrutinized. People who have lived lives above reproach may be sent to join the Buddha in the Land of Extreme
Felicity in the West, or they may go to the tenth court to be
allocated another incarnation on earth forthwith. But sinners
are sent on to visit each of the courts in turn, and in each their
conduct in certain particulars is judged, a punishment is decreed
if necessary, and the soul is carried off by hideous red-faced
devils into one of the adjacent hells, there to be subjected to the
prescribed tortures.

However, the worst of tortures eventually come to an end, and
the purged soul comes at last to the tenth court, where it is allocated the mode of its rebirth into its next life on earth. This may
be as a human being, as an animal, or, in the case of the un-
utterably base, such as those who in their last life refused to give
alms to wandering priests, as a *preta*, a demon destined to walk

the earth tormented by hunger or thirst, but for some reason—
such as being endowed with teeth like needles, or an immense
stomach and a very narrow alimentary canal—unable ever to
satisfy its appetites. All souls on their way back to earth have to
pass the house of Lady Meng, where they are given a dose of her
Broth of Oblivion, which wipes out all their memories of their
previous lives and of their experiences in hell. If a soul refuses to
drink, sharp blades shoot up from the ground beneath and all
around it, and a dose is forcibly administered by means of a
copper tube thrust down its throat. After partaking of Lady
Meng's broth, the oblivious souls are herded by demons onto
the Wheel of Fate, which carries them down to earth like a fair-
ground big wheel and pitches them once again into the lottery of
life.

This Buddhist vision of hell could be multiplied with variations
from Japanese, Indian, Sinhalese, and Tibetan sources, but a
detailed parade of their horrors would be at once unedifying and
tedious. Besides, the Buddha himself is said to have stated that it
would take 100,000 years to describe the tortures of the damned.

Farther west lies Persia (Iran), a country whose modern oil-
based economy flouts its ancient religion, in which one of the
greatest sins was to make holes in the earth which would afford
devils a passage to and from hell. The Christian world's finest
description of the afterlife, Dante's *Divine Comedy*, was antici-

Above: a section from a Buddhist Wheel of
Life painting showing scenes of punishment
and torment. Because there is no God in
Buddhism and therefore no one to oversee
the conduct of the faithful, a system of
rewards and punishment developed. The
Buddhist hell in particular is well
documented. Even so, the Buddha himself
declared that it would take 100,000 years to
describe the tortures of the damned.

Above: *The Boat of Dante*, by the French
painter Eugene Delacroix. Dante and his
guide Vergil are being rowed along the Styx
by Charon, ferryman of the Underworld.
The damned souls are everywhere in the
brown waters. They try to grasp the boat but
are repelled by Vergil. The description
appears in Dante's *Divine Comedy*, written
more than 650 years ago, in an age when the
Church demanded complete obedience and
acceptance of its dogmas: the purpose of
the human body was to provide an earthly
shelter for the eternal soul. The earth itself
was less important and no more real than
hell, purgatory, and paradise.

pated by some 2000 years in Persia, in the work of Arta-i-Viraf.
This author claimed to have separated his soul from his body
by taking a drug called *mang*, and then to have been shown
around heaven and hell by two angels, just as Dante was guided
by the Roman poet Vergil. His descriptions run to 101 chapters,
83 of which are devoted to hell and 9 to heaven, a ratio that
reflects the bias of the human imagination everywhere.

Arta-i-Viraf's guides took him first to the banks of a river
down which smoking souls floated, continually harassed by
hungry snakes and other reptiles, and explained that the river
was made up of the tears of mourners. This meant that the more
the living mourned the dead, the more the river swelled and the
harder it became for souls to cross the river, beyond which lay
heaven. The crossing was attempted by means of the Chinvat
bridge. This is a rather original conception: a bridge that is broad
for the innocent and narrows down for others in proportion to

their sins, until for the irredeemable reprobate it becomes as narrow as a razor and he can barely set foot on it before plunging into the river beneath. The river then carries him to the part of hell where he can be suitably punished for his sins.

In hell itself the writer witnessed the usual gruesome sights: a man who in life had persecuted true believers hanging from a tree by one leg and being skinned by devils; an ungrateful man forced by hunger to bite pieces out of his own arms; a disobedient wife suspended by hooks through her breasts; a man who had watered down milk being flogged with snakes; a liar with his tongue sticking out and covered with centipedes. For souls who had fallen marginally short of reaching heaven there was a special place called Nanistagan where their only suffering was "cold or heat from the revolution of the atmosphere," or exposure to climatic extremes.

In the Zoroastrian religion "good is the final goal of ill" and ultimately the Good Lord, Ahura Mazda, will prevail over the Evil One, Angra Mainyu. Hell itself will cease to be and the souls imprisoned in it will be released, and after finally being purged by fire they will achieve eternal happiness. Furthermore, until that day of deliverance Ahura Mazda will continue to visit the

The Orthodox Christian Hell

Left: the monster Geryon, from the 18th Canto of Dante's *Inferno*. Geryon was a type of fraud or malice, "His face the semblance of a just man's wore . . . the rest was serpent all." Dante and Vergil are carried on its back down to the eighth circle of hell where all kinds of fraudulent sinners are kept, and proceed to describe the torments of two kinds, the scourging by demons of those men who are seducers of women, and the immersion of flatterers in filth up to their necks.

infernal regions for the last five days of every year, to hear the confessions of the contrite and to relieve their sufferings. So the Persian sinner, however horribly culpable his misdeeds, could derive some comfort from the thought that there would come an end to his torments.

Not so the Christian. As we have seen, the early Hebrew afterworld, Sheol, was not at first a place of punishment at all. It was only after the Babylonian exile, when they had been exposed to Eastern and Zoroastrian ideas, that the Jews took up the idea. There is not a great deal about it in the canonical Old Testament, but there is a lot in the apocalyptic literature of the Apocrypha, written in the last 400 years B.C. Thus in the book of the prophet Enoch we read a description of "Gehenna," which goes: "There are all sorts of tortures in that place, savage darkness and impenetrable gloom; and there is no light there, but a gloomy fire is always burning, and a fiery river goes forth. And all that place has fire on all sides, and on all sides cold and ice; thus it burns and freezes. And the prisoners are very savage. And the angels terrible and without pity, carrying savage weapons, and their torture is unmerciful. And I said, Woe! Woe! How terrible is this place!"

Such descriptions abound in Jewish apocalyptic literature, and the tradition found its way into the Christian scriptures in many ways, culminating in the splendid and harrowing visions of the Book of Revelation. Those Christians who look only to the founder of their faith for scriptural truth, however, have only two brief passages to go on to maintain that Jesus preached hellfire and damnation. In the "Little Apocalypse" in Mark Chapter 9 there is: "If your eye causes you to sin, pluck it out; it is better for you to enter the Kingdom of God with one eye than with two eyes, to be thrown into hell." And in Matthew Chapter 25 there is a reference to "the eternal fire prepared for the devil and his angels," and a statement that the damned "will go away into eternal punishment, but the righteous into eternal life." Even if these statements were authentic sayings of Jesus—and many scholars believe that they are not—they would hardly constitute scriptural foundation for the elaborate and grotesque hells of medieval Christianity. That extraordinary distortion of the human imagination, which found expression in cathedral architecture and in the paintings of such as Peter Breughel and Hieronymus Bosch as well as in the stanzas of Dante's *Inferno*, took its authority and inspiration from visionary works of the early Christian centuries.

There was, for example, a 4th-century *Vision of St. Paul*, in which the evangelist visited hell and as a result of the horrors he saw there prevailed upon God to give sinners a few hours' respite from their torments every Sunday. Among the sights that appalled the saint were trees of fire from which sinners hung by hands, feet, ears, or tongue, a wheel of fire that scorched a thousand souls on each of its 1000 daily revolutions, and a smoking, stinking pit into which unbelievers were pitched headlong. Then there was the *Vision of Alberico*. Alberico, a boy of 10, described what he saw on a tour of hell on which he was conducted by St. Peter. One of the scenes he reported was of one-year-old babies boiling and writhing in fiery vapors fed with

Torture and Eternal Fires

Opposite: *The Four Horsemen of the Apocalypse*, an engraving done in the early 1500s by the German artist Albrecht Dürer. The Horsemen represent (left to right) Death, Famine, Pestilence, and War riding and trampling men and women, under the guidance of the angel of death. The bishop, bottom left, trampled by death's bony horse, falls into the open jaws of the Dragon of Hell.

Below: Saint Peter opening the gates of paradise, from a painting in the Rila Monastery, Bulgaria. In the paradise garden are (left to right) the repentant thief, Abraham, Isaac, and Jacob. The tiny figures in their laps are the souls of the blessed.

Above: an early 15th-century European Christian view of the Last Judgment when the righteous are separated from the damned, painted by the Italian artist Fra Angelico. In Chapter 25 of Matthew's Gospel Jesus gives a description of the last days when the world has ended and all souls must appear before him to be judged. "When the Son of Man comes in his glory and all the angels with him, then he will sit on his glorious throne. Before him will be gathered all the nations, and he will separate them one from another as a shepherd separates the sheep from the goats." He goes on to explain that the sheep, the righteous souls, are to inherit the kingdom prepared for them from the foundation of the world, and the goats, the damned, are to go into the eternal fire, prepared for the devil and his angels.

flaming coal, whose only sin was that they had died unbaptized. When Dante embarked on his literary labor of describing the seven circles of hell the only inspiration he needed was for the manner of his writing. The subject matter was provided for him in numerous works and traditions so widely disseminated in the Middle Ages as almost to be described as "popular."

One of the refinements exclusive to the Christian afterlife is the idea that one of the rewards of the righteous will be to enjoy the spectacle of the sufferings of the damned. No lesser authority than 13th-century Italian theologian Saint Thomas Aquinas described the idea: "That the saints may enjoy their beatitude more thoroughly, and give more abundant thanks for it to God, a perfect view of the punishment of the damned is granted them." Aquinas tried to justify this appalling idea of sadistic voyeurism by saying that the contemplation of the order of divine justice, no less than the fact of their own deliverance, must be a cause of joy to the blessed. But the 2nd-century Christian writer Quintus Septimus Tertullian attempted no apology for his anticipation of sheer vindictive satisfaction. He wrote: "How shall I admire, how laugh, how rejoice, how exult, when I behold so many proud monarchs, and fancied gods, groaning in the lowest abyss of darkness; so many magistrates, who persecuted the name of the Lord, liquifying in fiercer fires than they ever kindled against the Christians; so many sage philosophers blushing in red-hot flames with their deluded scholars; so many celebrated poets trembling before the tribunal."

Excommunication—expulsion from the communion of the Church—was a powerful weapon of the priesthood. With the threat of it even emperors and kings could be coerced or intimidated. To make it the more effective all priests and pastors were urged, in the words of the Catechism of the Council of Trent of 1563 to "very frequently press upon the attention of the faithful" the horror and fear of the eternal torments of the damned. That same council also instructed preachers to teach that even good men would not escape the tortures of purgatory, which differed from those of hell only in that they came to an end when the purged soul was ready for "the eternal country into which no defiled thing may enter." The idea of purgatory as a place of cleansing and purification had been expressed by many theologians, but the fact that the official pronouncements of the Church speak of *expiation* of sins—that is, of making payment or satisfaction for them—undeniably suggest a vindictive and unforgiving God. The doctrines of purgatory, of excommunication, of the inclusion of the unbaptized and of the virtuous heathen among the damned, of the legitimate joy of the righteous in the sufferings of sinners, and of the inexpiable nature of some sins and endlessness of the punishment for them have made the Christian concept of the afterlife more terrifying, more uncompromising, and more cruel than that of any other great religion.

The Aztecs of South America had a simple idea of the afterlife. Priests and nobles went to a comfortable heaven known as the Mansion of the Sun, but everybody else went to a gloomy place called Mictlan. Aztecs converted to Christianity in droves

The Concept of Purgatory

Below: the 16th-century Italian artist Giovanni Bellini's enigmatic painting *Allegory of Purgatory*. In Roman Catholic belief, purgatory is a place where souls suffer for a time after death on account of their sins. The Church points to Chapter 12 of Matthew's Gospel, where Jesus spoke of a sin against the Holy Spirit that would not be forgiven either in this world or the next, declaring that he would not have said that if no sin could be forgiven in the next world. But souls in purgatory feel joy as well as pain. They know their salvation is assured. Their chief pain is caused by the postponement of the Vision of God.

Moslem and Aztec Beliefs

when the Spaniards took over their country, for they believed that simply by being baptized they would be able to escape Mictlan and ensure themselves a place in heaven. One can only assume that the Spanish priests, in their zeal for converts, told the Aztecs rather less than half the story.

The Islamic concept of life after death is unique because it dwells more on the delights of heaven than on the torments of hell. It boasts a hell, to be sure, but neither in the Koran nor in subsequent Islamic theology is there any revelling in its horrors or controversy as to who will and who will not qualify for it. The tortures of the Islamic infernal regions lack the ingenuity and variety of those of more hell-bent faiths, and consist primarily of sundry forms of heat chastisement. The furnaces of hell, the Koran informs us, "cast forth sparks as big as towers, resembling yellow camels in color," and the damned "have garments of fire fitted unto them, boiling water poured on their heads," and are beaten with iron maces. It is clearly preferable to be a damned Moslem rather than a damned Christian, Hindu, or Buddhist, for not only are the torments less diabolical but

Right: the grim ruler of the Aztec world of the dead, Mictlantecuhtli, represented here as a grinning skeleton, and in the Aztec burial position. The realm of the dead was in the north—the direction of cold and darkness.

Left: demonic beings, or ghouls, of Moslem belief, from a Persian manuscript. According to Moslem belief the dead are resurrected in their graves by an angel and then they are examined about their beliefs in God and in the prophet Muhammad. The time of the resurrection was not disclosed to Muhammad by the archangel Gabriel— only that three blasts of a trumpet will herald it. After the judgment the good will enter paradise and the wicked will pass into hell. Hell is divided into seven compartments assigned to Moslems, Jews, Christians, Sabeans, Magians, idolaters, and hypocrites. All who profess the unity of God will finally be released, and unbelievers condemned to everlasting punishment.

also a sinner who goes on his knees in hell and sincerely vows repentance and begs forgiveness will be looked upon compassionately by Allah, the All Merciful.

If the torments of the Islamic hell are banal, the same must be said of the delights of its heaven. Christian critics have made much of the blatant and unashamed sensuality of the Moslems' paradise, and particularly of the delectable houris who will minister to men's needs there. In fact these houris are referred to in the Koran as "beautiful maidens, withholding their eyes from any but their spouses, and who no man shall have de-

Death's Happy Hunting Ground

flowered before them," so there is no ground for alleging that Islam proposes sexual license as one of the delights of heaven. In fact, few active pleasures are envisaged in the Moslems' paradise. The foreseen reward for the virtuous is an afterlife of repose, contentment, indulgence in rather showy extravagance, and languor. "Reclining in silken robes on bridal couches," says the Koran, "naught shall they know of sun or piercing cold; its shades shall close over them, and low shall its fruits hang down; the vessels of silver and goblets like flagons shall be borne around among them." Paradise itself is seen as a series of gardens through which rivers flow. There are rivers of incorruptible water, and rivers of fresh milk, of delicious wine, and of clarified honey. Fountains and great trees affording shade are abundant, and all kinds of luscious fruit are there for the picking. It is in fact a desert-dweller's dream of the ideal life, so completely different from the conditions of his life on earth that it is not so much a visionary version of heaven as a wish-fulfillment one.

The same is true of most heavens. The Egyptian Land of the Blessed was a fertile country resembling the Nile delta, where fruit ripened and flowers bloomed in perpetuity, and there was an abundance of wildfowl. The Teutonic Valhalla offered heroes the enjoyment of great feasts in a place cosily warmed by great fires, alternating with merry martial sports—a natural dream-world of dwellers in the drear and chilling north. Aboriginal Tasmanians as well as tribes of American Indians looked forward to going to Happy Hunting Grounds, where teeming game would guarantee invariable success in the chase. The concept of heaven, in the first instance, is a dream in which the physical hardships of earthly existence are alleviated and its deficiencies are amply catered for.

Buddhism tends to be rather more spiritual. The Chinese Land of Extreme Felicity in the West was portrayed as a place of refined, aesthetic delights. Enclosed by seven rows of terraces and seven rows of trees with branches laden with precious stones that sound musically in the gentle wind, it is a place where even the wondrously colored birds sing the praises of the Buddha and the

Right: a 5th-century A.D. painting on a rock face in Sri Lanka of two voluptuous females. They might well fit the description of the houris to be found in the luxurious paradise so graphically described in the Koran, the sacred book of Islam. Those chosen by Allah "shall recline on jeweled couches face to face, and there shall wait on them immortal youths with bowls and ewers and a cup of purest wine . . . with fruits of their own choice and flesh of fowls that they relish. And there shall be dark-eyed houris, chaste as hidden pearls. . . ." To increase the erotic pleasures of paradise each man is endowed with the sexual vigor of 100 others.

Holy Law, and where the extreme felicity of the blessed consists in perpetual contemplation of Buddha and performance of religious observances. Indian Buddhism concedes rather more to less pious ideas of felicity. It teaches the existence of 26 heavens, the first six of which afford the blessed the ultimate in sensual enjoyment. They live in palaces of solid gold decorated with precious stones, feed on *soma*, or what the Greeks called ambrosia, and have at their beck and call an entourage of beautiful girls who sing and dance divinely. In the higher heavens, however, to which all souls must ultimately graduate however reluctant they may be to do so, the satisfactions enjoyed are those of abstract meditation and listening to the divine voice of Buddha.

It is a truism that the experience of physical pleasure palls much sooner than does that of physical anguish, and that man soon becomes surfeited with it and longs for a change. This is no doubt a major reason why religious writings have rather less to say about the experience of heaven than about that of hell. The Christian idea of what that experience is like derives mainly from the description in Revelation: "I looked, and lo, in heaven an open door! And the . . . voice . . . like a trumpet, said, 'Come up hither, and I will show you what must take place after this.' At once I was in the Spirit, and lo, a throne stood in heaven, with one seated on the throne! And he who sat there appeared like jasper and carnelian, and round the throne was a rainbow that looked like an emerald. Round the throne were twenty-four thrones, and seated on the thrones were twenty-four elders, clad in white garments, with golden crowns upon their heads."

Understandably, the joys and pains of the afterlife as conceived by the different religions of the world are conceived in essentially physical terms. Such terms, taken literally, lead to contradictions and even absurdities which are the delight of the skeptics. There

Above: *The Buffalo Hunt*, by the 19th-century American painter George Catlin. Success in the hunt, which brought food, clothing, and a reasonable sense of security, might well have figured in some way in the Plains Indians' belief in the afterlife. A human being consisted of three parts—his body, his soul, and his ghost. The soul went to a kind of heaven while the ghost continued to share in the life of the living, so that a hunting party might consist of the hunters and a large number of ghosts who had come along to join in the excitement of the chase.

Right: a painting from a Tibetan Buddhist temple that renders the concept of an eternity of bliss into sexual terms. It shows an enlightened one (Boddhisattva) in union with his consort. The circles are symbols of completeness and eternity.

is, for example, the story of the Christian priest who preached the orthodox doctrine that in hell there would be "weeping and gnashing of teeth." When a quick-witted old lady pointed out that if she went there it wouldn't apply to her because she had no teeth, the resourceful priest replied: "They will be provided, my dear."

Nevertheless, such literal concepts of heaven and hell remained in the mind of ordinary Christians for centuries, even after the 17th-century French philosopher Descartes made theologically acceptable the idea that thought is the essence of the soul. But Descartes had delivered a mortal blow to those literal concepts, rather as modern, 20th-century space exploration has exploded the traditional idea that heaven is situated somewhere in the sky. Today, medieval concepts of heaven and hell are seen as the cruel and unfounded fabrications of a cynical priesthood aimed primarily at establishing and maintaining its power. But still the questions of the soul of man and of its ultimate fate are open and of concern to us all. For this reason, the teachings of the 18th-century Swedish mystic Emanuel Swedenborg, set out in his book *Heaven and Hell*, first published in 1758, have by no means been invalidated by the last 200 years of development in science and philosophy.

Swedenborg began with the astonishing claim that he had "been permitted to associate with angels, and to talk with them as with man; and also to see what is in the heavens, and what is in the hells." He realized that the claim sounded preposterous, that some people would say it was all fantasy, or that he had cynically made it up. "But," he wrote, "by all this I am not deterred, for I have seen, I have heard, I have felt." On several occasions, he said, he had been led through the experience of dying so that he would be able to relate what it was like for the enlightenment of mankind.

There are, Swedenborg wrote, a series of states that a person

Salvation or Damnation

Above: the 18th-century Swedish scientist, philosopher, and theologian Emanuel Swedenborg. A mystical thinker endowed with unusual mental fertility and inventiveness, Swedenborg claimed he had direct contact with angels and the supernatural. To Swedenborg, hell was the community of the spirits of evil men trying to force themselves on men's minds, destroying their freedom to choose between good and evil.

Left: a 19th-century "Sermon in a picture" painting of the *Broad and Narrow Paths*. The broad path, on the left, leads to damnation, the narrow path, on the right, to life and salvation.

Swedenborg's Unique Vision

Opposite: an English stained glass window by the 19th-century British artist Sir Edward Burne-Jones. It depicts a guardian angel. Belief that God assigns an angel to guard every person's body and soul has a long history. Plato mentions them in his *Phaedo*, and Chapter 12 of the Acts of the Apostles shows that they were believed in by the friends of Peter. Jesus mentioned them with reference to children (in Chapter 18 of Matthew's Gospel) and their function is described in Chapter 8 of the Book of Revelation.

Below: a red devil, part of a 16th-century English church window of the Last Judgment. Swedenborg's descriptions of angels and devils were based on the premise that thought is the essence of the soul—in which case the evil, malice, and sheer burning hatred of many of the inhabitants of hell has molded, and colored, their physical appearance.

goes through after death. In the first state he or she is in a kind of dream world, very like the physical world, and may not realize that he is dispossessed of his physical body. Full realization of this fact is the second state, when "Man, now a spirit, is let into the state of his interiors"—that is, he becomes what he truly is, identified with his essential self, which is determined by what he most intensely loves. This essential self has a tendency toward heaven or hell, an urge to transcend the self and relate to what is higher or to indulge the self in all its basest desires. This is the judgment, but it is nothing but a self-judgment, a recognition of the essential self, and a choice to take it where it will be most at home. "Man after death casts himself into hell, and not the Lord," wrote Swedenborg.

There are, according to Swedenborg, three levels of heaven. These are the natural heaven, the spiritual heaven, and the celestial heaven. They are not spatially separated, for there is no space in heaven, as there is neither time nor matter. The heavens are separated according to the levels of spiritual attainment of their inhabitants, for out of the body only those who are, as it were, on the same wavelength can communicate with each other and constitute a community. In the heavens "there is a communication of all with each and of each with all" and "things innumerable are in it in such order as can never be described," and in this sense of unity and communication the soul finds great joy. Although "the angels in the Lord's celestial kingdom far excel in wisdom and glory the angels who are in his spiritual kingdom," the demarcations are by no means fixed, and good spirits and angels can, through a process of continual purification, approach nearer to the state of perfection, which involves more profound and intimate communion with the divine.

Spirits that have consigned themselves to hell find themselves at first apparently welcomed by its other inhabitants, but this is only to put them off their guard. In hell all is separateness and self-seeking, "everyone desires to be the greatest, and burns with hatred against others," and "spirits are engaged in continual quarrels, enmities, blows, and fightings . . . There are thick forests in which infernal spirits wander like wild beasts, and there are underground dens into which those flee who are pursued by others." Devils, like angels, have forms determined by their dominant thoughts and passions, and "in general their faces are dreadful and void of life, but in some instances they are black, and in others fiery like little torches; in others they are disfigured with pimples, warts, and large ulcers; with some no face appears, but in its stead something hairy or bony, and with some only teeth are seen."

Swedenborg's visions of heaven and hell and his concept of the afterlife correspond not only with Descartes' idea that thought is the essence of the soul, but also with the discoveries of modern science. Scientists suggest that thought is a form of energy with moving and shaping power. Whether Swedenborg was, as he believed, permitted by God to learn these things, or whether he inferred them from his own imagination, may be debatable, but certainly his teachings make heaven and hell meaningful to our psychologically sophisticated age, which is more than can be said for the concepts taught by the orthodox religions.

Chapter 12
The Unresolved Mystery

Is there a God or gods? This fundamental question has teased or troubled mankind from the earliest times to the present day. The ancient Greeks, with their galaxy of gods and goddesses, also had philosophers who, by applying pure reason to the problem, again and again demonstrated that there were no gods. Similarly, since the early 19th century, rationalist philosophers, evolutionists, and other scientists have laid siege to orthodox Christianity, with devastating results. But the need for worship is deeply embedded in man's basic makeup. It refuses to be stifled with logical argument. This final chapter takes a look at this, greatest of all mysteries of the gods.

One evening in 1878 a group of young men were discussing religion in a doctor's home in London. One of them told a well-known anecdote about the self-confessed English atheist Charles Bradlaugh, who at a public meeting had taken out his watch and challenged God to strike him dead in five minutes if he existed and disapproved of atheists. The young men argued among themselves as to whether the story was true. One member of the group, the Irish playright and music critic George Bernard Shaw, remarked that even if Bradlaugh hadn't tried the experiment he should have done, and that he, Shaw, was prepared to try it himself, there and then. It seemed to him to be a scientific experiment of a simple and straightforward kind to test the "belief in violent interferences with the order of nature by a short-tempered and thin-skinned supernatural deity." So he took out his watch.

"The effect was electrical," wrote Shaw later. "In vain did I urge the pious to trust in the accuracy of their deity's aim with a thunderbolt, and the justice of his discrimination between the innocent and the guilty. In vain did I appeal to the skeptics to accept the logical outcome of their skepticism: it soon appeared that when thunderbolts were in question there were no skeptics." His host finally prevailed upon him not to attempt the experiment, and Shaw gave way, but he could not resist the characteristical impish remark that, although he hadn't uttered the challenge to the Almighty, he had thought it, so he might be under sentence

Opposite: blinded by a light that flashed from the sky Saul of Tarsus (the future Saint Paul) falls to the ground. He was on a mission to Damascus to arrest some Christians and bring them back to Jerusalem for trial when the extraordinary event occurred that changed his life. While blinded on the ground he heard a voice saying "Saul, Saul, why persecutest thou me?" The artist has here tried to convey the overwhelming power of God and the puniness of man.

Above: the British 19th-century freethinker and radical, Charles Bradlaugh. In an age when most people held religious beliefs Bradlaugh shocked English society with his self-confessed atheism.

Below: the Irish playwright and critic George Bernard Shaw at the age of 74. Shaw identified God with what he called a life force—life would evolve through all stages from an amoeba, through man, and eventually to God.

Below right: Thomas Henry Huxley, the British biologist, who coined the description of his religious beliefs as "agnostic"—that only material phenomena can be the subject of real knowledge and that knowledge of a Divine Being, immortality, or the supernatural is impossible.

of death just the same. But the five minutes passed without any dramatic manifestation of God's wrath.

The events of that evening in 1878 were typical of the times. Emotions ran high in the debate about the existence and nature of God in the late 19th century. As early as 1811, the young poet Shelley had been expelled from the University of Oxford for declaring himself an atheist and for publishing a pamphlet to that effect called *The Necessity of Atheism*. The English philosopher and economist John Stuart Mill had shocked the pious by declaring that, in view of all the suffering and misery in the world, God could not after all be either all-powerful or all-loving. In Germany, the philosopher Friedrich Nietzsche had declared categorically with even greater impact that "God is dead." Another English philosopher and biologist, T. H. Huxley, invented the word "agnostic," from Greek words meaning "not knowing," to describe those like himself who maintain that they know nothing of these things other than purely material phenomena, and that a Creator or any other form of First Cause is unknown and apparently unknowable. Huxley was viciously attacked for his stand. One churchman said the term agnostic was just another word for infidel, which he said was "an unpleasant, indeed an awful thing" to confess to be, while another attacked him as a "cowardly agnostic." Huxley replied it was immoral to attempt to intimidate a man from saying what he sincerely believed. He in turn attacked "the pestilent doctrine" of the churches "that honest disbelief in their more or less astonishing creeds is a moral offense . . . deserving and involving the same future retribution as murder and robbery." The debate engendered a good deal of invective, wit, mockery, and indignation as entrenched orthodoxy took its stand against the assaults of sharp-shooting "freethinkers." An enjoyable time was had by all, possibly even by God Himself, who, if he was not above taking an interest in such things, might have been at least gratified by the degree of ingenuity, sincerity, and passion that human beings brought to the discussion of his existence.

Agnostics and Fundamentalists

Left: a woodcut illustrating the teaching of John Calvin, the 16th-century French reformer, that the Bible, not the Church, is the infallible word of God. As the critics of religion became more numerous and more outspoken in the 19th century, the Bible became a battleground of rival scholarship —those who wished to prove that its writings were simply a historical record, versus those who believed that the writings were part of the Divine revelation to men.

The fundamentalist belief that the Bible was literally God's word to man was one of the first casualties in the battle. One critic remarked that if God had supported the fundamentalists he would have done something like arranging the stars in the sky so that they spelt out the first verse of St. John's gospel.

Without some such impressive demonstration, their beliefs were gradually eroded by scholars who at last began to study the Bible for what it is—an anthology of the writings of a particular people over a period of about 1000 years. Their studies during the century drew attention to the numerous contradictions, anomalies, and inconsistencies within those writings. The idea that an omniscient God had employed a series of Jewish writers to act as his personal amanuenses or scribes had to be revised.

So had the traditional "proofs" of the existence of God. The ancient belief that everything must have a cause and therefore there must have been a First Cause of everything, a Creator of the universe, simply did not stand up. The argument had always begged the question, Who created the Creator? For to maintain that he just existed and always had existed would in fact invalidate the basic belief that everything must have a cause, and the idea of an infinity of creators was simply absurd. To add to these difficulties, the new science of biochemistry and the formulation of the theory of evolution made it easier, as Shaw said, to believe that the universe made itself than that a maker of the universe made himself. As Shaw wrote, "the universe visibly exists and makes itself as it goes along, whereas a maker for it is a hypothesis."

The traditional "argument from design," which maintained that the presence of order and design in the world implied the existence of a designer, was also undermined by evolution theory. Although, as the 18th-century theologian William Paley had pointed out, the existence of that ingenious contrivance, a watch,

God the Creator?

Below: God as the world's great architect.
This illustration from an Anglo-French
biblical history shows God creating the
Universe with a turn of his compass. It was
the evolutionary theory that undermined
the argument that the presence of order and
design in the world implied the existence of
a designer.

implied the existence of a watchmaker, the analogy didn't hold
for organic as distinct from mechanical things. In the 1850s, the
English naturalist Charles Darwin had demonstrated that a
process of "natural selection" operated in nature. He had shown
how over a period of time and through numerous mutations
nature eventually produced organisms perfectly adapted to their
environment, simply because they were the fittest to survive
within it and *not* because they had been designed specifically for
the purpose.

Another so-called proof of the existence of God was the argument known as the "ontological" argument. Formulated by
Saint Anselm, an 11th-century archibishop of Canterbury, the

argument ran along the lines that, because the human mind can conceive of a being that possesses all imaginable qualities in perfection, and that those qualities must inevitably include the quality of existence, this proves that God must exist. Generations of Christians had been convinced by this somewhat complex argument. But in the 18th century the German philosopher Emmanuel Kant had taken this argument for God's existence apart with devastating ease. He pointed out first that existence is in any case not a quality in the same category as power, knowledge, or goodness. Kant clinched his own argument by declaring that he could very easily formulate the idea of 300 coins jingling in his pocket, but that his doing so by no means whatsoever meant that they existed.

Left: giraffes, seen here silhouetted against an African sunset, are often quoted as more obvious examples of natural selection—the main process of evolutionary change put forward by the 19th-century British naturalist Charles Darwin (above, in a cartoon dated 1859).

So by the 19th century both the traditional proofs of God's existence and belief in it became for many thinking Europeans anachronisms unworthy of consideration let alone the consent of enlightened minds. And several of those enlightened minds applied themselves to the task of explaining how the idea had arisen in the first place. Anthropologists, psychologists, and philosophers contributed ideas from their several viewpoints to a discussion about the true nature of God. The general trend of their arguments discounted completely the supernatural and set out to show that God was "nothing but" something quite natural —a revered ancestor, a father-figure, a personification of forces in nature that man needed to control, or a projection of man's own highest self-image.

This kind of fundamental discussion about the true nature of God was new in Christian Europe. But the ancient Greek philosophers had repeatedly disputed and reassessed the nature of their gods. Much of what the ancient Greeks had said was naturally familiar to 19th-century scholars well versed in Greek literature and thought. One of the earliest Greek thinkers had remarked that, if horses had hands and could paint, "they would paint the forms of gods like horses." What Xenophanes was suggesting was simply that the gods his own contemporaries looked up to

Above: the 18th-century German philosopher Immanuel Kant. He proposed that all knowledge required an ingredient derived from nature.

Above: a carved ancestor figure from the Solomon Islands in the Pacific Ocean. The basis of ancestor worship lies in a feature found in most human societies—the commemoration of the dead.

and made sacrifices to were nothing but idealized men and women. Another Greek philosopher, Euhemeros, had put forward the idea that the gods were originally great warriors, benefactors, and other distinguished humans. A third, Empedocles, according to legend, had announced that he himself was a god and had acquired a devoted following who believed that he could teach them how to control the climate, heal the sick, and raise the dead. Few of these precedents escaped the attention of the 19th-century critics of religion in their search for the real nature of God. One of them, indeed, the English philosopher Herbert Spencer, took his ideas directly from Euhemeros, and developed a theory of religion as nothing more than ancestor worship which gained wide acceptance in his day, over 2000 years after it was first put forward.

"Anything which transcends the ordinary," wrote Spencer, "a savage thinks of as supernatural or divine; the remarkable man among the rest. This remarkable man may be simply the remotest ancestor remembered as the founder of the tribe; he may be a chief famed for strength and bravery; he may be a medicine-man of great repute; he may be an inventor of something new. And then, instead of being a member of the tribe, he may be a superior stranger bringing arts and knowledge; or he may be one of a superior race predominating by conquest. Being at first one or other of these, regarded with awe during his life, he is regarded with increased awe after his death; and the propitiation of his ghost . . . develops into an established worship. There is no exception, then. Using the phrase ancestor-worship in its broadest sense as comprehending all worship of the dead, be they of the same blood or not, we reach the conclusion that ancestor-worship is the root of every religion."

The popularity of Spencer's idea in its day was partly due to the fact that it was in line with evolution theory. So, too, were the anthropomorphic ideas later put forward by Sir James Frazer in his monumental study of religion, magic, and folklore, *The Golden Bough*, first published in 1890. In primitive human societies, and by implication at the dawn of religion, Frazer argued, both men and gods were believed to possess supernatural powers, and therefore the distinction between them had been blurred. Men had believed they could bribe or coerce the gods to do their will, and had lived on a more or less equal footing with them. Then in course of time men had become aware of the immensity of the universe and of the powers of nature, and had felt their own insignificance and impotence in relation to them. The gods, therefore, they now identified, not with themselves, but with the forces that controlled nature. They looked to them as exclusive possessors of the supernatural powers that they had once believed they too shared. Sacrifice and prayer entered religion at this stage. Magic became regarded as a black art because it was an encroachment upon the domain of the gods. At a still later stage men began to recognize the principles of natural law. As a result the idea of the elemental forces as personal agents became obsolete, and magic, being based on a recognition of the principle of cause and effect, reemerged to prepare the way for science, as alchemy led to chemistry. Finally science clearly demonstrated that belief in the gods was based

Ancestor Worship

Left: it was Herbert Spencer, the 19th-century British philosopher, who put forward the idea that ancestor worship was at the root of every religion during the great debate about science and religion of the 18th and 19th centuries. He vigorously upheld the scientific and naturalistic view of the world against supernaturalism. He thought of primitive peoples as childlike, emotional creatures whose attachment to their parents developed into a religion after their deaths.

Left: a painted board or "henta" from the Nicobar Islands in the Indian Ocean. It depicts a white man with a magical umbrella together with numerous symbols of European bounty and power. It was during the late 1800s that a strange religious manifestation occurred among the islands on the trade routes. They have at their heart the awaited arrival of a ship or airplane loaded with consumer goods such as refrigerators, radio sets, and furniture.

God the Father or Father Figure?

Right: a citizen of 15th-century Bruges consults a witch. According to 19th-century scholars witchcraft and magic belonged to a stage in man's development before belief in the powerful deities that controlled the forces of nature. In fact, belief in witches and witchcraft existed alongside belief in all-powerful gods. In Christian Europe in the 11th century Pope Gregory VII condemned the burning of women for supposed crimes such as causing storms and disease. Belief in witchcraft received a fresh impetus, however, when Crusaders brought back books of Jewish and Arabic magic, and later the exaggerated teachings of the Albigensians on the principle of evil also contributed to keeping the beliefs alive.

almost entirely on ignorance and superstition.

This type of argument, in which the authority of step-by-step logic joined forces with the authority of evolutionism (which had started as a theory and soon became a dogma), was often put forward in the debate about religion. So many people were impressed by its logic or found it agreed so well with their own opinion that few troubled to ask if it was based on sound premises. Men who believed themselves to be the end-product of the evolutionary process assumed that they were automatically endowed with knowledge of the stages through which human beings had evolved. They therefore assumed that the mind of the "savage" was an open book to them. As we have seen in an earlier chapter, this assumption was criticized by the Scottish scholar Andrew Lang in his book *The Making of Religion*, first published in 1898. Lang's study of the "High Gods of Low Races," and his demonstration that the concept of an ethical Supreme Being came before that of a ghost-god or a magician-god undermined Frazer's argument completely. But in time Lang's arguments languished and Frazer's flourished, for the latter's supported and were supported by evolutionism and rational man's conviction of his own enlightenment and supremacy.

Psychological theories are generally more difficult to prove or disprove than anthropological ones. It is probably for this reason that the biggest gun leveled at God and religion at this time was aimed and fired by Austrian psychologist Sigmund Freud.

The metaphor of God the Father had been used by the Old

Testament Prophets, particularly Isaiah and Ezekiel, and extensively by Jesus. In Christianity the image of God as a benevolent, caring, sometimes stern but always forgiving father-figure was widely preached and frequently represented in Christian art. The idea that man stands in relation to God as a child does in relation to his father, looking to him for guidance, protection, provision of the essentials of life, and for an understanding and forgiving love, had long been held without it occurring to people generally that God was nothing but a substitute father, a wishful projection of man's sense of insecurity and dependence. Freud not only pointed this out, but also brought to the interpretation of religion his own rather specialized, not to say eccentric, view of the relations of fathers and sons. "God the Father once walked upon the earth in bodily form and exercised his sovereignty as chieftain of the primal human horde until his sons united to slay him," Freud wrote, and he insisted that the motive behind this patricide of the "son horde" was to take by force the place of the father in the affections of women. The myths of Ea's murder of Apsu and Cronus's mutilation of Uranus, and the usurpation of Ea and Cronus in their turn by their sons Marduk and Zeus, may seem at first to bear out Freud's theory, but as the first chapter suggested, these myths may be more plausibly regarded as symbolizing the struggles involved in the creation of order out of a primordial chaos.

Freud applied his sexual theory to his interpretations of the origin of religious ideas and practices in the individual as well as in history. In his most elaborately written-up case history, that of

Below left: a 17th-century Dutch painting of Christ blessing the children. The faithful of both Old and New Testament were encouraged to look upon God as a father. Christ himself taught his followers to pray "Our Father" to God.

Below: Sigmund Freud, the Austrian neurologist and founder of psychoanalysis, photographed in 1922. To Freud, God was nothing more than a substitute father. His preoccupation with the sex-instinct led him further to say that all religion is simply a sublimation of that instinct.

Above: a child's drawing of a tree. A tree motif often appears in dreams and can have a wide variety of meanings. It might symbolize evolution, physical growth, psychological maturity, sacrifice, or death (Christ's crucifixion on the tree). It might also be a phallic symbol and many other things.

a wealthy young Russian who went to him for psychoanalysis in 1910, Freud attempted to demonstrate that religion was simply a form of obsessional neurosis. Factors involved in the young man's illness were the infantile traumas of seeing his parents making love, being genitally aroused and seduced by his sister, imagining his father to be fonder of his sister than of him, and a dream of wolves which he feared would eat him. When his mother and governess started reading the gospel stories to him he was perplexed by the question whether Joseph or God was Christ's real father and worried by the fact that God had let Christ suffer so cruelly. He began to identify himself with Christ and his father with God. His perplexity and worries led him to the conclusion that the relation between father and son was not as intimate as he had imagined, and caused him to have mixed feelings, of love and hate and dependence and fear, about both God and his father. His psychological situation was further complicated by the fact that he felt guilty about these feelings. His seduction by his sister caused him to direct his own developing sexual feelings toward other males, and he entertained the thought of a sexual relationship between Christ and his Father, and felt all the guiltier for this blasphemy. "A violent defensive struggle against these compromises," Freud wrote, "then inevitably led to an obsessive exaggeration of all the activities which are prescribed for giving expression to piety and a pure love of God. Religion won in the end."

This is the briefest summary of a very complex analysis, given as an example of the kind of ideas that were tremendously influential in rationalizing and explaining away religion and the God-concept in the early 20th century. There was no anthropological evidence for Freud's sexual theory of the origins of religion, and no justification for his generalizing about those origins on the basis of the data gleaned from a few pathological studies. Nevertheless, his views gained wide acceptance among people who already believed that both God and religion were out of date.

Freud's one-time disciple and colleague, the Swiss psycho-

Right: the Swiss psychologist Carl Gustav Jung (fourth from the right). Also in the photograph are some of the tribesmen of Mount Elgon, Kenya. Jung's firsthand study of primitive societies led to many of his most valuable psychological insights. He considered religion the principal factor of integration in human life—the loss of which often led to neurosis.

Jung and the Need for God

Left: the medieval concept of God (the supernatural world) embracing and controlling the natural world—the universe, portrayed as circles, and man himself. To Jung, God was an archetype, an irrepresentable, unconscious, pre-existent form that is part of the very structure of the psyche (or soul, or mind) of man. He emphasized the psychological safeguards of dogma and ritual and insisted on the importance of symbolism in mental health.

logist Carl Gustav Jung, whom Freud begged with an extraordinary show of passion never to abandon the sexual theory, not only abandoned it but vehemently opposed it. Jung described as "psychologism" the argument that "if God is anything, He must be an illusion derived from certain motives, from fear, for instance, from will to power, or from repressed sexuality." He considered it as naive as the materialist view that because God could not be discovered in the heavens he had never existed. Jung himself was a man with mystical leanings. He had matured through undergoing religious experiences and religious perplexities, and for him "God was . . . one of the most certain and immediate of experiences." Psychology, he said, could no more prove the objective existence of God than it could disprove it, but anyway proof was not important. "The idea of an all-powerful divine being is present everywhere, if not consciously recognized, then unconsciously accepted, because it is an archetype."

"God is subtle, but He is not malicious...."

Jung defined an *archetype*, a concept central to his psychology, as "an irrepressible, unconscious, pre-existent form that seems to be part of the inherited structure of the psyche [soul or mind] and can therefore manifest itself spontaneously anywhere, at any time." For Jung, the statement that God is an archetype is a strictly scientific one, verifiable by psychology and anthropology, and it is enough to refute all forms of other psychological explanations because it establishes "that 'God' already has a place in the part of our psyche which is pre-existent to consciousness and that therefore He cannot be considered an invention of consciousness."

Jung stressed that he did not put forward his observations as a proof of the existence of God. All they prove was "the existence of an archetypal image of the Deity, which to my mind is the most we can assert psychologically about God." But this was not to say that God was nothing but a subjective, psychical reality. Modern physics had made it clear that the relations between the subjective and objective worlds were far more complex than earlier science had allowed, indeed that in the last analysis the distinction between them might vanish, and certainly that it was naive to maintain that the objective alone was real. Physicists had found that they could not pursue their researches into the sub-atomic world without taking into account how the act of

Right: Albert Einstein, the great German mathematical physicist. His theories of relativity revolutionized physics. In his First (or Special) Theory of Relativity, Einstein demonstrated that time and space are not absolute but relative to the observer and that matter and energy are the same thing. The concept of a dynamic, intelligent principle at work in the world did not conflict with advanced scientific discoveries.

observation is a factor that determines events in that world. "This means," wrote Jung, "that a subjective element attaches to the physicists's world-picture, and secondly that a connection necessarily exists between the psyche . . . and the objective space-time continuum." In his later years he sought to explain the connection by developing his theory of synchronicity with the co-operation of the German physicist Wolfgang Pauli. Did Jung then believe that there is a God? It is not easy to give a definite answer, but he did write that "archetypes must have a non-psychic aspect." When put in the context of Jung's concept of God as an archetype, this comes close to a statement that God does indeed have an existence independent of the mind of man.

Twentieth-century physicists, in fact, have on the whole been less coy about talking about God than other intellectuals. When the English astrophysicist Sir James Jeans stated that in the light of the discoveries of physics the universe was beginning to look more like a great thought than a great machine, the fact that a thought cannot exist without a thinker did not escape the religious-minded. They were delighted to find support for their convictions coming from scientific people, their former inveterate foes. Further support came from the greatest of scientists, Albert Einstein, who said that he had discovered the theory of relativity because he was "so strongly convinced of the harmony of the universe," and left no ambiguity about his belief as to where that harmony originated. "I cannot believe that God plays dice with the cosmos," he declared, and "God is subtle, but he is not malicious." Relativity theory established that harmony and mathematical law were more basic constituents of the universe than matter, and indeed matter virtually disappeared when physicists probed its fundamental nature, a situation which was summed up by the English astronomer Sir Arthur Eddington; "The stuff of the world is mind-stuff." Einstein's relativity equation had demonstrated that matter and energy are the same thing, so the concept of an intelligent, dynamic principle continually at work in the universe in no way conflicted with the findings of the most advanced science. God had found his way back into human minds by a route so unexpected that it had been left quite unguarded by the anti-God party. Although he had had to relinquish the trappings of divinity, such as the throne, the beard, and the thunderbolt, his omniscience and omnipotence remained undiminished.

If Jung's psychology and the discoveries of physics made the idea of God again acceptable to the mind of 20th-century Western man, this did not generally reconcile him to the religious institutions of Western culture. Many people in our world who confess themselves religious and believers in God do not profess the Christian faith or follow its observances. Recent years have seen the emergence of many exotic cults, a spreading of Eastern religions to the West, and a revival of the ancient practice of God-seeking through the taking of mind-altering drugs.

Mind-altering drugs have played a part in many religions. Professor John Allegro has made out something of a case for early Christianity having been a drug-based religion in his book, *The Sacred Mushroom and the Cross*, first published in 1970. The use of such drugs for altering consciousness is not necessarily a

Below: a mushroom stone from Central America of around A.D. 300–600. The head on the base is thought to represent a shaman possibly under the influence of the hallucinogenic mushroom or, alternatively, the guardian spirit of the sacred plant. In most shaman-based religions, especially those still found in Asia, Australia, Africa, and North and South America, narcotics and alcohol are used to trigger trance states.

Above: the British singers and instrumentalists known as "The Beatles," with Maharishi Mahesh Yogi. The Maharishi, educated as a physicist, turned to meditation as a means of "enhancing his ability to make broad human contributions." Exotic-seeming Eastern religions and cults became popular in the West in the 1960s and early 1970s especially among the young.

dangerous or evil practice, but as several of Allegro's opponents have pointed out it results more often in delusional than in religious experiences when used by people of whose culture it is not a part. Two of his opponents do, however, relate one case in which the subject of their controlled experiments with drugs underwent a profound and life-transforming religious experience which he described in terms of an encounter with God. They defend the use of psychedelic (the word means "mind-manifesting") experience, under expert supervision and guidance, as a possible and even valuable means for individuals to seek the encounter with the divine.

As expert guidance through the psychedelic experience is difficult to obtain, "chemical ecstasy" is likely to remain a byway to God and never to become one of the major routes. In recent years Eastern religions have become a more popular way, particularly among the young. The young American philosopher Jacob Needleman has some pertinent things to say about this development in his book, *The New Religions*, first published in 1970. He maintains that in Western culture "The whole idea of the psychological effort of turning to God was set in terms of morality rather than cosmically determined psychodynamics. Man inappropriately estimated his resistance to this turning in terms of blameworthiness because he did not see this resistance

The Need for God in Today's World

Left: when Western Christians pray they used to use the simple method of closing their eyes to indicate a turning toward the invisible world of the spirit, and God. It also helped to cut off distractions.

as rooted in the laws governing the great scheme of nature."

Needleman's term "cosmically determined psychodynamics" implies that there is a means of effecting a change in the psyche, a "turning to God," in a manner that harmonizes with the laws that govern the cosmos, and it implies also some kind of connection between the inner and outer worlds, the subjective and objective, such as Jung maintained existed. He continues: "Within man is a finer quality of life which becomes obscured by the attractions of the isolated intellect and the concomitant force of individual desires. This finer quality is divine since it is finer than our ordinary mind, it may be said to be more intelligent, more conscious, as well as more loving and more powerful. Moreover—and this is crucial—the universe *requires* that man in some measure come in touch with this finer quality of life."

The idea that God needs man in order to fulfill his purposes is not alien to Western thought, but it is not developed in orthodox Christianity. As Needleman implies, Christianity has tended to stunt human growth by construing man's relation to God in terms of morality. Morality is the by-product of the religious life, not its goal. Buddhism teaches the Noble Eight-Fold Path to Enlightenment, but a man does not follow the paths of Right Thinking, Right Conduct etc. in order to please God or secure his own salvation, but in order to live and grow in harmony with

Gods as Spacemen?

the purposes of the universe. To practice meditation is to put oneself in harmony with those purposes, and to be energized by that harmonious adjustment. When Western man prays he does not generally do so with this understanding but rather conceives himself as a humble petitioner before the throne of Omnipotence. The present interest in meditation and in Eastern religions is a good thing if only because it indicates that Western man is coming round to the understanding that religion is participation in the activity of God, and that the universe as a whole is affected by what happens in its smallest part.

Finally there are the exotic cult religions of the modern world. Such religions have flourished in the West in all ages, but the modern age has probably seen a greater crop of exotics than most, at least in recent centuries. Such men as Maharishi Mahesh Yogi, L. Ron Hubbard, Meher Baba, Mohammed Subuh, and Guru Maharaj Ji have attracted immense followings by teaching variations on basic and universal religious ideas or disciplines. Some have been regarded by many of their followers as incarnations of God. But perhaps the cult that raises the most interesting question concerning the subject of this book is that of the Space God—not yet a new religion but with all the ingredients of one, including prophets and miracles.

Literature about Unidentified Flying Objects (UFOs) and extraterrestrial civilizations is voluminous and has been building up steadily since the beginning of the modern spate of "sightings" of spacecraft in 1948. In the 1970s an interesting new theme has come into this literature. "Was God an Astronaut?" asked Erich von Däniken in his book, *Chariots of the Gods?*, and others have taken up his theme. This proposes that many passages in the scriptures of the world's religions are in fact descriptions of encounters with beings from outer space. No doubt beings possessed of advanced technologies who appeared suddenly among primitive people would be regarded by them as gods. We have the example of the 16th-century Spanish conquistador Hernando Cortes, who was regarded by the Aztecs of Mexico as a reincarnation of their sun-god, Quetzalcotl. But the question whether the high gods of the world's religions were deified cosmic visitors must remain for the present one of the many unsolved "mysteries of the gods." There is in this literature a certain eagerness to believe the proposition true, but people of thoughtful and religious disposition might as fervently wish it untrue, because it would impoverish somewhat the religions of mankind, with all their inspiring and intriguing aspects, if their gods turned out after all to be nothing but spacemen.

Left: envoys of the Aztec emperor Montezuma presenting gifts to Hernando Cortes. To the Aztecs Cortes was the reincarnation of their sun-god Quetzalcotl. There are those who argue that all our literature about gods was inspired by extraterrestrial visitors not from the supernatural world but from another planet somewhere in the universe. They argue with great ingenuity that many passages in the sacred scriptures of the world's religions are in fact descriptions of encounters with beings from other worlds. If Cortes was treated as a god, how much more overwhelming to the imagination of the ancients must a space vehicle have been. It is an intriguing thought.

Index

References to illustrations are shown in italics.

Picture Credits